Robert
R Juller
Brussels.

LETTERS
1922-1966

KARL BARTH
~
RUDOLF BULTMANN
LETTERS
1922-1966

Edited by
BERND JASPERT

Translated and Edited by
GEOFFREY W. BROMILEY

WILLIAM B. EERDMANS PUBLISHING COMPANY
GRAND RAPIDS, MICHIGAN

255 Jefferson Ave. SE, Grand Rapids, Mich. 49503

Printed in the United States of America

Translated from *Karl Barth-Rudolf Bultmann: Briefwechsel, 1922-1966,* V, Vol. 1, of the *Karl Barth Gesamtausgabe*

Library of Congress Cataloging in Publication Data

Barth, Karl, 1886-1968.
Karl Barth-Rudolf Bultmann letters, 1922 to 1966.

Translation of: Briefe. Bd. 1. Karl Barth-Rudolf Bultmann Briefwechsel, 1922-1966.
Includes bibliographies and index.
1. Barth, Karl, 1886-1968. 2. Bultmann, Rudolf Karl, 1884-1976. 3. Theologians—Switzerland—Correspondence.
4. Theologians—Germany (West)—Correspondence.
I. Bultmann, Rudolf Karl, 1884-1976. II. Jaspert, Bernd. III. Bromiley, Geoffrey William. IV. Title.
V. Title: Barth-Bultmann letters.
BX4827.B3A4 1981 230'.044'0922 [B] 81-17246
ISBN 0-8028-3560-0 AACR2

CONTENTS

TRANSLATOR'S PREFACE

The letters in this collection document an important, complex, and fascinating theological relationship. We see what seems to be an initial solidarity gradually eroding until it is finally replaced by a rift that would have a decisive impact on theology for the rest of the century. Nowhere can one trace this development, or see the reasons for it, or perceive its personal implications, more fully or intimately than in this correspondence and the supporting documents. Yet if the letters show plainly how brittle was the original agreement and how unavoidable the later breach, they also bear eloquent and heartening testimony to the depth and persistence of personal friendship that protected Barth and Bultmann from the bitter hostility that marked and marred the break of Barth and Brunner. Recognizing the impossibility of agreement, Barth good-humoredly compared their debate to the encounter of a whale and an elephant. And it is fitting that in the last communication Bultmann should offer brief but affectionate greetings to Barth on his eightieth birthday.

In the English translation of the letters it has not been thought necessary to offer every letter or document in full, since many of them contain matters of practical or academic or political interest that do not directly advance the main argument. Specialists who need the complete texts will in any case consult the Swiss original, and general readers will, we believe, find all the more important material as it was written, with a precis of all the rest, and all in the original order. The extensive notes have undergone some abridgment, but not to the exclusion of any individual or any significant data. On the other hand, the English version retains the complete indexes of the Swiss edition except where abridgment has led to the elimination of a few unimportant entries.

G. W. BROMILEY

Pasadena, Michaelmas 1981

PREFACE TO THE FIRST EDITION

This edition of the correspondence of Karl Barth and Rudolf Bultmann was planned independently of the general edition of Barth's works undertaken in 1970. At the suggestion of the Barth commission, however, and with the agreement of Bultmann, it is now published as part of the general edition. It contains all the available letters and postcards that the two theologians exchanged in several decades of friendship and theological discussion: 30 letters and 33 postcards written by Bultmann (1922–1966) and 25 letters and 10 postcards by Barth (1923–1963). Unfortunately, 11 letters and postcards by Barth were lost in the mails in 1969 and have not so far been recovered.

The surviving material by Barth is in the possession of Rudolf Bultmann and that written by Bultmann may be found in the Barth archive in Basel.

Barth and Bultmann first met when Barth was a student in Marburg in 1908 and 1909, and they became better acquainted at the open evenings at the home of Martin Rade, whose journal *Die Christliche Welt* Barth helped to edit in 1909. Bultmann became particularly friendly with Barth's brother Peter, who is mentioned more than once in the letters. Peter Barth wrote the joint postcard from the Aarau Conference (21 March 1911) which is the first written contact between Barth and Bultmann. Thirteen years later Barth greeted Bultmann on a card sent by Eduard Thurneysen from Pany in the Grisons (15 August 1924). These two cards, and that signed by Bultmann which R. Imberg sent to Barth from Grindelwald (14 April 1952), have not been included in the present collection.

For the early period of the intellectual exchange between Barth and Bultmann no letters have thus far been discovered. It may be assumed that they corresponded after the well-known Tambacher Tagung of 1919, in which they both participated, but no trace of any such correspondence has remained. Their real interaction begins only after the first communication from Bultmann reproduced here.

The gaps in letters between them may be explained by the fact that they continually met for discussions, especially when Barth was teaching in Göttingen, Münster, and Bonn. Even when Barth had to settle in Switzerland in 1935 because of political developments in Germany, Bultmann tried to keep in touch by means of occasional visits to Basel, which the party authorities viewed with suspicion. Even these sparse contacts were rendered impossible by the outbreak of World War II in 1939. Undoubtedly, their approaches to National Socialism, which agreed in general but differed in detail, helped to separate the two no less than their theological differences, which began in the middle twenties but led to an open breach only after the war, when Barth responded to Bultmann's famous demythologization program (1941) with his equally famous "attempt to understand him" (1952). Beyond all the material differences, however, the two remained good friends to the very end.

A few months after the end of World War II, Barth made fresh contact with Bultmann and visited him in Marburg (31 August 1945). Bultmann paid Barth a return visit in Basel (21 September 1948) and came to see him again a few times.

This book may rightly be described as a theological exchange, since both authors deal constantly with the central themes of Christian theology and practice. Their approaches are only partially the same, but even where they differ the one is always trying to understand the standpoint of the other. This desire for unimpaired understanding was the presupposition of the open, often severe, yet always fair dialogue conducted in the letters. Perhaps for those who did not know Barth and Bultmann personally as teachers, the letters are for this reason a better key to their theological positions than many volumes of secondary literature about them.

In relation to this edition of the letters the following points may be noted. The spelling and punctuation have been retained except for commas, which have been brought into line with present practice. The spelling and punctuation in documents in the appendix have been kept in their original form.

Peculiarities like *i* for *ü* (*gleichgiltig*) or *ie* for *i* (*giebt*) have been retained, as has also Barth's use of *als* for *wie,* the form *sodass,* and the use of the capital in *Alle* (for *alle*). A few slips, however, have been quietly corrected.

The headings of the letters and postcards have been standardized with the name and address of the writer on the left and the (place and) date of writing on the right. [Since in the Swiss edition the writer's address appears in the position reserved for the *recipient's* address in

English correspondence, that address has been omitted in the English version.]

Obscure abbreviations in the text have been expanded without references; names of people or journals that remain abbreviated in the text are given in full in the notes.

Notes that Barth and Bultmann themselves appended to words or statements in the text are in parentheses at the relevant points. Editorial emendations are in square brackets.

All the Greek and Latin quotations are very short, and most of them should be understandable without translation. [In a few cases a rendering has been supplied in the English edition.]

The editor's notes, especially those that are biographical, are composed in such a way that even nontheologians can get a clear picture of the historical background of the individual letters. [These notes have sometimes been shortened in the English version.]

This volume would not have been possible without the generous consent of Professor Bultmann, who at first modestly resisted the publication of his letters but then agreed on the understanding that the exchange would perhaps help many students to understand both Barth's theology and his own. First of all, then, we owe thanks to Dr. Bultmann for his permission to publish this material.

I then want to thank the Barth commission and especially Mrs. Nelly Barth (Basel) for their spontaneous agreement to the publication. I am particularly indebted to another member of the commission, Mrs. Franziska Zellweger-Barth (Basel), who helped me tirelessly with the original letters and documents and also provided detailed biographical and bibliographical information. Without her I could not have done the work.

Third, I must mention my wife, Renate Jaspert, who carried much of the burden of preparing the manuscript and the indexes. In addition I am grateful to many others, especially, in addition to those mentioned in the notes, Norbert Andernach, Hilde Dammshäuser, Erich Dinkler, Antje Lemke-Bultmann, Erna Schlier, Ernst Wolf, Winfried Zeller, Dieter Zellweger, and Elisabeth Zilz.

I am particularly grateful to Dean Otto Kaiser (Marburg) for permission to consult the minutes of the Marburg Theological Faculty.

Finally I want to express to Professor Max Geiger and Mr. Marcel Pfändler of the Theologischer Verlag, Zurich, my sincere thanks for some valuable hints and for their friendly cooperation.

BERND JASPERT

Marburg, 20 January 1971

ABBREVIATIONS

AGK	*Arbeiten zur Geschichte des Kirchenkampfs*
Anfänge, I	*Anfänge der dialektischen Theologie,* Vol. I: *Karl Barth, Heinrich Barth, Emil Brunner,* ed. J. Moltmann, 2nd ed. (Munich, 1966; ET *The Beginnings of Dialectical Theology* [Richmond, 1968]).
Anfänge, II	*Anfänge der dialektischen Theologie,* Vol. II: *Rudolf Bultmann, Friedrich Gogarten, Eduard Thurneysen,* ed. J. Moltmann, 2nd ed. (Munich, 1967; ET Richmond, 1968).
Bekenntnisse 1933	Kurt Dietrich Schmidt, *Bekenntnisse und grundsätzliche Äusserungen zur Kirchenfrage des Jahres 1933* (Göttingen, 1934).
Bekenntnisse 1934	Kurt Dietrich Schmidt, *Bekenntnisse und grundsätzliche Äusserungen zur Kirchenfrage des Jahres 1934* (Göttingen, 1935).
BEvTh	*Beiträge zur Evangelischen Theologie*
BFChTh	*Beiträge zur Förderung christlicher Theologie*
Briefwechsel	*Karl Barth–Eduard Thurneysen: Ein Briefwechsel aus der Frühzeit der dialektischen Theologie* (Munich-Hamburg, 1966; ET *Revolutionary Theology in the Making* [Richmond, 1964]).
CD	Karl Barth, *Church Dogmatics,* ed. G. W. Bromiley and T. F. Torrance (Edinburgh, 1956ff.).
CW	*Die Christliche Welt*
DtPfrBl	*Deutsches Pfarrerblatt*
EvTh	*Evangelische Theologie*
Exegetica	*Rudolf Bultmann, Exegetica. Aufsätze zur Erforschung des NT,* selected and edited by E. Dinkler (Tübingen, 1967).

FRLANT	*Forschungen zur Religion und Literatur des A und NT*
Ges. Vorträge; I	Karl Barth, *Das Wort Gottes und die Theologie* (Munich, 1924; ET *The Word of God and the Word of Man* [London, 1978; New York, 1957]).
Ges. Vorträge, II	Karl Barth, *Die Theologie und die Kirche* (Munich, 1928; ET *Theology and Church* [London, 1962]).
Ges. Vorträge, III	Karl Barth, *Theologische Fragen und Antworten* (Zollikon, 1957).
GuV, I–IV	Rudolf Bultmann, *Glauben und Verstehen: Gesammelte Aufsätze* (Tübingen, 1933–1965; ET Vol. I: *Faith and Understanding* [London and New York, 1969]; Vol. II: *Essays Philosophical and Theological* [London and New York, 1955]).
HNT	*Handbuch zum NT,* ed. H. Lietzmann, G. Bornkamm.
HZ	*Historische Zeitschrift*
JR	*Journal of Religion*
KJ	*Kirchliches Jahrbuch für die Evangelische Kirche in Deutschland*
KuM, I and II	*Kerygma und Mythos,* Vol. I, ed. H. W. Bartsch (Hamburg, 1948); Vol. II, ed. H. W. Bartsch (Hamburg, 1952). ET (essays from both I and II) *Kerygma and Myth* (London, 1953).
KuD	*Kerygma und Dogma*
Meyer K	*Kritisch-exegetischer Kommentar über das NT,* ed. H. A. W. Meyer
RGG[2]	*Die Religion in Geschichte und Gegenwart,* 2nd ed. (1927–1932).
RKZ	*Reformierte Kirchenzeitung*
SThZ	*Schweizerische Theologische Zeitschrift*
TDNT	*Theological Dictionary of the NT,* ed. G. Kittel, G. Friedrich, tr. G. W. Bromiley (Grand Rapids, 1964ff.).
ThBl	*Theologische Blätter*
ThEx	*Theologische Existenz heute*
ThLZ	*Theologische Literaturzeitung*
ThR	*Theologische Rundschau*
ThZ	*Theologische Zeitschrift*
ZNW	*Zeitschrift für die neutestamentliche Wissenschaft und die Kunde der älteren Kirche*
ZSTh	*Zeitschrift für systematische Theologie*
ZThK	*Zeitschrift für Theologie und Kirche*
ZZ	*Zwischen den Zeiten*

1

Marburg, 9 April 1922

Honored Colleague, or, if you will permit me, Dear Mr. Barth,

This last week I have sent my review of your *Romans* to Rade.[1] Since it is fairly long, there is some doubt as to how soon it can be printed, unless 1700 M[arks] can be found to increase the usual length of *CW* by half a sheet. Since I assume that you can no more lay your hands on this sum than I can, we shall have to wait a while, and I will provisionally entrust my thanks for your book to this card; perhaps you will like them better in this form than in my critical observations. In my review, of course, I have restrained my own objections and wishes in order to concentrate on reaching an understanding if at all possible. Not that I wanted to keep them from you! I hope rather that we can have a more intensive exchange on the matter itself. Will you be paying another visit to Marburg?

Yours sincerely,
R. BULTMANN

[1]Martin Rade (1857–1940) served pastorates in Schönbach (Oberlausitz) and Frankfurt and later taught at Marburg. He helped to found *Die Christliche Welt* in 1886 and was its editor until 1931. As may be seen from Bultmann's card of 25 May 1922 (No. 2), Rade let Barth have a copy of Bultmann's review before it was printed. Barth sent it back with some desired corrections that are known to us only from Bultmann's card of 25 May, since Barth's answer to the card of 9 Apr. has not yet been found. The review appeared in *CW*, 36 (1922), 320–323, 330–334, 358–361, and 369–373 (*Anfänge*, I, 119–142), and Barth replied to it in the preface to the third edition of his *Romans*. In *CW*, 34 (1920), 725–731 and 738–743, Bultmann had said of the first edition of *Romans* (1919) that while he welcomed its "religious culture-criticism," he could find in its positive contribution no more than arbitrary support for the Pauline Christ-myth. As he saw it, Barth's judgment on liberal theology applied in the same measure to Barth himself. Forty years later, in the preface to a Zurich reprint of the first edition of his *Romans* (1963), Barth said that for a while the second edition brought Bultmann and himself fairly close together, and this is borne out by the correspondence.

2

Marburg, 25 May 1922

Dear Mr. Barth,

Now that my essay on your book has come out,[1] it is time to thank you for your letter.[2] If I do not do this more explicitly it is partly because I would like to see you personally to discuss "either/or thinking." I do not really understand you, for to the extent that either/or thinking aims at clarifying concepts I cannot abandon it. I agree that the clarifying of concepts can and often does do violence to the matter itself, but I cannot give up the obligation of conceptual clarity on this account. I do not think you would want this, and if not, the point of your opposition needs to be elucidated. I am especially exercised about your rejoinder on faith and logos; this seems to me to be the most important thing, and it is here, I think, that the greatest danger arises for you, as is confirmed by the fine essay by your brother on ethics and eschatology in the *Kirchenblatt,*[3] Brunner's little book (*Erlebnis, Erkenntnis, Glaube?*),[4] and that of Natorp (*Individuum und Gemeinschaft*).[5] Just two points regarding my essay: 1) I have gladly cut out the shadowboxing, which was not aimed at you personally but at what you said; and 2) I have shortened the note on Jülicher[6] (though the part I have dropped did not say that you always agreed with him but that you were led by him to greater precision and a few alterations); I could not cut it out altogether (I discussed it with Rade). It is meant for my students, among whom I do not want to leave the impression that we should take philological exegesis less conscientiously than Jülicher does.[7] In the hope of future cooperation,

Yours sincerely,
Rudolf Bultmann

[1]See No. 1, n.l.

[2]Not yet found.

[3]P. Barth, "Ethik und Eschatologie," *Kirchenblatt für die reformierte Schweiz,* 37 (1922), 18.

[4]E. Brunner, *Erlebnis, Erkenntnis und Glaube* (Tübingen, 1921, 1923).

[5]P. Natorp, *Individuum und Gemeinschaft. Mit einem Anhang: Vom echten Tod* (Jena, 1921).

[6]Adolf Jülicher (1857–1938) was Professor of NT and Early Church History at Marburg from 1889 to 1923 and taught both Bultmann and Barth.

[7]For the shortened note see *CW*, 36 (1922), 373, n. 4: "Barth will partly gather from what is said and will partly state himself that, in relation to both the historical-philological exposition and the material evaluation of Romans and Paul, I agree in large measure with what Jülicher said about the first edition in this journal (*CW*, 34 [1920], 29 and 30)." Cf. A. Jülicher, "Ein moderner Paulus-Ausleger," *CW*, 34 (1920), 453–457 (*Anfänge,* I, 87–98).

3

Marburg, 31 July 1922

[Bultmann informs Barth that he will be passing through Göttingen with his eldest daughter (four years old)[1] on 14 Aug. and wonders if it might be possible to spend a day there, but does not want to cause domestic disruption.]

[1]Antje Lemke-Bultmann (b. 27 July 1918), now a professor of library science in the United States.

4

Oldenburg, 10 September 1922

[Bultmann thanks Barth for a card[1] and says that in Barth's absence he passed through Göttingen by night. Bultmann hopes now to see Barth in Elgersburg[2] if Barth is able to come.]

[1]This has not so far been found.

[2]Elgersburg (Thuringia) was the site of the annual meeting of the "Friends of the Christian World," 2–5 Oct. 1922. Both Barth and Bultmann participated, the former giving an address on "The Word of God as the Task of Theology" on 3 Oct. (*CW,* 36 [1922], 858–873 [*Anfänge,* I, 197–218]). For Barth's account of the meeting cf. his letter to Thurneysen, 7 Oct. 1922, *Briefwechsel,* pp. 93–96.

5

Marburg, 25 October 1922

[Bultmann uses an opportunity to send greetings and to press Barth to come to address the Theological Society,[1] a request he had meant to make of Barth at Elgersburg.[2] He offers to put him up unless he prefers to stay with Rade. He suggests that the main value of the visit would lie in personal discussion.]

[1]Bultmann wrote this note on the back of the official invitation to address the Theological Society sent by a student, Heinrich Schlier, who urged Barth to come at least to discuss his Elgersburg address if not to give a special lecture.

[2]Cf. No. 4, n. 2.

6

Marburg, 31 December 1922

Dear Mr. Barth,

Sincere thanks for sending me a copy of the new edition of *Romans.*[1] I am glad that you are coming to Marburg at the end of January[2] and hope that we shall then be able to clarify many matters. But I should like to express my thanks for your book before that and to reply to what you say against me in the preface.[3]

It seems to me that your response makes two points. The first is that the expositor must be faithful to the author. I agree with your statement on p. xxii that one cannot do justice to an author if one does not venture out with this hypothesis and enter into this relationship of fidelity to him. We should indeed write *with* him and not *about* him. But if "with him" does not mean "in psychological sympathy with" but "under the guidance of the matter itself," this might mean not only tacitly or explicitly elongating or shortening the lines drawn in a specific text (p. xxiii) but also correcting them. Is this to speak *about* Paul? If you want to say so, then so be it, but then the "bad taste" of mingling "with Paul" and "about Paul" is posited by the approach to the task and is just as little an error of taste as is Gundolf's distinction between "primal experience" and[4] "cultural experiences." Naturally there can be no question of going on to speak "about Paul" when things become too lively for us, but faithfulness to the author may be demonstrated by sometimes having to correct the material into which we are led by him. The criterion is the matter itself and not the contemporary analogy. Yet a reference to the Jewish, popular Christian, or Hellenistic world of thought may help to clarify the issue, just as my criticism of the earlier works of Gogarten or the first edition of *Romans*[5] may help to make me aware that I find touches of romanticism in places, or as my criticism of the second edition[6] may alert me to traces of the transcendental philosophy of Cohen. In this question I cannot at root see any difference between your exegetical approach and mine, great though the differences may be in exegetical practice. Behind these is a deeper difference which is not in my view a material one but a difference in "cultural experience." It has become increasingly plain to me that you have no inner relationship to history such as you so strongly have toward idealistic philosophy. As Plato's philosophy leads to the limit of the human, so does history in, for example, Wilhelm v. Humbold. And where historical criticism is practiced as a method of continual questioning, not to establish causal connections but in the service of self-reflection, it leads from hypothesis to hypothesis and on to the question of the final hypothesis. For me Hellenistic mysticism or Jewish legalism is not just a matter of historical interest by means of which I can "explain" some of the sayings of Paul (though exegesis can sometimes use this formulation), but these phenomena represent intellectual attitudes which, as students wrestle with the sources, draw them into debate with such attitudes and force the students to ask decisive questions.

A brief illustration which for reasons of space I had to leave out of my review. I find in Romans a big break which obviously does not concern you, namely, in the relation between 1:18–3:18 and 3:21ff. The difficulty lies in 3:19f. V. 19 seems to draw its conclusion from what precedes but the reason advanced in v. 20 is surprising. ἐξ ἔργων νόμου does not arise in relation to the Gentiles, and according to ch. 2 the sin of the Jews lay in transgression of the law, whereas in v. 20 we find the same thoughts as in 5:20f. and 10:2–4. Hence the negative substructure (1:18–3:18) does not support the positive continuation (3:21ff.). I should say that here the older and earlier Paul is speaking, while 1:18–3:18 reproduces the schema of Hellenistic-Jewish propaganda preaching. I should attempt to clarify the basic thought, asking how far it leads and in what relation it stands to Paul's faith preaching, and with these questions, which in the first instance relate to historical material, I have in truth posed the question of the principial point of Jewish, Stoic, and true Pauline thinking, and I am not refusing to ask whether and how far all this can be understood in connection with the matter itself (p. xxi).

It is more difficult to relate to your other thought, namely, that the πνεῦμα Χριστοῦ cannot be viewed as competing with other spirits (p. xxi). Yes—and no. Your question regarding where one can say for certain that the πνεῦμα Χριστοῦ is speaking is by no means an absurd one. For one can in fact do this. As it is no accident that you chose Romans rather than the Pastorals or that Paul is a witness to the πνεῦμα Χριστοῦ rather than Musonius or the author of περὶ κόσμου, so from the fact that the πνεῦμα Χριστοῦ cannot be coordinated with other spirits one may infer that the words of Paul might be testimony to this πνεῦμα to differing degrees, and some of them might not testify to it at all. And your statement that it is only other spirits that come to *words* in Romans seems to me to lead to the ridiculous conclusion that one can either expound every word that is spoken or written as testimony to the πνεῦμα Χρ. or one can expound none at all. If this conclusion may not be ridiculous from one standpoint, but quite correct, it is not true from the standpoint of the exegesis of Romans. For witness has to be expounded as witness. And this is impossible if faith is not also a process and position. The witness of faith also appears as *litera,* and as such stands alongside other utterances, forming a "standpoint." This does not alter anything. It does not call in question the miraculous character. One may still say that the *litera* is the concealing husk and agree that there is no *litera* which does not echo something of the voice of other spirits. But even though Christ's spirit is the crisis in which everything finds itself, including the testimony of faith, only the fact that there are testimonies of faith gives point to the task of exegeting Romans. I am not arguing here that criticism does not often make mistakes and that there are extremes which do not take the relationship of fidelity seriously; but I believe that the fact that Christ's spirit cannot be coordinated with other spirits, but is the crisis of everything, does not reduce to absurdity the criticism of which I spoke in my review.—

Perhaps we can talk some more about these matters. Thanks for sending me your sermon,[7] which is for me a welcome proof of the emptiness of Niebergall's[8] statement that in your view of things no more preaching is possible (which was naturally not meant in the same sense as what you said about the impossibility of the task of theology in your address at Elgersburg).[9] We spoke about this address at the last evening gathering of the "Friends of the Christian World," and some abysses opened up—not least in the case of Rade. I will not conceal from you that he found the reason for your disqualification of the prophetic in your (supposed) lack of understanding, failure to understand the prophets being linked to a lack of moral presuppositions on the part of the hearers, though this can hardly apply here! For my part I would simply ask whether the attack of your group on Schleiermacher is not due to the fact that you have all read the *Reden* in the edition of Otto with its, in my view, totally misleading notes.[10] I myself put Schleiermacher in the sequence from Jeremiah to Kierkegaard. Yes, I do. And the sign whose absence you assert—the attack on Christianity—is surely clear enough in the *Reden*. And one should not be led by the romantic terminology or phrases such as "feeling" to overlook or undervalue statements like the one which says that one can tell about the origin of religion only in the story of a miracle (p. 268 of the first edition), or that religion begins in man with some memorable occurrence (pp. 273f.), or that religion can begin only with a fact or not at all (p. 278), where the context leaves no doubt as to the meaning. Naturally I will not invalidate in the case of Schleiermacher the duty of criticism which I recommend in the case of Paul.

I hope we have a good time together again when you visit Marburg. Every best wish to you and your family for the New Year,

With sincere thanks
and greetings,
Yours,
R. BULTMANN

[1]K. Barth, *Der Römerbrief*, 3rd ed. (Munich, 1922; ET *The Epistle to the Romans* [London, 1935]).

[2]Barth's note to this effect, if he wrote such, has not been found.

[3]Preface to the third edition, most of which is a reply to Bultmann's criticism of the second edition; cf. No. 1, n. 1.

[4]This is not legible in the MS.

[5]Cf. No. 1, n. 1.

[6]Ibid.

[7]K. Barth, "Der Name des Herrn. Predigt," *Reformierte Kirchenzeitung*, 49 (1922); rpt. in K. Barth and E. Thurneysen, *Komm Schöpfer Geist! Predigten* (Munich, 1924, pp. 24–35; ET *Come Holy Spirit* [New York, 1933], pp. 24–35).

[8]Friedrich Niebergall (1866–1932) taught practical theology in Heidelberg after 1903 and in Marburg after 1922.

[9]Cf. No. 4, n. 2.

[10]F. Schleiermacher, *Über die Religion. Reden . . .*, ed. R. Otto (1899; 5th ed., 1926). The English translation is based on the Otto edition.

7

Marburg, 8 September 1923

[Bultmann uses an opportunity to send greetings to Barth,[1] to say how pleased he will be if Barth can visit Marburg, and to thank him for his essay on the problem of ethics,[2] the second part of which he regards as very valuable.]

[1]He wrote these lines beneath a letter of Heinrich Schlier to Barth inviting the latter to a discussion at Marburg on the 15th or 22nd of September.

[2]K. Barth, "Das Problem der Ethik in der Gegenwart," *ZZ*, 1 (1923), No. 2, 30–57 (Ges. Vorträge, I, 125–155); cf. Barth's letter to Thurneysen, 7 December 1922, *Briefwechsel*, 93f.

8

Marburg, 16 September 1923

[Thanking Barth for his card,[1] Bultmann urges him to stop off at Marburg for a chat.[2] He also wants to warn Barth against the appointment of a certain Strunck.[3] He expresses the hope that during the vacation he will be able to get to work on his commentary on John.[4] In his lectures on John he has had Heiler in the audience, who was incensed at the elimination of a mystical interpretation.[5] Bultmann would like to spend some time in Göttingen in order to use the library and get the advice of Lidzbarski and Reitzenstein.[6] He wonders when Barth will be back from Switzerland.]

[1]This has not been found.

[2]Barth was unable to accept the invitation to Marburg; see No. 7, n. 1.

[3]Friedrich Heinrich Wilhelm Strunck (b. 1900) took his first theological examination in Marburg in the winter semester 1923/24.

[4]This commentary was published eighteen years later (Göttingen, 1941).

[5]Friedrich Heiler (1892–1967) was Professor of the Comparative History and Philosophy of Religion at Marburg.

[6]Mark Lidzbarski (1868–1928) and Richard Reitzenstein (1861–1931). On the basis of the Mandaean sources made available by these scholars, Bultmann was interested in the Gnostic background of John's Gospel; cf. his essays in *Exegetica,* pp. 10–35, 55–104, 124–197, 230–254.

9

Göttingen, 9 October 1923

[In this letter Barth suggests the name of Erik Peterson[1] as a possible successor for Jülicher at Marburg,[2] and wonders if Rade might already have advanced his name.[3] He admits that Peterson had written little apart from his dissertation,[4] but attributes this to the seriousness with which he took theology. Students spoke well of him, and Barth found him the only person of theological interest at Göttingen apart from Hirsch.[5] He was not a member of the Barth-Gogarten group and had not even read the copy of *Romans*[6] that Barth lent him. Hence there is no conspiracy to take revenge on Jülicher for his opposition to Barth.[7] He confesses to Bultmann that he has again passed through Marburg (with his wife and children)[8] without stopping. He speaks of his present confusion of interests and is sure that Bultmann must have laughed that in a recent article he used footnotes.[9] He awaits the reaction of his "historical friends"[10] to this venture into historical theology. He mentions a rumor that Gogarten is being considered for Giessen[11] and tells of his own plans to lecture on Schleiermacher in the winter,[12] then on Augustine in the summer of 1924,[13] and on dogmatics the following winter.[14] In a postscript he asks humorously about a conference at Weimar in which Bultmann had taken part: *Est* Deus in nobis?[15]]

[1]Erik Peterson (1890–1960) taught NT and early church history at Göttingen, became a professor in Bonn in 1924, and later, as a Roman Catholic (1930), taught Christian archaeology in Rome (from 1934).

[2]Cf. No. 2, n. 6.

[3]Cf. No. 1, n. 1.

[4]E. Peterson, Εἷς θεός, "Epigraphische, formgeschichtliche und religionsgeschichtliche Untersuchungen" (diss., Göttingen, 1920); cf. *FRLANT,* 24 (Göttingen, 1926).

[5]Emanuel Hirsch (b. 1888) was Professor of Church History at Göttingen after 1921 and Professor of Systematic Theology after 1935.

[6]The reference is probably to the 2nd or 3rd edition.

[7]Cf. Jülicher's criticism of the 1st edition of *Romans* (1919) in *CW*, 34 (1920), 453ff. Barth replied in the preface to the 2nd edition, and F. Gogarten replied in "Vom heiligen Egoismus des Christen . . . ," *CW*, 34 (1920), 546–550 (*Anfänge*, I, 99–105).

[8]Nelly Barth (née Hoffmann, b. 26 Aug. 1893) and Franziska (b. 13 Apr. 1914), Markus (b. 6 Oct. 1915), Christoph (b. 29 Sept. 1917), and Matthias (b. 17 Apr. 1921). Hans Jakob was born one and one-half years after this journey (6 Apr. 1925).

[9]K. Barth, "Ansatz und Absicht in Luthers Abendmahlslehre," *ZZ*, 1 (1923), No. 4, 17–51. *ZZ* was founded in 1922 by Karl Barth, Friedrich Gogarten, Eduard Thurneysen, and Georg Merz.

[10]Behind this statement lies Barth's criticism of the historical method, his own aim being to penetrate "through the historical to the spirit of the Bible which is the eternal Spirit" (1st ed. of *Romans*, p. v). He undoubtedly has Adolf von Harnack in view; cf. *CW*, 37 (1923), 6–8, 89–91, 142–144, 244–252, 305f. (*Anfänge*, I, 323–347); also A. von Zahn-Harnack, *Adolf von Harnack* (Berlin, 1951), pp. 412–418; D. Braun, "Der Ort der Theologie . . . , " in ΠΑΡΡΗΣΙΑ (Zurich, 1966), pp. 11–49; E. Fascher, "Adolf von Harnack und Karl Barths Thesenaustausch von 1923," in *Frage und Antwort. Studien zur Theologie und Religionsgeschichte* (Berlin, 1968), pp. 201–231.

[11]Friedrich Gogarten (1887–1967) held pastorates in Stelzendorf (Thuringia) after 1917 and Dorndorf after 1925. He also taught systematic theology at Jena, and later became a professor at Breslau in 1931 and at Göttingen in 1935.

[12]He taught a four hour course on Schleiermacher and a one hour course on 1 John.

[13]He never gave this series, but instead taught a three hour course on Christianity and a one hour course on Philippians.

[14]He taught a four hour course on Christianity and a one hour course on Colossians.

[15]At this conference on the Society for Modern Christianity, Prof. Karl Bornhausen of Breslau had given an address on the theme "Est Deus in Nobis? (Idealismus und Christentum)"; cf. *CW*, 37 (1923), 734–743.

10

Marburg, 31 October 1923
(really 30 October 1923; cf. n. 4)

[Bultmann expresses his interest in Peterson but the names have already gone to Berlin,[1] and he is only the third on the list, although on the strength of his dissertation[2] Bultmann would have put him second. He has not yet had a chance to read Barth's historical essay in *ZZ*[3] since he has had to give a lecture (yesterday)[4] to visiting colleagues from Leiden. He again warns Barth against Strunck[5] and says that he is doing what he can for Gogarten at Giessen.]

[1]To the Prussian Ministry of Science, Art, and Culture.

[2]See No. 9, n. 4.

[3]No. 9, n. 9.

[4]According to Rade's account in *CW*, 37 (1923), 724, Bultmann gave this address (cf. *Exegetica*, pp. 55–104) on 29 Oct., so that he must have dated his letter wrongly. The visitors were William Brede Kristensen, Karel Hendrik Roessingh, and Hans Windisch.

[5]See No. 8, n. 3.

11

Göttingen, 8 January 1924

[In this letter Barth encloses a letter from F. Siegmund-Schultze[1] and asks what has been going on in Marburg to agitate him so much.[2] He has heard something from students (including Strunck)[3] but would like direct word from Bultmann himself before replying. As regards Strunck, he had a glowing recommendation from Otto[4] but when Barth read Bultmann's last letter[5] he "sank without a trace" and someone else was appointed. Barth asks about a projected lecture in Marburg about which he has heard in a letter from Rade.[6] He asks Bultmann to assemble criticisms in an article for *ZZ*.[7] In a postscript he assures Bultmann that Strunck knew nothing about his letter.[8]]

[1]This letter was written on 5 January 1924; see Appendix, No. 1.

[2]Friedrich Siegmund-Schultze (1885–1969) worked in the Inner Mission, became Honorary Professor for Youth Affairs at Berlin University (Faculty of Philosophy) in 1926, emigrated to Switzerland in 1933, helped in refugee work, became Director of the Dortmund Seminar for Social Pedagogy in 1948, founded the ecumenical archive in Soest, Westphalia, in 1959, and for several decades edited various ecumenical journals and literary series.

[3]See No. 8, n. 3.

[4]Rudolf Otto (1869–1937) taught in Göttingen and Breslau and was Professor of Systematic Theology at Marburg from 1917 to 1929.

[5]Bultmann's letter of 31 Oct. 1923; see No. 10.

[6]Martin Rade wrote to Barth on 31 Dec. 1923 telling him that he viewed with sympathy his influence on the students, but feared the threat—if only the threat—of a clique. He was tensely awaiting Bultmann's projected lecture and did not think that Barth would agree with him even in essentials. This lecture bore the title "Die liberale Theologie und die jüngste theologische Bewegung" (*GuV*, I, 1–25). Barth in his circular letter of 4 Mar. 1924 tells how he and twelve students paid a sudden visit to Marburg for the occasion and how he and Bultmann sat in the theological seminar the following morning smoking their pipes like two rabbis. He thinks that Marburg has now become a point on the map of Central Europe that can be viewed with satisfaction. For Rade, Bultmann is a historical unbeliever, who "despairing of everything has fallen into our arms" (cf. *Briefwechsel*, p. 151).

12

Marburg, 9 January 1924

Dear Mr. Barth,

That Siegm.-Sch.[1] and many of those who heard his lecture here were plunged into agitation seems to me to have been the best result of this rather weak address, which was impressive only in the first half, in which S. Sch.[2] told us about his own experiences and work. In the second part, which dealt first with opposition to the social work of the church, the followers of K. Barth were included among those who emancipate themselves from social duties. S. Sch., it is true, regarded this appeal to you as a misunderstanding. This misunderstanding, however, was not proved to be such, but was simply asserted, and S. Sch. did not deal at all with the problems that can give rise to it. S. Sch. himself obviously does not grasp these problems, it being axiomatic for him that the church is pledged to social work; and though he would probably deny it, there lies behind his statements—unelucidated and unexplained—the idea that "for the sake of the church and its existence" the church must do social work if it is not to perish. When at first no one entered into debate, I spoke up to clarify this issue somewhat, in relation to many discussions with my students; that is, I spoke up in order to show how problematic it all is. I said that social work should not be done as auxiliary work or as an attempt to cure all kinds of social ills, but that it is possible only on the basis of real knowledge, that it presupposes a clear program of what should be, that is, a political and economic program, and that we should not obscure the seriousness and responsibility of social work by hiding this. I then said that the task of the church can be only the proclamation of the Word, that the Word proclaimed is the Word of judgment and grace and has nothing directly to do with a social ideal, and that even the best social program or the most ideal state of human society is not itself the kingdom of God but stands "under crisis." I said finally that the theologian, too, has every reason to take social problems[3] seriously, because as a member of human society he has a duty in this area like everyone else; for proclaiming the Word is not just preaching on Sundays in empty city churches, but proclaiming it where and in such a way that it will be heard, working at social problems being part of this. In any case, however, social work as such is not the office of the church.

The discussion became heated when Rade and Niebergall[4] spoke after me. The former was half annoyed by what I said and half distressed that everything would now be taken from the church when it has already lost so much in the modern world; it is now desired that it should be restricted to the Word!! Niebergall spoke sarcastically about sin and grace—that it is a comfortable Christianity which sets us in sin today and in grace tomorrow. Rade spoke as though he had never read Troeltsch's Social Teachings[5] and has no idea at all of the problems; Niebergall as though he had never read the New Testament or Luther. S. Sch. went completely off the rails in his closing statement, saying that it was brutal to want to preach a sermon to the hungry wife of a worker, etc.

You note that I have not advocated quietism, but simply tried to show that proclamation of the Word is the one office of the church; I not only emphasized the seriousness of social work but also attempted to bring out the full compass of it. I believe, of course, that I am at one with you in basic thinking in this field.

That the Strunck affair turned out as it did is probably for the best. He tells me that he has the prospect of an appointment with Wernle.[6]

I have been asked by the Theological Society to give a lecture on Barth-Gogarten and liberal theology (the subject not yet fixed).[7] One source among others for liberal theology is provided by the "morning devotions" in *Christl. Welt.*; you will see that my intentions in relation to liberal theology are not good. For the rest, my criticism of your *Romans* is not yet at rest; I am rereading it for my course.[8] I have many other positive and negative things to say beyond what I said in *Christl. Welt,* and have begun to collect my thoughts in an essay which I will be pleased to send you for *ZZ.* But I am in no hurry and it can wait for a while.[9] Perhaps I will tell you about my lecture

With sincere greetings and good wishes for the New Year,

Yours,
RUDOLF BULTMANN

[1]Cf. No. 11, nn. 1 and 2.
[2]Siegmund-Schulze.
[3]The MS here replaced an original "duties" with "problems."
[4]Cf. No. 6, n. 8.
[5]E. Troeltsch, *Die Soziallehren der Christlichen Kirchen und Gruppen* (Tübingen, 1912).
[6]Paul Wernle (1872–1939) taught NT at Basel beginning in 1897, and became Professor of NT in 1900 and of Church History in 1901.
[7]Cf. No. 11, n. 6.
[8]A four hour course on Galatians and Romans.
[9]The essay was never written.

13

Göttingen, 15 April 1924

[Barth thanks Bultmann for a copy of his essay "Die liberale Theologie und die jüngste theologische Bewegung."[1] He asks him to send a copy to Wernle, keeping his own for the widow of Wilhelm Bousset.[2] He recalls with pleasure his visit to Marburg[3] but wonders if the picture of two rabbis smoking their pipes among serious theological students will look so good from a heavenly standpoint. He mentions a possible visit by Bultmann to Göttingen and hopes to get advice from him on the teaching of dogmatics,[4] in relation to which he has lodged a complaint against the faculty in Berlin.[5] He does not know how it will all end and needs comfort. Schlatter[6] has graciously asked him to take part in some "big theological maneuvers" in Bethel. He asks how the commentary on John is going and how Bultmann will "draw the diagonal" between Walter Bauer[7] and himself.]

[1]Cf. *GuV,* I, 1–25.

[2]Marie Bousset; the NT scholar Wilhelm Bousset had died in 1920.

[3] 6 Feb. 1924; cf. No. 11, n. 6.

[4]Cf. Barth's letters on this to Thurneysen, *Briefwechsel,* pp. 143ff.

[5]Cf. Barth's letters to Thurneysen, *Briefwechsel,* esp. pp. 143f., 146f., 155f., 160f. He had probably told Bultmann about the dispute when he was in Marburg on 6 Feb. 1924; it concerned the use of the word "dogmatics" in the title of his lectures. He had told Thurneysen how matters stood in a letter dated the previous day, 5 Feb. 1924. Cf. Appendix, Nos. 2 and 3.

[6]Adolf Schlatter (1852–1938) was Professor of NT in Greifswald in 1888, Berlin in 1893, and Tübingen in 1898. He reviewed the 2nd edition of Barth's *Romans* in *Die Furche,* 12 (1922), 228–232 (*Anfänge,* I, 142–147).

[7]W. Bauer, *Das Johannesevangelium, HNT,* 2/2 (Tübingen,1912; rev. ed., 1925 [*HNT,* 6]; 3rd ed., 1933).

14

Marburg, 18 April 1924

[Bultmann thanks Barth for his card and says of his essay that many, like Rade, will probably conclude that what is essential has already been said, and they will ignore the rest, which is wrong[?].[1] Not much is to be expected of the older generation. He, too, has good memories of Barth's visit. He cannot come to Göttingen for the vacation, since he has to go to Breslau for a lecture, but he hopes to spend between eight and fourteen days there in the summer. The Theological Society is thinking of asking Ragaz[2] to give an address in the summer semester, and Bultmann wonders if he will come and if he has something worthwhile to offer. He mentions his essay on Paul's ethics in the next issue of *ZNW.*[3]]

[1]This word is illegible. The editor suggests "*verkehrt.*"

[2]Leonhard Ragaz (1868–1945) was pastor at Basel minster beginning in 1902, co-

founded and directed the "Religious Social Movement" in 1906, and was Professor of Systematic and Practical Theology at Zurich from 1908 to 1921.

[3]"Das Problem der Ethik bei Paulus," *ZNW*, 23 (1924), 123–140 (*Exegetica*, pp. 36–54).

15

Göttingen, 25 April 1924

Dear Mr. B.,

I realize with horror that I have neglected to answer your card. Naturally the Marburgers should have Ragaz come. There may be much against him, but he is at any rate a type that is worth knowing, and the students should wrestle with him no matter to what banner they pledge allegiance. I am having some poor days, as always before the beginning of a semester, but especially this time. One can just as easily rack one's brains about correct dogmatics as about perpetual motion. O confounded history, if only one might flee into a desert and put one's head in the sand! In addition there is the quarrel with the faculty mandarins, so that I cannot even announce anything and begin.[1]

Yours sincerely,
KARL BARTH

[1]See No. 13, n. 5.

16

Marburg, 4 July 1924

[Bultmann thanks Barth for the book of his[1] sent by Miss Haas.[2] Heidegger[3] is to lecture on "History and Time"[4] on Friday evening (the twenty-fifth). He hopes Barth can come and stay until Sunday evening.]

[1]*Die Auferstehung der Toten* (Munich, 1924; ET *The Resurrection of the Dead* [New York, 1933]).

[2]Erna Haas, who later married Heinrich Schlier, was a student at Marburg from 1921 to 1925, with a break at Göttingen in 1924. According to a letter received from her (12 June 1970), the summer of 1924 saw a lively exchange between Bultmann and his students on the one hand and Barth and his students on the other, each group visiting the seminars and lectures of the other.

[3]Martin Heidegger (b. 1889) was Professor of Philosophy at Marburg from 1923 to 1928 and had a close working relationship with Bultmann; they remained friends even after Heidegger left Marburg; cf. Appendix, Nos. 39 and 40. On Heidegger's influence on Bultmann and Barth, and on theology in general, cf. F. Traub, "Heidegger und die Theologie," *ZSTh*, 9 (1932), 686–743; J. Macquarrie, *An Existentialist Theology! A Comparison of Heidegger and Bultmann* (London, 1955); G. W. Ittel, "Der Einfluss der Philosophie M. Heideggers auf die Theologie R. Bultmanns," *KuD*, 2 (1956), 90–108; H. Ott, *Denken und Sein . . .* (Zollikon, 1959); H. G. Gadamer, "Martin Heidegger und die Marburger Theologie," *Zeit und Geschichte*, ed. E. Dinkler (Tübingen, 1964), pp. 479–490; *The Theology of Rudolf Bultmann*, ed. C. W. Kegley (New York, 1966), including the essays by J. Macquarrie, "Philosophy and Theology in Bultmann's Thought," pp. 127–143, and G. Harbsmeier, "The Theology of Rudolf Bultmann and its Relation to Philosophy," pp. 144–152, with Bultmann's "Reply," pp. 273–276; *Heidegger und die Theologie . . .*, I, ed. G. Noller (Munich, 1967); *Neuland in der Theologie . . .*, I: *Der spätere Heidegger und die Theologie* (Zurich, 1964).

[4]Incorporated into *Sein und Zeit* (Halle, 1927; ET *Being and Time*, 1962).

17

Göttingen, 15 July 1924

[Barth would like to visit Marburg but is too busy and gathers from Rade's objections that he is no longer welcome. He is not clear how he can usefully enter into debate with Heidegger, whom he does not know. He wonders if they might meet at a third place. Miss Haas seems to have communicated to Bultmann the "darkest parts" of his lectures.[1]]

[1]In the summer semester of 1924 Barth was lecturing on the prolegomena to Christianity and gave his students some materials which, with those of the 1924/25 winter semester, would be a preliminary form of the *Dogmatik im Entwurf* of 1927.

18

Marburg, 18 July 1924

[Bultmann tries to persuade Barth to come to Marburg for at least a day; he suggests that the sacrifice of time will be worth it and he does not think Rade's objection should be taken to mean that Barth is not welcome as a guest. Heidegger wants him to come, and the fact that Barth does not know Heidegger is all the more reason that he should do so, as it is high time they got to know one another.]

19

Göttingen, 28 July 1924

[Barth encloses a letter from O. Urbach.[1] He has had a difficult time and is glad to be going on vacation, from which he will return in the second half of September.]

[1]See Appendix, No. 4.

20

Oldenburg, 25 September 1924

[Bultmann thanks Barth for his card[1] and speaks of his return on the midday train from Hanover.]

[1]Not yet found.

21

Marburg, 24 January 1925

[Bultmann thanks Barth that, as he has learned from Bielfeld,[1] he is to stay with Barth when giving a lecture in Göttingen. He agrees that there should be no debate[2] after the lecture but asks for some group discussion the following day. Some students and Heidegger plan to come with him. He cannot send on a copy of the lecture (for a response) since it exists as yet only in note form and will not be ready until after he has delivered it in Marburg on 1 February. He will not focus on differences between Barth and himself, but will pose the basic question of the possibility of understanding history in general and will then go on to deal with theological exegesis, which is, in Barth's words, "an impossible possibility." Only incidentally will differences from Barth become explicit. Bultmann ends by referring to a lecture which Brunner[3] had given and which he regarded as very weak; Heidegger had criticized it dreadfully.]

[1]Walter Bielfeld, a theological student at Göttingen, had spent the winter semester of 1923 under Bultmann. He later became a pastor at Wilhelmshaven. He had written to Bultmann on 21 Jan. 1925 inviting him to stay with Barth when he came to address the Theological Society. Because of Barth's delicate situation at Göttingen, Bultmann was asked to avoid any open rift that might weaken his position, the idea simply being

to have a response to the lecture, for which purpose Barth desired a copy as soon as possible.

[2]Bultmann's address, "Das Problem einer theologischen Exegese des NT," was printed in *ZZ*, 3 (1925), 334–357 (*Anfänge*, II, 47–72).

[3]Emil Brunner (1889–1966), after a period of teaching in England, was Professor of Systematic and Practical Theology at Zurich from 1924 to 1953. His lecture on "Die Menschheitsfrage im Humanismus und Protestantismus" was published in *ThBl*, 4 (1925), 53–58, under the title "Gesetz und Offenbarung. Eine theologische Grundlegung."

22

Göttingen, 26 January 1925

Dear Mr. Bultmann,

I do not know whether my instinct was right when—hastily through the student Bielfeld—I made my request to you. Obviously, and rightly so in the light of relations at Marburg, it will seem rather strange to you. But you can have no idea how complicated the situation is here. The faculty will be like a wall against both of us; Hirsch, who is always present on such occasions, will do everything he can to set us against one another; and finally the students will listen to you all ears, and afterwards—as happened just recently when Tillich[1] was here (not[2] my students, but the plebs who are very numerous here)—will demand with stamping and shuffling of feet that I say something about the matter. You will have to reckon with incomparably more opposition (taken to be self-evident) on the one side and more stupid sensation-seeking on the other than in Marburg or Giessen. Something of the mood of a gladiatorial fight or a duel usually seems to be in the air on these occasions. I suppress myself as often as I can. But when *you* come and speak on *this* subject[3] I cannot do so, nor will it do that we should discuss only in a small group the following day (as can and should *also* happen, but first the other). And what I really want is that we should *agree* to present a common front to opponents, to let the students see only as much of our differences as we see fit, to "play ahead of the ball," as the football world says. This is what I had in mind with my solemn sounding proposal of a response. I am *not* a good debater, at least not in an *arena* in which one can count on *ill* will on more than one side, and I do not want to be surprised by trains of thought which, as often happens, I do not properly understand at a first hearing, so that I will be *provoked* into an answer which in the ears of Hirsch etc. will appear hostile to you only by following my own line. This must not happen. It may be that the situation will finally let me be silent, but because this may not happen I would rather consider the matter in advance. An explicit outline of your lecture—the sooner the better, of course—will do very well for this purpose. If it turns out that my contribution is not needed or that we can put off discussion for a smaller group, all the better. (I have no urge to speak and have enough to do on my own!) But if it's worth doing, it's worth doing well. And we should not provide Göttingen with a show!

After the event on the sixth you will sleep, not without some amusement, in the same bed that Graf Hermann Keyserling[4] will sleep in on the night of the fifth. It is another "impossible possibility" that *he* (who is speaking to the literary society on the evening of the fifth), snatching at an invitation that was made out of courtesy last summer, should do missionary work in Göttingen from *my* house! Eight days later Günther Dehn[5] will be in the same place. He, too, is speaking to the theologians, his theme being religious socialism,[6] another risky subject for me. It is a pity that I cannot invite Heidegger to something too. But at the moment I have only this *one* bed for famous people. I am looking forward to you all coming with real anxiety. You are all so much cleverer than I am. Yet you are sincerely welcome (only you must solemnly promise, in Heidegger's name too, that you will not disturb the peace of my lecture early on Saturday; it is unfortunately the one on Colossians, at which I do not want you *in any circumstances* to be present!).

Will you reply to Windisch?[7] Was the passage in Harnack's centennial article[8] in *Theol. L. Zeit.* directed against you or against me?

With sincere greetings,

Yours,
KARL BARTH

[1]Paul Tillich (1886–1965) was Professor of Systematic Theology and the Philosophy of Religion at Marburg in 1924, then became Professor of Evangelical Theology at Dresden in 1925, Professor of Philosophy at Frankfurt in 1929, and in 1933 left Germany for political reasons and taught at various American schools.

[2]In the MS Barth here replaced an original "less" by "not."

[3]See No. 21, n. 2.

[4]Hermann Graf Keyserling (1880–1946) was a philosopher who founded a "School of Wisdom" in 1920 which had some influence on the contemporary intellectual life of Germany. In a letter to Thurneysen (*Briefwechsel,* p. 182) Barth called his lecture a "very poor address on eastern and western wisdom" (25 Feb. 1925).

[5]Günther Dehn (1882–1970) was a pastor in Berlin from 1911 to 1930, founded the League of German Religious Socialists in 1919/20, became Professor of Practical Theology at Halle in 1931, was suspended in 1933, taught at the school of the Confessing Church in Berlin in 1935, was imprisoned for illegal teaching, became a pastor in Ravensburg in 1942, and became Professor of Practical Theology at Bonn in 1946.

[6]The subject of Dehn's address was "Von Stöcker zu Kutter—Ein Beitrag zur Frage des Öffentlichkeitswillens der evangelischen Kirche." In a letter to Thurneysen (15 Feb. 1925, *Briefwechsel,* p. 183) Barth calls it "a solid lecture" which made "a real impression

on the students." It was disturbed only by a Christian Socialist pastor who was "hard of hearing (both physically and mentally)" and "who had never heard of Kutter ('Where does the fellow live?')."

[7]H. Windisch, "Das Problem des paulinischen Imperativs," *ZNW*, 23 (1924), 265–281. Bultmann made no public reply.

[8]A. v. Harnack, "Ein Wort der Erinnerung," *ThLZ*, 50 (1925), 1–40.

23

Marburg, 3 February 1925

Dear Mr. Barth,

With stiff fingers—for today I had to cycle to Kirchhain[1] and back to address the Pastors' Conference on recent research—I will dash off a few lines to you. I am so overworked that I cannot possibly tell you explicitly about my lecture. And I see no other possibility than to send you a first sketch of it,[2] which, of course, the earlier it is the further it will be from the definitive form (which is not yet available). In some places it will be fragmentary and in others unintelligible, but it will at least show you in what direction my thoughts are moving and with what concepts I am operating. I hope that the pages will be legible; the only unusual abbreviations are *sd* for *sondern* ["but"] and *viell.* for *vielleicht* ["perhaps"]. The manuscript will differ most from the oral lecture in the conclusion, especially as I shall try to show the connection or identity between historical (exegetical) and systematic theology, which in distinction from preaching is always incomplete, i.e., critical. Here I suspect that a difference between us will come to light: the difference between preaching and theology. But only the expert will see it, for I shall not mention your name. I fully hope that we can present a united front. And if Heidegger comes, as I hope, Hirsch may experience something. But you must treat this in strict confidence. It would be a good thing if the news that H. is coming were not to get around in Göttingen. So that we may have time to reach an agreement the evening before the lecture, I will take the express on Friday which, if I am not mistaken, reaches Göttingen shortly after 12; this means that you will have to provide lunch, i.e., if it is convenient for your wife; if not I will find something to eat at the Krone or somewhere.

I am looking forward to seeing you again and hope we shall have a useful discussion,

Yours sincerely,
R. BULTMANN

[1] 15 km. (almost 10 miles) east of Marburg.

[2]This sketch has not been found. Concerning the lecture, which Bultmann delivered on 6 Feb. 1925, Barth wrote Thurneysen on 15 Feb. 1925 (*Briefwechsel*, p. 183) that it was very good and that Hirsch opposed it with manifest lack of success. Some thirty to forty students came from Marburg and Berlin who later gathered for an extra discussion with Barth. There was then a second public discussion and a series of private talks in which differences were discussed. Bultmann accused Barth of a lack of sobriety and Barth replied that Bultmann thought along much too anthropological-Kierkegaardian-Lutheran (plus Gogartian) lines ("to speak about God is to speak about man"), was still too eclectic in relation to the Bible, and had not yet broken free from the shell of history. But these were all differences that could be usefully discussed further. Bultmann, for Barth, was too close to Gogarten, though this was ten times better than Holl: anything but that!

24

Marburg, 21 April 1925

[Bultmann first says that he is thinking about Barth's wife and the little J.-J.[1] and then issues two invitations to Barth. First, in the name of the Pforta Society,[2] he asks him to address a conference to be held 3–6 August[3] on the general theme of nationality. Meinecke of Berlin[4] and Tillich[5] have been selected as speakers on the first day (nationality and history) and Hauer of Tübingen[6] as the other speaker on the second day (nationality and religion). Bultmann hopes that Barth will come, since some members of the group favor Gogarten and himself, but others want to avoid the issue, and Barth's coming should force a decision. He realizes that participation will mean some sacrifice but thinks it may be worth it, and asks for a prompt reply. The second request relates to a vacation course on eschatology (27–29 April). Baumgartner[7] is to lecture on Daniel, Bultmann himself on eschatology and apocalyptic in primitive Christianity,[8] and Hermelink[9] on medieval and modern apocalyptic sects. So far, however, those invited to give the fourth lecture, on eschatology in faith and doctrine, including Frick of Giessen,[10] have all declined, and Pastor Schafft[11] (of Cassel) is anxious that Barth should be asked. Although realizing that the notice is much too short, Bultmann as dean[12] urges Barth to come and if necessary simply use a chapter from his lectures on dogmatics.[13] All expenses will be paid. He closes the letter by mentioning the publication of his *Jesus* and wonders what Barth will think of it.[14]]

[1]Jean Jacques, i.e., Hans Jakob Barth, b. 6 Apr. 1925.

[2]This society (the Pforta-Kreis) was founded in 1921, and was primarily directed by Wilhelm Heitmüller. It held conferences and local group meetings and aimed to unite

young and old, not in a dogmatic front, but in a process of growth and deepening by personal contact.

[3]In Naumburg.

[4]Friedrich Meinecke (1862–1954), a historian, taught in Strassburg (1901) and Freiburg (1906) and was then professor in Berlin from 1914 to 1929. In 1948 he helped to found the Free University of Berlin.

[5]See No. 22, n. 1.

[6]Jakob Wilhelm Hauer (1881–1962) was a historian who later took a leading part in the German Faith Movement (1933).

[7]Walter Baumgartner (1887–1970) was Professor of OT at Marburg in 1916; he was at Giessen in 1920, and from 1929 to 1958 he was at Basel. For his Daniel lecture cf. "Das Buch Daniel," *CW,* 39 (1925), 675–677, 724–726, 776–787, 819–828; published, with some slight revision, as a monograph (Giessen, 1926).

[8]Not published.

[9]Heinrich Hermelink (1877–1958) taught in Kiel and Bonn and was then Professor of Church History at Marburg after 1916.

[10]Heinrich Frick (1893–1952) was Professor of Practical Theology at Giessen (1924), then of Systematic Theology and Religious Knowledge (1926), and held the same post in addition to being Professor of Missions at Marburg after 1929.

[11]Hermann Schafft (1883–1959) edited the journal *Neuwerk.*

[12]Bultmann was at this time Dean of the Faculty of Theology.

[13]On 4 May Barth began his summer semester lectures in Dogmatics II, 6: "The Doctrine of Reconciliation, §27: The Faithfulness of God."

[14]*Jesus* (Berlin, 1926). Barth made a brief reference to it in a letter to Thurneysen, 15 Feb. 1925 (*Briefwechsel,* p. 183).

25

Marburg, 19 July 1925

[Bultmann has had to put off staying with Küper[1] in Baltrum but expects to be in Langeoog from 4 August. He hopes they can meet in B. and L.[2] since there are many matters to discuss. Hess[3] has brought a manuscript of Barth's Prolegomena,[4] but he has not read it and will not do so without Barth's permission. He has sent his Göttingen lecture in emended form to Merz;[5] he still has doubts about it, but it should contribute to discussion. He likes Peterson's recent essays[6] and hopes to take up the issues raised.[7] He also expects Barth to reply to them.[8] In his classes he is now dealing with I Cor. 15 and has some quarrel with Barth,[9] as will become apparent in an essay in *ThBl.*[10]]

[1]Rented rooms for the vacation.

[2]Baltrum and Langeoog.

[3]Hans-Erich Hess studied with Bultmann in the summer semester of 1923, then with Barth; he later worked in Darmstadt.

[4]Cf. No. 17, n. 1.

[5]This lecture, "Das Problem einer theologischen Exegese des NT," was published in *ZZ* (ed. Merz), 3 (1925), 334–357 (*Anfänge,* II, 47–72). Cf. No. 23.

[6]E. Peterson, "Der Lobgesang der Engel und der mystische Lobpreis," *ZZ*, 3 (1925), 145–153; also "Über die Forderung einer Theologie des Glaubens. Eine Auseinandersetzung mit Paul Althaus," *ZZ*, 3 (1925), 281–302; also *Was ist Theologie?* (Bonn, 1925; *Theologische Traktate* [Munich,1951], pp. 9–43).

[7]Cf. R. Bultmann, "Die Frage der 'dialektischen' Theologie (Eine Auseinandersetzung mit Peterson)," *ZZ*, 4 (1926), 40–59 (*Anfänge*, II, 72–92). Cf. also Bultmann's review of Peterson's *Was ist Theologie?* in *CW*, 39 (1925), 1061f.

[8]Barth answered Peterson in his lecture "Kirche und Theologie" (Göttingen, 7 Oct. 1925 and Elberfeld, 23 Oct. 1925), which was published in *ZZ*, 4 (1926), 18–40 (Ges. Vorträge, II, 302–328). Peterson heard the lecture in Göttingen and on 11 Oct. 1925 wrote to Bultmann that he did not think Barth had answered his arguments. He was not thinking of becoming a Roman Catholic. He found no substance in the rejoinder of Althaus in *Theol. Literaturblatt*. He thought Althaus, like Hirsch, was more of a politician than a true theologian. Yet he did not want to become involved in personal animosities, but simply to engage in clear and calm discussion.

[9]The reference is to Barth's *Die Auferstehung der Toten* (Munich, 1924).

[10]Cf. Bultmann's "Karl Barth, 'Die Auferstehung der Toten,' " *ThBl*, 5 (1926), 1–14 (*GuV*, I, 38–64).

26

Marburg, 29 September 1925

[Bultmann thanks Barth for a card,[1] congratulates him on his appointment to Münster,[2] takes it that he is following Smend,[3] wonders if he is going over to practical theology (which he would regret if Barth were not also teaching dogmatics and NT), and says he could wish that it might help to improve things in G.[4]]

[1]This has not been found.

[2]In May 1925 Barth was invited to join the theological faculty at Münster. He was also approached about succeeding Hermann Kutter at Neumünster, Zurich (*Briefwechsel*, pp. 202f.). This approach, along with letters from Kutter and Rudolf Schlunck (Appendix, Nos. 5 and 6), caused Barth to ask the Göttingen authorities what they had in view for him in Prussia, and he was offered a personal chair at Münster. While he did not want the move, which would take him further from Switzerland, he welcomed the financial advantages and in July accepted the call to become Professor of Dogmatics and NT Exegesis. He would have liked Thurneysen to follow him in Göttingen (cf. *Briefwechsel*, pp. 207, 210ff.).

[3]Julius Smend had been Professor of Practical Theology at Münster after 1914 and became Professor Emeritus in 1926. In 1927 Barth received a regular appointment as the successor of Georg Wehrung.

[4]Göttingen. Bultmann was hoping that a regular professorship might be found for Barth to keep him in Göttingen.

27

Baltrum, 11 August 1925

[Barth notes that the one kilometer of water that Bultmann's wife has put between them is a bigger gap than that between Marburg and Göttingen. He wonders if Bultmann can get over, an added attraction being the presence of Wilhelm Loew.[1] He takes a poorer view of Peterson on a second reading.[2] He will not be teaching practical theology at Münster but will teach dogmatics and NT exegesis. In the winter he will be lecturing on John's Gospel and would like information on the Mandaeans from the proofs of Bultmann's *John* if these are available.[3]]

[1]Wilhelm Loew (b. 1887) was later Professor of Practical Theology at Mainz.

[2]Cf. No. 25, n. 6.

[3]This commentary was planned by Bultmann but was not published until 1941. There was some reference to the Mandaeans in his *Jesus* (in the section "John the Baptist and Jesus"), and he had written a longer essay on "Die Bedeutung der neuerschlossenen mandäischen und manichäischen Quellen für das Verständnis des Johannesevangeliums," *ZNW*, 24 (1925), 100–146 (*Exegetica*, pp. 55–104), which he sent to Barth in September; cf. No. 29.

28

Langeoog, 22 August 1925

[Bultmann is sorry that he has not been able to see Barth, and since he wants to talk to him[1] he wonders if he can spend a day with Barth in Göttingen on his return journey around 11–13 September. He will need accommodation for one of the children as well; his wife and another of the children[2] will stay with a friend.[3] A sofa will be enough for him, but if he is asking too much Barth is to say so. Joh. Müller, whose *Jesus* he has roughly handled in a review,[4] has written to say that Barth has sent him a note in acknowledgement; Bultmann finds this puzzling and asks for clarification.]

[1]I.e., before Barth moves to Münster (in October).

[2]The two children are Antje (7) and Gesine (5). The third daughter, Heilke (1½), had stayed at home with her grandmother.

[3]Benedicte Henke, Göttingen.

[4]J. Müller, "Jesus, wie ich ihn sehe," *Grüne Blätter*, 27 (1925), 1–96 (later published as a book). For Bultmann's review, cf. Appendix, No. 7, and for Müller's letter Appendix, No. 8.

29

Marburg, 23 September 1925

[Bultmann hopes that things have gone well in Münster.[1] He is working on his reply to P.[2] and will soon send a draft, though he is not hurrying. He hopes Barth will approve of it and thinks he can incorporate the theses of Thurneysen.[3] It will not be enough to correct P.'s misunderstanding of their dialectic, but they must also go into the question that he raises, that of the formation of theological concepts. He will thus draw on his essays in *ZZ.*[4] He sends personal greetings and thanks for the days in Göttingen.[5] In a postscript he says that he will send on his Mandaica.[6]]

[1]Bultmann had visited Göttingen in the middle of September.
[2]Peterson; see No. 25, nn. 6 and 7.
[3]The reference, according to a communication from Thurneysen (12 July 1970), is to an unpublished reply to Peterson, the MS of which has not been found.
[4]Cf. No. 25, n. 6.
[5]Cf. No. 28.
[6]Cf. No. 27, n. 3.

30

Göttingen, 25 September 1925

[Barth thanks Bultmann for the Mandaica[1] and the card. He, too, is wrestling with Peterson and his brilliant pamphlets, which put them all in the same corner as Herrmann.[2] He wonders if Bultmann knows in what sense Peterson is using such terms as "act," "fulfillment," and "concrete," or how he relates the antithesis of faith and mysticism in the first essay to the schematisms of the third,[3] or whether theology is identical with the talk of the church, or what is meant by the *qua jure* of revelation. He has bought a house in Münster, but the sale of their present house has fallen through. There are all kinds of rumors about his lecture on the seventh.[4] He dare not think about John and eschatology.[5]]

[1]Cf. No. 27, n. 3; No. 29.
[2]Wilhelm Herrmann (1846–1922) was Professor of Systematic Theology at Marburg from 1879 and had taught both Barth and Bultmann.
[3]The reference is to Peterson's "Der Lobgesang der Engel und der mystische Lobpreis," *ZZ*, 3 (1925), 141–153, and *Was ist Theologie*? (Bonn, 1925), a monograph which Barth describes here as the third essay.
[4]Barth's lecture at Göttingen on 7 Oct. 1925; cf. No. 25, n. 8.
[5]Barth was preparing for his winter semester lectures on John's Gospel and eschatology (Dogmatics III/7: "The Doctrine of Redemption").

31

Marburg, 19 October 1925

[Bultmann has taken longer to send his draft than he expected.[1] He has had to visit Halle for the Faculty Conference,[2] taking the chance to see Gogarten too. Meanwhile Barth has given his lecture and debated with

Peterson. Perhaps he will no longer wish to amplify or correct Bultmann's reply. Bultmann will publish it on his own responsibility, preferably in *ZZ*. Having had in view a joint answer, he has worked in Thurneysen's theses, but wonders if he should now omit or alter them.[3] He has tried to avoid personal feelings and to aim simply at clarification and the promotion of discussion, sharing with P. a common concern for the task of formulating authentic theological concepts. He will still welcome Barth's comments but asks for prompt return of the draft, since he wants it for an evening discussion of P.'s work[4] at the beginning of the semester.]

[1]Cf. No. 25, n. 7. With reference to this essay Barth wrote to Georg Merz on 25 Oct. 1925 (*Briefwechsel*, p. 220) that it was a fine piece and should appear with Barth's own reply, which it supplements, since the double answer should and would "act like a fiery cross."

[2]Bultmann participated in this conference (7–8 Oct. 1925) as Dean of the Faculty of Theology at Marburg.

[3]Cf. No. 29, n. 3. It is plain that the original idea had been a joint reply to Peterson, but Barth had assumed from Bultmann's card of 23 Sept. 1925 that the latter now wanted to act on his own (cf. Barth's letter to Thurneysen, 4 Oct. 1925, *Briefwechsel*, pp. 215f.).

[4]E. Peterson, *Was ist Theologie?* (Bonn, 1925).

32

Münster, 26 October 1925

[Barth tells Bultmann that his MS arrived half an hour before he left to give the lecture against Peterson at Elberfeld.[1] He has now been in the clerical and Anabaptist nest of Münster for three days. He is tired of buying and selling houses and will soon have enough experience to become a realtor himself. His essay on Peterson draws a wider circle than Bultmann's but has the same center. Merz asked for it immediately after 7 October and it is being printed. Barth has sent him Bultmann's too and would like them to come out in a single booklet or in the same edition of *ZZ*.[2] Merz will probably choose the latter course.[3] Kaiser[4] favors booklets and there will be a wide distribution in *ZZ*. The theses of Thurneysen should be retained (with acknowledgements). Loew has read the essay in Remscheid and likes it, saying that the man with the violet socks[5] will have difficulty evading our cross-examination. Barth, too, has handled him mildly, but with an opening blast against those (he has in mind Stange,[6] Hirsch, Althaus,[7] etc.) who think he can be dismissed with silence or laughter. Barth has remained good friends with him but has gained the impression that *W.i.Th.?*[8] has its source in a mad whim and in spite of the seriousness of the problem is culpably superficial. In a postscript he expresses interest in how Gogarten will fare with his first steps on the slippery academic slope.[9] He also tells Bultmann he will refrain from sending[10] letters written only on one side now that he has learned what Bultmann does with such missives.[11]]

[1]Cf. Barth's detailed description of this trip in his letter to Thurneysen on 25 Oct. 1925 (*Briefwechsel*, pp. 218–220).

[2]*Zwischen den Zeiten.*

[3]K. Barth, "Kirche und Theologie," *ZZ*, 4 (1926), 18–40 (Ges. Vorträge, II, 302–328); R. Bultmann, "Die Frage der 'dialektischen' Theologie," *ZZ*, 4 (1926), 40–59 (*Anfänge*, II, 72–92).

[4]Chr. Kaiser Verlag, Munich.

[5]Erik Peterson.

[6]Carl Stange (1870–1959), Professor of Systematic Theology at Göttingen.

[7]Paul Althaus (1888–1966) taught systematic theology at Göttingen in 1914 and became Professor of Systematic Theology at Rostock in 1919 and at Erlangen in 1925.

[8]*Was ist Theologie?*

[9]Friedrich Gogarten began to teach systematic theology at Jena in 1925.

[10]In the MS Barth here replaced an original *schreiben* by *schicken.*

[11]Bultmann used the blank sides for notes for lectures, addresses, and essays.

33

Münster, 3 December 1925

[Barth notes with satisfaction that Bultmann will be in Danzig in January.[1] He speaks well of Bishop Kalweit.[2] He hopes to meet Bultmann in Hanover or Berlin[3] and to shorten the rest of the journey with some pipes of tobacco. Negotiations about housing are still not settled. He is exegeting John but has so far reached only v. 15. He is noting Mandaean parallels, but with little profit, since the text is for him more remarkable than anything that stands behind it. The essays in reply to Peterson will soon be published together.[4] He has added to his own a note that they arose independently and had not been compared.[5]]

[1]This was for a continuation course for pastors and teachers of religion (4–8 Jan. 1926, see Appendix, No. 9) directed the first two days by General Superintendent Kalweit. Barth lectured on Phil. 3 and Bultmann on the significance of NT eschatology. Other lecturers were Heinrich Rendtorff of Leipzig (on the church, baptism, and confirmation) and Hans Schmidt of Giessen (on the New Year Festival in the Psalms, the question of alcohol in the OT, and the problem of suffering in the OT).

[2]Bultmann underlined the reference to Kalweit.

[3]According to an oral communication from Bultmann (7 May 1970) they met in Berlin and had a meal before proceeding together to Danzig.

[4]Cf. *ZZ*, 4 (1926), 18–40 and 40–59; see No. 25, nn. 7 and 8.

[5]ZZ, 4 (1926), 18, n. 2: "The work by Bultmann which follows arose independently of this essay and was not compared with it prior to printing."

34

Marburg, 10 December 1925

[Bultmann writes in haste to say that he has accepted the Danzig engagement for both of them.[1] He suggests Berlin as the place to meet. He has to rush off to a seminar where Dr. Krüger[2] will be speaking on Barth's exegesis of Rom. 5:12–21[3] and his relation to transcendental philosophy.]

[1]After receiving the letter of 2 Dec. 1925 from Pastor Schneider of Posen (see Appendix, No. 10) Barth seems to have told Bultmann he would accept the invitation to Danzig in a letter that has not so far been found.

[2]Gerhard Krüger (b. 1902) was a student and friend of Bultmann's who taught philosophy in Marburg from 1929 and became Professor of Philosophy in Münster in 1940, Tübingen in 1946, and Frankfurt in 1952, then retiring to Heidelberg.

[3]Krüger's criticisms of Barth's exegesis were published one and one-half years later under the title "Dialektische Methode und theologische Exegese. Logische Bemerkungen zu Barths 'Römerbrief,' " *ZZ*, 5 (1927), 116–157.

35

Marburg, 24 December 1925

[Bultmann intends[1] to go to Berlin on the third and then take the night train to Danzig at 10:45. He would like Barth's approval so that he can reserve two sleeping berths. This will make the journey less tiring. He proposes that they should skip Rendtorff's lectures on the morning of the fourth[2] and visit the castle at Marienburg instead. In[3] Danzig he will be staying with a cousin.[4] He will be coming by way of Göttingen (where Barth is now spending Christmas with his family) and should be there at 12:28, then in Berlin at 6:55. Antje has the measles and he expects the other two will soon follow,[5] but there is no reason for anxiety.]

[1]This word is illegible in the MS.

[2]Cf. No. 33, n. 1.

[3]Illegible in the MS.

[4]Karl Ramsauer.

[5]Gesine and Heilke.

36

Marburg, 29 December 1925

[As Barth has pointed out, they do not need to travel to Danzig until the fourth. Bultmann will arrive in Göttingen at 12:23 and they will go together to Berlin, arriving at 6:59. They will travel by sleeper to Marienburg, first having a meal in Berlin,[1] then leaving at 10:45. They can spend some time in Marienburg. Bultmann will bring with him the proofs of his review of Barth's I Corinthians.[2]]

[1]Cf. No. 33, n. 3. This card was in answer to a communication of Barth's that has not been found so far.

[2]R. Bultmann, "Karl Barth 'Die Auferstehung der Toten,' " *ThBl,* 5 (1926), 1–14 (*GuV,* I, 38–64).

37

Marburg, 10 December 1926

Dear Mr. Barth,

I was genuinely sorry to hear of your accident while on vacation.[1] Mr. Bröking[2] has told me that you are now better and conveyed your greetings to me. I ought to have thanked you long since for your work on the "Christian life."[3] I like it better than you did my *Jesus,*[4] as I heard from Pastor Haake.[5] The more I agree in pretty well all essentials with what you say (at least I think I do) the more I am concerned finally and definitively to get at the difference which comes out in every possible detail. Perhaps it will help us to reach an understanding if I briefly examine your statement that you do not understand what I am after in my book.

I thought the purpose was clear even though I intentionally did not discuss the problem in the book. You cannot ascribe to me the misunderstanding that with my exposition I thought I could show what the Christian proclamation of Jesus ought to be. Instead my book has (among other things) a definite purpose in tackling the problem which can be described as that of the relation of John to the synoptists or as the question how it is to be understood (not causally explained) that the proclaimer Jesus becomes the proclaimed Jesus Christ. I have the impression that you do not see this problem, which to me seems to be a true theological problem, indeed, *the* problem of NT theology in general. (It can also be called the problem of the incognito of Christ.)

The problem arises very simply out of an exegesis of John itself. Here Jesus is presented as the revealer who—reveals what? *That he is* the revealer. Now do not think that my point is that he should reveal *something,* that his "Word" should have an intelligible content which one can understand, know, and possess, so that one will no longer need him as the revealer. Not at all; one does not go to Jesus as a teacher or hierophant *for something;* one comes to *him.* Nevertheless the Word became *flesh,* a *someone* who has said *something.* The synoptists tell us about this someone and something. It makes no difference here that in Christian proclamation the synoptics are heard as *Christian* talk about Jesus, or, historically formulated, are seen in a Pauline or Johannine light. They still do not talk about Jesus in the same way as Paul and John. They do not simply say, as John does, that Jesus presented himself as the revealer; instead they tell us *how* he did so, which John does *not.* This fact seems to be brought out most clearly, and the problem presented most pressingly, when with the help of historical criticism one tries to show *what,* then, Jesus said. The result may be formulated as follows: Jesus appears as a prophet. This settles the incognito question. In Kierkegaard it seems that the incognito is an x, and it is not clear why what is said about Jesus cannot be said about any individual that God has very arbitrarily and randomly chosen as one in whom to conceal the Logos. But to ask how far the incognito can go is forbidden, not only in the sense (Kierkegaard, too, sees *this*) that the incognito should not be a limited one in which clever people can see something (e.g., in which the messianic consciousness of the historical Jesus may be seen, as Brunner[6] would have it) but also in the sense that one should not speculate whether the incarnate one might have been different, e.g., might have been a woman, because we do in fact have a specific person *whom* God has chosen. What can and must be asked, however, is what we are saying when we say that *this* person is chosen. And as I see it the answer must be that the relationship of law and gospel is evident here. (Does not the "law" come out quite correctly in my presentation?) I naturally realize that Kierkegaard is fundamentally right when in the *Philosophical Fragments* he says that the tradition about Jesus is adequately presented if one says that "we have believed that in such and such a year God showed himself in the lowly form of a servant, lived among us, and taught, and then died" (Diederichs, 1925, pp. 94f.). And my presentation of the proclamation of Jesus does not in the least aim to have Jesus appear as the Christ (I even allow for the possibility of showing that the historical Jesus did not regard himself as the Messiah). In fact, however, the synoptists hand down *more* than

Kierkegaard regards as necessary, and since this *more* is in fact handed down, I view it as a concern of theology to be interested in this more and to present it.

It is a pity that—for the time being at least—we cannot clarify the issue in oral give and take. I would be pleased if you could tell me what your objections are. I hope that you will be more in agreement with my review of Hirsch,[7] which will appear in *ZZ,* than you were with my book.

You will now have fully recovered, I hope. Good wishes to you and yours for Christmas. We hope that things are going well, and my wife sends sincere greetings to you all; please pass them on to the children.

Would you propose Gogarten as a successor for Wehrung?[8] I suppose that most of your colleagues will think that alongside you they should have a different and "nondialectical" person. This seems to me to be very foolish. I liked your contribution to Barathrum.[9]

Yours,
R. BULTMANN

[1]In the autumn of 1926 Barth had had a fall at the "Bergli" in Oberrieden.

[2]No information could be discovered about Bröking.

[3]K. Barth, *Vom christlichen Leben* (Munich, 1926; ET *The Christian Life,* London, 1930).

[4]R. Bultmann, *Jesus* (Berlin, 1926; ET *Jesus and His Word,* 1934).

[5]Of Varel/Oldenburg.

[6]Cf. E. Brunner, "Geschichte oder Offenbarung? Ein Wort der Entgegnung an Horst Stephan," *ZThK,* 6 (1925), 266–278, esp. 272ff.

[7]R. Bultmann, "Zur Frage der Christologie," *ZZ,* 5 (1927), 41–69 (*GuV,* I, 85–113). At the beginning of the review Bultmann says that it is a discussion rather than a review, p. 41 (85).

[8]Georg Wehrung (1880–1959) was Professor of Systematic Theology at Münster from 1920 to 1927, at Halle from 1927 to 1931, and at Tübingen after 1931.

[9]The critical column initiated for short notices, etc.; in *ThBl,* 5 (1926), 7. Bultmann probably has in mind the extract from Barth's essay in *ZZ,* 4 (1926), 385–403 ("Geschichtliche und übergeschichtliche Religion im Christentum?"), which appeared in *ThBl,* 5 (1926), 270.

38

Marburg, 6 January 1927

Dear Mr. Barth,

I do not know how to thank you better for sending your Christmas sermon[1] than by sending you my own Christmas address to the students,[2] though only as a loan, since I would like it back. If you find reading the MS too much of an imposition please return it unread. (I use few abbreviations and apart from those that are readily understandable, only *sd.* for *sondern* ["but"], *viell.* for *vielleicht* ["perhaps"], and *zus.* for *zusammen* ["together"]).

You will perhaps answer the letter I wrote before Christmas[3] when you have read my review of Hirsch in *ZZ.*[4] Since I know that I agree with you in what you say about Christmas, I do not see what your real problem is with my *Jesus.*[5] Formally you do not make it easy for readers of the *Münch. N.N.*[6] and perhaps it is not just a formality if I think that your use of "history" is not appropriate. As it seems to me, and as Gogarten desires,[7] in relation to the naturalistic science of "history," which does not really speak about history, we will have to develop genuine histor. categories (cf. Yorck in correspondence with Dilthey!).[8] There is no "history" in general (any more than there is σάρξ) but only a concrete, qualified history in which we actually stand, which we *are.* I hope that things are going well with you and that you celebrated Christmas and have begun the New Year in good health and spirits.

With sincere wishes and family greetings,

Yours,
R. BULTMANN

[1]K. Barth, "Die Fleischwerdung des Wortes," *Münchener Neueste Nachrichten* (25 December 1926).

[2]Unpublished.

[3]No. 37.

[4]Cf. No. 37, n. 7.

[5]No. 37, n. 4.

[6]*Münchener Neueste Nachrichten.*

[7]E.g., in *Ich glaube an den dreieinigen Gott. Eine Untersuchung über Glauben und Geschichte* (Jena, 1926).

[8]*Briefwechsel zwischen Wilhelm Dilthey und dem Grafen Paul Yorck von Wartenburg, 1877–1897,* ed. Sigrid von der Schulenburg (Halle, 1923).

39

Marburg, 21 April 1927

[Bultmann says that K. L. Schmidt[1] has put him in the picture regarding a possible doctorate for Thurneysen at Marburg, but already there are enough on the list for the university anniversary in August,[2] and he sees three difficulties: 1) the list cannot be enlarged; 2) *one* Swiss is enough; and 3) it is Thurneysen. He will try in six months when Otto[3] will be in India. Things might be quicker and easier in Jena, and he has asked

Schmidt to try there.[4] He finds increasing mistrust and opposition in Marburg but has a good following and enjoys the fellowship and friendship of Heidegger.[5] He is sorry to hear so seldom from Barth and fears Barth might be dropping him. In the differences between Gogarten and himself on the one side and Barth on the other he believes the old Lutheran-Calvinist opposition is still at work, but thinks that the agreement is really greater and decisive. He asks Barth not to regard him as unteachable but to write. Does he not agree with his criticism of Hirsch and objections to Herrmann?[6] He hopes, too, that he will approve of his condemnation of Bruhn in the Barathrum.[7]]

[1]Karl Ludwig Schmidt (1891–1956) was Professor of NT at Giessen in 1921, at Jena in 1925, at Bonn in 1929, and at Basel in 1935.

[2]The quatercentenary of the foundation of the Philipps University of Marburg was celebrated 29–31 July 1927.

[3]See No. 11, n. 4.

[4]The letter to Schmidt has not survived; Schmidt burned all his letters and papers (according to a communication from Franziska Zellweger-Barth, 9 June 1970).

[5]See No. 16, n. 3.

[6]For Hirsch see No. 37, n. 7; for Herrmann see *ZZ*, 5 (1927), 57ff. (*GuV*, I, 101ff.).

[7]W. Bruhn, *Vom Gott im Menschen. Ein Weg in metaphysisches Neuland* (Giessen, 1926). For Bultmann's criticism cf. *ThBl*, 6 (1927), 108. For Barth's reaction cf. his epilogue to the essay "Ludwig Feuerbach," *ZZ*, 5 (1927), 11–40 (Epilogue, 33–40).

40

Münster, 28 April 1927

Dear Mr. Bultmann,

Do not take amiss my stiffnecked silence. You do not do so, and I am really grateful for this. Look, it is simply that at the moment—and this will perhaps go on for some time—I do not see my way through all that does in fact seem to be up in the air between you, Gogarten, and me. That it is up in the air has been made much clearer to me by Gogarten's book[1] than it was by yours[2] last fall, and a visit that I paid him eight days ago in Dorndorf[3] has strengthened this impression, even though our meeting was very friendly. In some way the old controversies between the Lutherans and the Reformed, which were never settled, do cause us difficulties on both sides and will perhaps come to a head in a great explosion *within ZZ*. But for the moment, apart from all the tactical reasons which may make sense, I feel a need to work as thetically as possible and to give you and Gogarten time to develop more clearly what you are after. Later will be the time for debates if they are unavoidable. Provisionally I do not want to advance any stupid questions or objections (just as I learned little from investigations such as the one that G. Krüger devoted to me),[4] but would rather pursue my own course as you all are doing—and Gogarten so brilliantly. If we were in the same place we could clarify or expedite many things by talking face to face, and I hope the time will soon come again when we shall have the chance to do this, although the visit to Dorndorf has shown me that a personal encounter does not guarantee a real encounter. In our case spatial distance makes it necessary that (with a certain quiet confidence in a fellowship that has been proved often enough and is obviously present on the broadest lines) we should put up with one another, though in detail we cannot do this without some wrinkling of the brow on both sides. Be sure, then, that I have no intention of giving you up, even though I may be silent for so long, as I have been this winter, though not for material reasons. I am happy and grateful that you do not give me up!

Thanks for your communications regarding Thurneysen. I understand perfectly. Do you think there will be any point in approaching Karl Heim, since they are celebrating an anniversary in Tübingen this summer and they may not yet have awarded the usual wreaths?[5] I do not want to do this if in your judgment the attempt is perhaps hopeless from the start. But as you will know through K. L. Schmidt, it is a matter of finding Th.[6] a position as quickly as possible by way of a doctorate.

Please greet your family for me. All is well, at least *kata sarka,* which is no little thing when there are several children.

Yours sincerely,
KARL BARTH

I again send a festival piece (the catchy title is not mine) from the paper which has engaged me for such occasions.[7] It is questionable whether I ought to be doing this, especially as the paper is so nationalistically German! I was pleased to read the festal poem for Rade and also to see that you gave a festal address![8]

[1]See No. 38, n. 7.
[2]Bultmann's *Jesus*; see No. 37, n. 4.
[3]Gogarten was at this time pastor of Dorndorf, and also taught at Jena.
[4]See No. 34, n. 3.
[5]Karl Heim (1874–1958) was Professor of Systematic Theology at Tübingen after 1920.
[6]Thurneysen.
[7]K. Barth, "Öffne mir die Auge, dass ich sehe Wunder an deinem Gesetz," *Mitteilungen zur Förderung einer Deutschen Christlichen Studentenbewegung,* 15 Jan. 1927.
[8]Cf. *An die Freunde,* No. 86 (1927), p. 994. This poem was written by a certain Jahnow for the fortieth anniversary of *CW* on 4 Apr. 1927 and printed in *An die Freunde,* No. 86, cols. 997f.

41

Marburg, 1 May 1927

[Bultmann thinks Thurneysen could be suggested at Tübingen, but not for the anniversary. He will see what he can do if he hears that Schmidt can do nothing soon at Jena. He thanks Barth for the rest of his letter and agrees to proceed as he suggests. But he would welcome a personal meeting and asks about the summer. He himself will be at home working while his wife takes the children to Langeoog for six weeks at the beginning of August. Can Barth come for a few days, perhaps on his way to Switzerland? In October he will be going to Oldenburg for fourteen days and might perhaps go by way of Münster. He wishes Barth a good semester and notes that they will be lecturing on the same theme.[1]]

[1]During the summer semester of 1927 Barth gave a course on Galatians (using the commentaries of Luther and Calvin) (two hrs.) and Bultmann gave a course on Luther's commentary on Galatians (two hrs.).

42

Marburg, 26 May 1927

[Bultmann has just read the *Berneuchener Buch* and thinks Barth should write a reply, since in the preface he is given some responsibility for its contents.[1] He recognizes the good will of the authors and many good things, but thinks the book as a whole is poor stuff, contains too much declamation, has no feeling at all for the Reformation, and uses the speculations of Tillich so irresponsibly that it ought to be publicly refuted by Barth. He quotes from Luther's 1516–1517 Galatians[2] the statement that Christ's teaching in the gospel gives us a clearer knowledge of the law and a better knowledge of sin so that we may seek grace the more ardently. He wonders if this remarkable thought is one that Luther often championed or developed more broadly. He is to speak in Zurich on 13 and 14 June.[3]]

[1]*Das Berneuchener Buch. Vom Anspruch des Evangeliums auf die Kirchen der Reformation*, ed. by the Berneuchener Conference (Hamburg, 1926). On the basis of preparatory work by Wilhelm Thomas, the book was given its final form by Ludwig Heitmann, Karl Bernhard Ritter, and Wilhelm Stählin. The preface pays tribute especially to Paul Althaus, Karl Barth, Friedrich Brunstäd, and Paul Tillich.

[2]Ed. H. von Schubert (Heidelberg, 1918).

[3]The theme of this unpublished address was "Die theologische Bedeutung der historisch-kritischen Arbeit am NT."

43

Münster, 24 July 1927

[With apologies and reliance upon Bultmann's good will Barth has at last read and is returning his Christmas address.[1] He can find no objection to it; rather, more positively, he has read it with unreserved joy and gratitude. He hopes it might be used in the Christmas number of *ZZ*. He himself plans to publish there a Christmas sermon by Calvin[2] and he thinks the two voices might profitably be heard together. He is writing to Georg Merz[3] and will suggest this to him. Bultmann should thus keep hold of the MS if he has not already made other arrangements for it.[4] He does not envy Bultmann the centenary celebrations.[5] He is more tired than usual and is looking forward to a vacation in Wernigerode. The question of Wehrung's[6] successor, or rather of his own, since he has succeeded Wehrung, has not yet been settled. The faculty wants to "supplement" Barth with a nondialectical Lutheran, and after Elert's refusal those in view are Schmidt of Halle, Schmidt-Japing, and Heinzelmann,[7] any of whom he would welcome.]

[1]Cf. No. 38.

[2]K. Barth, trans., "Predigt über die Geburt Jesu Christi von Johannes Calvin," *ZZ*, 5 (1927), 465–478.

[3]Editor of *ZZ*.

[4]It was not in fact published.

[5]See No. 39, n. 2.

[6]See No. 37, n. 8.

[7]Werner Elert (1885–1954) was Professor of Historical and Systematic Theology at Erlangen after 1923. Friedrich Wilhelm Schmidt (1893–1945) taught at Halle and was later called to Münster. Johann Wilhelm Schmidt-Japing (1886–1960) taught in Bonn. Gerhard Heinzelmann (1884–1951) was a professor in Basel.

44

Marburg, 27 September 1927

[Bultmann invites Barth to address the Theological Society on the church (in Protestantism).[1] The aim is not just to have a celebrity; this will be part of a series on the church. K. L. Schmidt has spoken on the church in early Christianity; there will be lectures on the Orthodox, Roman Catholic, Reformation, and Enlightenment views; finally he hopes Barth will speak about the Protestant concept of the church. Bultmann thinks that only external reasons should lead to a refusal, and he would be personally very glad if Barth would come. He is pleased that Barth turned Bern down.[2] He is looking forward to *Dogmatics*, I.[3] Merz could not use his Christmas address this year.[4] For 1928 he has sent an essay on eschatology in John's Gospel, the revised third part of his Danzig lectures of 1926.[5] He can tell Barth some amusing things about the recent theological conference.[6] He wishes him and his a good Advent season.]

[1]See Appendix, No. 11.

[2]On 24 Oct. 1927 Barth had received by telegram an invitation to join the Faculty of Theology at Bern. He laid down some conditions (13 Nov. 1927) which Bern would not accept, mainly for theological reasons. He thus rejected the call.

[3]K. Barth, *Die christliche Dogmatik im Entwurf*, I: *Die Lehre vom Worte Gottes. Prolegomena zur christlichen Dogmatik* (Munich, 1927). It may be gathered from Bultmann's letter of 8 June 1928 (No. 47) that Barth had sent him a copy in 1927. A projected second edition was never published, so that Bultmann's comments, which have never been found, could not be considered. Five years later, with different theological presuppositions, Barth published *CD* I, 1 (Munich, 1932).

[4]See Nos. 38, 43.

[5]R. Bultmann, "Die Eschatologie des Johannes-Evangeliums," *ZZ*, 6 (1928), 4–22 (*GuV*, I, 134–152). On the Danzig courses see No. 34, n. 1, and cf. *ThBl*, 6 (1926), 50.

[6]At the first German Evangelical Conference at Eisenach (18–21 Oct. 1927) Bultmann read a paper (21 Oct.) on "Die dialektische Theologie und das NT"; cf. *Deutsche Theologie I. Bericht über den ersten Theologentag zu Eisenach (Herbst, 1927)*, ed. A. Titius (Göttingen, 1928), pp. 98–107. The paper was published under the title "Die Bedeutung der 'dialektischen Theologie' für die ntliche Wissenschaft," *ThBl*, 7 (1928), 57–67 (*GuV*, I, 114–133).

45

Münster, 24 May 1928[1]

Dear Colleague,

I have heard from Munich[2] that you have sent there a letter which is very critical of my *Prolegomena*.[3] Why did you not write such a letter directly to me? I know that because of my own dilatoriness in relation to Marburg I did not deserve it. But if I do not care in the least what most people say about my book, if I simply laughed obstinately at even the good passages in the treatment in the last issue of *Theol. Lit. Zeitung*,[4] it is for me so important that I should know *your* precise reservations, even though I suspect their location, that I would ask you to repay my evil—my silence and my refusal to let myself be catechized publicly at the place of correct concepts[5]—with good, and tomorrow, when the Whitsuntide vacation begins, not to deny me a little exposition of your most important charges.

With sincere greetings to your wife (my own would join me in this but is spending the whole summer in Switzerland),

Yours,
Karl Barth

[1]The date of the postmark.
[2]From Georg Merz, editor of *ZZ.*
[3]See No. 44, n. 3.
[4]O. Ritschl had reviewed Barth's book in *ThLZ,* 53 (1928), 217–228.
[5]Cf. Nos. 29, 31, 46, 47, 48.

46

Marburg, 26 May 1928

Dear Mr. Barth,

News at second hand should always be tested critically to prevent misunderstanding. The situation is that on 28 April I wrote a letter to you[1] and also a whole set of pages of critical comments on your *Dogmatics,* which were to accompany the letter as soon as they could be typed. In the meantime the number of pages increased, but the lady whom I wanted for the job became sick and then had too much to do. I ask you, then, to be patient a little longer. Naturally I wrote my critical comments from the very first for you and me. For you—not in order to "catechize" you from the place of correct concepts (I am not sure why you construe the invitations to Marburg in this way; they had their source in a sincere desire to learn from you in debate; was it really so bad the previous time in our seminar?), but 1) as thanks for the gift; 2) to learn better from you; 3) to make myself better understood by you; and 4) to warn you, indeed, to implore you not to ignore several questions (including that of correct concepts) any longer, since this can only do harm to the cause which—I am convinced—is our common one. For the rest, I have not yet sent my critical comments to Munich; I have simply put in a letter to Merz something of what you will soon have before you in much greater compass. My wife thanks you for your greetings and reciprocates them.

With sincere greetings and a request that you think of Marburg more kindly,

Yours,
RUDOLF BULTMANN

[1]This letter was not sent.

47

Marburg, 8 June 1928

Dear Mr. Barth,

Here is the first part of my critical comments on your *Dogmatics.* In the meantime my letter of 28 April[1] has become too outdated to send. From it I repeat that I wrote my comments to *thank* you, as *critical* thanks. I agree that there is now no real dogmatics among us, and I view your book as a beginning of true dogmatic work. You will not expect me to enumerate all my points of agreement with it, especially your understanding of the task and your orientation of dogmatics to preaching. But I have many doubts about the execution. The criticism (*yours*) often outweighs the positive presentation. Even the criticism should, of course, be more comprehensive. I am sorry that you do not enter into critical debate with your friends, especially Gogarten. But I understand that you have worked out this first "outline" without regard for companions of whom you are obviously not sure. In a second edition you should not hesitate to take issue with Gogarten.

What is more important is that you have failed to enter into (latent but radical) debate with modern philosophy and naively adopted the older ontology from patristic and scholastic dogmatics. What you say (and often only *want* to say) is beyond your terminology, and a lack of clarity and sobriety is frequently the result. You have a sovereign scorn for modern work in philosophy, especially phenomenology. What point is there in saying occasionally that the dogmatician must also be oriented to philosophical work if the presentation finds no place for this orientation, and indeed if pp. 403–407 show that philosophical work is not taken seriously, as standing under responsibility to the question of truth? It seems to me that you are guided by a concern that theology should achieve emancipation from philosophy. You try to achieve this by ignoring philosophy. The price you pay for this is that of falling prey to an outdated philosophy. For because faith is the faith of a *believer,* i.e., an existent person (I can also say: because the justified person is the *sinner*), dogmatics can speak only in existential-ontological terms; but these (springing out of an original understanding of existence) are worked out by philosophy. Now if the critical work of philosophy, which is ongoing, and which is being done today with renewed awareness and radicalness, is ignored, the result is that dogmatics works with the uncritically adopted concepts of an older ontology. This is what happens in your case. It is right that dogmatics should have nothing whatever to do with a philosophy insofar as this is systematic; but it is also right that it must learn from a philosophy that is a critical (ontological) inquiry. For only then does it remain free and make use of philosophy as a helper of theology; otherwise *it* becomes the maid and philosophy the mistress. There is no alternative; it must be either maid or mistress. Your planned ignoring of philosophy is only apparent. Naturally lordship or servanthood applies to the forming of concepts. But if dogmatics is to be a science, it cannot avoid the question of appropriate concepts.

Your attacks on Wobbermin, Schaeder,[2] etc., are as relevant as they are amusing. But are you not in some sense fighting ghosts? Is not our real opponent to be found elsewhere today? The Barathrum is really enough for Wobbermin and Schaeder, etc. But Tillich, the Berneuchener, the Gundolfians, and the value philosophy of Max Scheler (from which there are, of course, many positive things to learn)—here are the real enemies today (though they are always the same in essence). In my view a dogmatics must have the coming generation in mind in relation to both pastors and congregations. What are the thoughts that live today behind our educated people and in our papers? Must theology always arrive after the event?

Please do not take my strenuous appeal amiss, nor the apodictic form in which my individual observations are couched. This is partly due to my temperament and partly in the interests of brevity. I need hardly stress that I have learned, and learn, and hope still to learn many decisive things from you. In relation to you I am the recipient, the student, albeit a critical student. More important than the criticisms are the thanks that I owe you, and the criticisms themselves have their source in the conviction that I am at one with you in the concern that you represent in your *Dogmatics*.

With my wife I send sincere greetings,

Yours,
RUDOLF BULTMANN

[1]See No. 46, n. 1. On Bultmann's comments, which were not found in Barth's papers, see No. 44, n. 3. On 12 June Barth wrote to his wife Nelly that Bultmann had

sent him "a whole mass of papers with comments on my Dogmatics which amount to this: I am doing the right thing but do not have the right concepts with which to do it."

[2]See *Die christliche Dogmatik,* passim.

48

Münster, 12 June 1928

Dear Mr. Bultmann,

It was a solemn moment when yesterday I opened your letter and the other document with your comments, fully aware that for the first time I would be reading some objections to my *Dogmatics* that I could not avoid considering very seriously. My sincere thanks for the great trouble that you have taken and that must not be for nothing. I will ponder the details a third and fourth time if a second edition of the volume is called for.[1] I see well enough that you draw attention to points where revision is needed and is possible on the basis of my presuppositions. But for all my willingness in details—apart from the fact that your detailed proposals unmistakably apply to the whole—I doubt whether it will be possible even to come close to satisfying you, because what you want of me finally amounts to no more and no less than an alteration of the intellectual habitus with which I approach such work, and involves ultimately the wish that the wild and crooked tree that I appear to be in your eyes (this is how I suddenly came to see myself in the light of your criticisms) should be given a more pleasing shape by an upright pole placed alongside it. It could well be that with the basic objections that you make, especially in your letter, you are simply touching on my *limitations,* i.e., demanding of me things which it may be right to demand of me but which I cannot achieve with the natural bent of my working potential. I simply say that this could be, and you must reckon with the fact that it may finally be so if you are not to become cross with me.

For example, perhaps it is simply not in me to debate with Gogarten. Possibly this would simply heap one misfortune upon another. I see and understand that he is ultimately on the same side, although there are many things that I do not see and understand clearly. I am glad that he is there, for I can see that he can speak to people to whom I have no access, and many times I have received from him a catchword that says something to me and helps me. For the rest he is quite a different creature of the good Lord from what I am; I would find it hard to deny that he is not congenial to me *kata sarka,* since he plans his essays and books in a way that would be intolerable to me, and above all I find in and behind him everything that is abhorrent to me in Luther. But I do not think I have any commission to bring all this to light in a debate, the less so as things seem to be much the same in his attitude to me. One day a young student seeking the licentiate may write a fine work about the kinship and differences between us, but so far the thing for both of us seems to be that each should take friendly note and knowledge of the work of the other but not be disturbed by it.

It might also be that what you want of me in relation to philosophy is not for me. I will not defend in principle what you call my ignoring of philosophical work. It is possible that someone else can do better in achieving a sober terminology than I can. But the fact is that no philosophy influences me in the way that Heidegger's obviously does you, so that I am compelled to measure my thinking by your standard and to give to it the appropriate soberness. It is also a fact that I have come to abhor profoundly the spectacle of theology constantly trying above all to adjust to the philosophy of its age, thereby neglecting its own theme. It is also a fact that the defect of older theology was never clear to me at the point where Harnack's *Dogmengeschichte* lays its finger, that the Platonism or Aristotelianism of the orthodox was not a hindrance to my (shall we say apparently) perceiving what was at issue and therefore to adopting the older terminology into my own vocabulary without identifying myself with the underlying philosophy. And it is finally a fact that in and spite of all the abandon with which you obviously see me operating I have been understood very well (for caution's sake shall we again say: apparently) by more than one professional philosopher[2] in what I was saying or trying to say, so that the question arises whether it is true that I have buckled on the armor of a particular philosophy of the schools. In *Romans* and now in the *Dogmatics* my path has in fact been that, with reference to the matters that I saw to be at issue in the Bible and the history of dogma, I have reached out on the right hand and the left for terms or concepts that I found to be the most appropriate without considering the problem of a preestablished harmony between the matter itself and these particular concepts, because my hands were already full in trying to *say* something very specific. And if, as I admit, there is something gypsylike about this procedure—so that I have never made a principle of it or recommended it for imitation—the anxious question is whether I can be successfully domesticated or whether it would be worthwhile for me to spend the rest of my life acquiring an unambiguous terminology from the phenomenologists. What of *importance* would I really be gaining thereby? When the essay of your student Krüger[3] was published last summer, I was inclined to view the whole art as unrewarding, so little did his academic expertise seem to produce a better exposition of Rom. 5:12f. I admit that your criticism of my *Dogmatics* sheds some light, but again I do not see that insofar as the relevant passages are weak they are so only because I do not have the correct concepts and not because I have not achieved a true perception, so that—no matter whether in these or any other concepts—I cannot say what ought to be said. I understand it perfectly if to you, pressed by your own particular concern, this seems to be the confession of a terrible dilettantism. I do not deny that your concern is justified, and therefore I must seem to be a dilettante from your particular standpoint. But Gogarten seems to be a dilettante to me as soon as he ventures even a single step out of the narrow house of his conceptuality and purports to be an expositor, e.g., of the Apostles' Creed.[4] My own concern is to hear at any rate the voice of the church and the Bible, and to let this voice be heard, even if in so doing, for want of anything better, I have to think somewhat in Aristotelian terms. Too academic a terminology would stand in my way, as it undoubtedly hampers Gogarten, in his final chapters,[5] from hearing and causing to be heard anything more than *his* belief in the triune God. This, mark you, is where I stand, and the anxious question is whether I am to be dislodged in the way you desire or whether, so long as I do not do too much harm, you will tolerate me in the admitted weakness of what I am and am not.

I would have to reply along similar lines in relation to Scheler, the Gundolfians, etc. Will you and Gogarten please make it your task to deal with such people? So far as I can see among students and at pastors' conferences and in the church press, Schaeder, Wobbermin, etc., are unfortunately far from being ghosts.

Please do not take all this as wicked obstinacy and impenitence. I realize how fine it would be for me if I understood the craft that with such admiration I see you practising, and how useful it would be if I could debate with Gogarten—but it might be that the value of your "appeal" is that it brings to light limitations which I may not be able to overcome. All the same, it is a real pity that your criticism is not a public one, so that the question might be put equally to all to whom it applies. I now anxiously await the second section of your comments.

With sincere greetings to you and yours (my wife is spending the whole summer in Switzerland),

Yours,
KARL BARTH

[1]No second edition was published.

[2]Barth originally wrote "in what I was trying to say" after "philosopher," but then

changed the order. (In the German text "in what I was saying or trying to say" now comes after the verb *verstanden worden bin.*)

[3]See No. 34, n. 3.

[4]Cf. F. Gogarten, *Ich glaube an den dreieinigen Gott. Eine Untersuchung über Glauben und Geschichte* (Jena, 1926).

[5]Ibid.

49

Marburg, 24 June 1928

Dear Mr. Barth,

Sincere thanks for your letter. Unfortunately I must ask you to wait a little for the continuation of my comments (there is no hurry), since I have been delayed by my wife's sickness and other things. Your letter made me above all very sorry again that we so seldom see each other. An oral meeting would be much more fruitful. Your brother Peter[1] delighted me recently with his visit, unfortunately too short.

Yours sincerely,
RUDOLF BULTMANN

[1]Peter Barth (1888–1940), minister of Laupen in 1912, and of Madiswil (Bern canton) in 1918, was a son-in-law of Martin Rade (Marburg) and editor of Calvin's *Opera selecta.*

50

Marburg, 22 July 1928

[Bultmann is sorry for the delay in sending his further comments in view of the review of M. Müller in *ThBl.*[1] He asks Barth not to be vexed by this review. As he has learned from Gogarten, Müller has switched his allegiance back to Grisebach,[2] so Barth must not see Gogarten behind the review. He has considered publishing his comments, since he has in view *positive* criticism, but would have to edit them to give them more of the character of friendly debate. But he will do this only with Barth's permission and asks for his reaction. He wishes Barth's desire for "critical agreement" were as great as his own. He has just received a letter from Gogarten that calls Müller's review a poor piece of work.[3]]

[1]H. M. Müller, "Credo, ut intelligam. Kritische Bemerkungen zu Karl Barths Dogmatik," *ThBl*, 7 (1928), 167–176; cf. Barth's *CD* I, 1, pp. 224, 230ff.

[2]Eberhard Grisebach (1880–1945) taught philosophy at Jena after 1913. His main work, *Gegenwart. Eine kritische Ethik*, came out in 1928. For his debate with Brunner cf. E. Brunner, "Grisebachs Angriff auf die Theologie," *ZZ*, 6 (1928), 219–232, and his reply, "Brunners Verteidigung der Theologie, " *ZZ*, 7 (1929), 90–106; cf. Barth, *CD* I, 1, pp. 13, 184.

[3]This letter has not been found.

51

Münster, 24 July 1928

Dear Mr. Bultmann,

Sincere thanks for your lines. Directly after reading Müller's review I wrote Gogarten,[1] yet not for a moment with the idea, oddly espoused by Peterson, that Gogarten was behind what was revealed by the poisonous nature of the relevant section of the essay,[2] but to ask him for information about this promising young man. There is something clever in this work as in most of his that I have read, but as a whole it is a youthful effort comparable to the scratching of one's name on a lookout tower or the like. Thus I am not really vexed but simply surprised to note that, having no sooner been compared to Flacius Illyricus, I am found to be "principially catholic" and neo-Protestant. But all this must take its course.

There is something in your charge that I have no great desire for critical understanding. So then—and I greatly desire this—you must direct your public review more to the people than to me, for I cannot promise with a good conscience that I will be brought into debate by it. It is connected with the constitutional faults that I mentioned last time that often I simply cannot enter into discussions because I am otherwise occupied at the time and can meet the relevant objections in a promising way only at a later stage. Often an objection has been indirectly removed by what might be said later without any connection to it and often it has been silently withdrawn later by its author. You must not think that I do not hear what you are saying—this summer Marburg leaves me breathless with the increasing number of students from you, including the great-grandson of old Hase[3] and cheerful Gretel Herrmann[4] with the bobbed hair. All things sink in eventually and will *perhaps* bear fruit sixtyfold or a hundredfold if I can make anything of them. But my processes of assimilation are longer than they should normally be, and I am grateful to anyone who does not take offence at me for this reason. Perhaps it is connected with what the good H. M. Müller calls my catholicity that I feel so helpless against the Marburg method of turning everything on its head and leaving it standing there, that I cannot venture on certain either/ors, cannot accept the prohibition of certain aspects, cannot at once take any of my various irons out of the fire, no matter how much someone may at the moment have against me from his *one* standpoint. Yet it is still true that I would welcome it if you would publish your objections. For how can I fail to approve if everything, yes, everything that can be said by perceptive people by way of correction or opposition or perhaps refutation is in turn said to everybody. At issue is the matter itself and the public teaching of the church in the broadest sense, and whether I can and will reply is secondary. In this sense even Müller's essay—incalculably—is welcome to me; something came "out of it" which *had to* come, if only the hint of the *possibility* of viewing my "catholicity" from a higher standpoint, and understanding it as a stage, and seeing all our zeal on the same level as that of revolutionary generals in China. From a heavenly standpoint this is undoubtedly how things are even though H. M. Müller himself has not supposedly spoken from heaven.

Where are you spending the vacation? And how is your wife doing?

With sincere greetings,

Yours truly,
KARL BARTH

[1]See No. 50, n. 1. For Barth's letter to Gogarten see Appendix, No. 12.

[2]For Müller's review see No. 50, n. 1. Erik Peterson told Barth in a letter (1 July 1928) that he did not like the review and thought that "if Gogarten has anything against you he should say it himself and not send this young man to the front. The level of this *recensio* is no different from that of O. Ritschl. If there is opportunity, I will support you. I do not like the rigidity of Gogarten and Grisebach."

[3]Hans Christoph von Hase (b. 1907), great-grandson of the historian Karl August von Hase and cousin of Dietrich Bonhoeffer, spent the summer semester of 1925 studying chemistry and physics at Göttingen, but under Barth's influence switched to theology. He was with Bultmann in Marburg from the summer semester of 1927 to the winter semester of 1927–28, then went to Barth in Münster for the summer semester of 1928. It was Hase's father who introduced Bonhoeffer to Barth's theology. Hase stated in a letter to the editor of this volume (22 May 1970) that for financial reasons he had to return to Berlin in 1925 and spent much time with Bonhoeffer discussing Barth, but Bonhoeffer had first learned about Barth through his father in Waldau; his father had read the second edition of *Romans* in 1922 or 1923, and was fascinated by it, though not to the point of total agreement. Since it was at this period that Bonhoeffer opted for theology, Hase was sure that his father had discussed Barth with him. Bonhoeffer's biographer, Eberhard Bethge, does not think, however, that Bonhoeffer came to know Barth until 1924–25 (letter to the editor, 15 June 1970; cf. *Dietrich Bonhoeffer. Theologe, Christ, Zeitgenosse* [Munich, 1970], pp. 102f.). Hase's letters to his cousin from Marburg in 1927–28 were important in introducing the latter to Bultmann's theology and giving him personal insights, e.g., into Bultmann's enthusiasm for Kierkegaard and Luther's Galatians, the influence of Heidegger, and the significance of the slogans "faith" and "existence." Hase thought that when he returned to Barth in 1928 he probably got on

Barth's nerves by breaking into his solid biblical theology with Marburg concepts, but Barth preserved his good humor and did not take it amiss. It is surprising that there is only posthumous reference to Bonhoeffer in the Barth-Bultmann letters, even though Barth and Bonhoeffer knew each other personally after 1931, and all three were prominent in the church conflict.

[4]Gertrud Herrmann studied theology at Marburg in the winter semester of 1927–28, at Münster in the summer semester of 1928, and then at Marburg again in the winter semester of 1928–29.

52

Marburg, 9 December 1928

[Bultmann writes about the possible transfer of Lieb[1] to Marburg as a tutor in church history. He hopes this will work out since he values Lieb highly. He has written out further comments on the *Dogmatics* during the summer, and Erna Schlier (née Haas)[2] will type them. But he has made his essential points in the material already sent.[3] He is disappointed that Rade is so unteachable, having imagined that his reply to Rade's essay on the venture of faith[4] would clarify matters. He congratulates Barth on not having to lecture the next semester.]

[1]Fritz Lieb (1892–1970) taught systematic theology at Münster after 1924. The transfer to Marburg fell through, but he became a professor at Bonn, was deposed in 1933, emigrated to Paris in 1936, and was a professor at Basel from 1936 to 1962 (with a brief interruption).

[2]See No. 16, n. 2.

[3]See Nos. 44ff.

[4]M. Rade, "Wagnis des Glaubens," *CW*, 42 (1928), 545f.; Bultmann's response was "Der Glaube als Wagnis," *CW*, 42 (1928), 1008–1010; G. Wobbermin replied to Bultmann with "Wagnis im Glauben," *CW*, 42 (1928), 1188f. Bultmann's reference presupposes a prior letter from Barth which must also have made a plea on Lieb's behalf, but which has not so far been discovered.

53

Marburg, 7 March 1929

[Bultmann has learned from Török[1] of Hungary that Barth will soon be going to Switzerland and wonders if he will call in at Marburg and stay as long as possible. If he wants to come incognito Bultmann will not tell anyone. But it is an urgent necessity that they should see one another.]

[1]István Török (b. 1904) studied with Barth and after 1930 taught systematic theology at various schools in Hungary. He wrote (in Hungarian) a book called *The Beginnings of the Theology of Karl Barth* (Pápa, 1931).

54

Marburg, 14 November 1929

[Bultmann has just learned from Berlin that Becker and Richter[1] are inclined to call Gogarten to Münster to succeed Barth if Barth will vote for him.[2] He has been told to telegraph[3] but is also writing this hasty note which may arrive in time before the faculty meeting. Bultmann assumes that Barth will in fact support Gogarten and hopes that the latter will finally achieve a professorship,[4] especially in view of their association before and in Eisenach.[5] Rade has been no help, since he does not understand why Bultmann and Gogarten despair of the modern situation in theology. He advises Barth not to compromise, since even if there is the expected opposition to Gogarten, his vote will carry the day and will thus "save Gogarten and render a decisive service to German theology."]

[1]Becker was Minister of Science, Art, and Culture in Berlin, and Richter was an official in the ministry.

[2]Barth had been invited to succeed O. Ritschl at Bonn in the summer semester of 1930.

[3]Bultmann telegraphed at 4:10 P.M. on 14 Nov. 1929: "Berlin wants you to vote for Gogarten, Bultmann."

[4]Gogarten was now teaching at Jena.

[5]Bultmann and Gogarten had spoken at the autumn conference of the Society for Modern Christianity at Eisenach (2 Oct. 1929), the theme being "Truth and Certainty." Karl Fischer of Lauenstein (Saxony) was the third speaker (in place of Karl Aé of Dresden, who was ill). For a discussion of the addresses cf. *An die Freunde*, 94 (1929), 1080–1098; for an account of the conference cf. *CW*, 43 (1929), 1018–1026; for Gogarten's address cf. *ZZ*, 8 (1930), 96–119; for the address that Aé had prepared cf. *CW*, 44 (1930), 618–625. Bultmann planned to make use of his material in his projected *Theologische Enzyklopädie*.

55

Münster, 23 November 1929

[Barth acknowledges Bultmann's telegram and letter; he has also heard from two other sources.[1] He asks Bultmann for a draft of his case for Gogarten[2] or a summary of the main points from memory. He would like it as soon as possible. He closes with family greetings.[3]]

[1]A telegram from Gogarten (14 Nov. 1929 at 3:55 P.M.) and a telephone call from Karl Ludwig Schmidt of Bonn.

[2]See No. 56.

[3]The original of this letter has not been found, and the copy used here has no address or signature.

56

Marburg, 25 November 1929

[Bultmann sends the draft that Barth has requested.[1] He hopes he can read it and would like it back. He says that he was not too happy sending the telegram, for, much as he would like Gogarten at Münster, he had no wish to interfere and did so only when he heard from Berlin. He asks about the report that Rade had said in Switzerland that he doubts Gogarten's soundness of judgment.[2] He cannot let this pass, since, if true, it amounts to defamation. Gogarten may speak vehemently, as at Eisenach, but this is a virtue which will cause offence only in a Pharisaic group like Modern Christianity. Bultmann's wife agrees that Gogarten did not go beyond the bounds of decorum.]

[1]Bultmann's draft has not survived. Barth worked hard on behalf of Gogarten, making contact with Wilhelm Zoellner, General Superintendent of Westphalia, Horst Michael of Charlottenburg, and K. L. Schmidt of Bonn, as may be seen from the letters sent to Barth by Zoellner on 27 Oct., Michael on 13 Nov., and Schmidt on 21 Dec. 1929 (with a copy of his letter to Grimme at the ministry, 17 Dec. 1929).

[2]See No. 54, n. 5. Rade was in Basel on 7 Oct. 1929 for a conference of the Friends of the Christian World.

57

Marburg, 3 February 1930

[Bultmann has just read "Quousque tandem . . ." in the new issue of *ZZ*.[1] He has seldom been so grateful to Barth as for this summons. He hopes it will be heard and not just become a sensation. He is sorry Barth could not stay on for a second day in Marburg[2]—many would have liked to hear him a second time and Bultmann would have liked some discussion.]

[1]K. Barth, "Quousque tandem . . . ?" *ZZ*, 8 (1930), 1–6 (reprinted as "Der Götze wackelt" in *Aufsätze, Reden und Briefe von 1930 bis 1960*, ed. K. Kupisch [Berlin, 1961], pp. 27–32).
[2]On 20 Jan. 1930 Barth had given a lecture to the Marburg Theological Society on "Theological and Philosophical Ethics."

58

Münster, 5 February 1930

Dear Mr. Bultmann,

Many thanks for your friendly card. It is high time for me to tell you and your wife how glad and grateful I was to be in your house again. I would be delighted any time to share a pleasant pipe and a good talk with you. If my departure on the Thursday caused some disappointment, I am sorry. But repeating the same lecture in the same place would have been so unsatisfying an affair that I was glad to be able to escape. I would rather come back to you and the people at Marburg on another occasion. Now I must admit that actually, when I look back on our private talks and the public discussion, I went away from Marburg worried most about the essay on Kuhlmann[1] which you read to me, and I have not yet properly recovered. What I heard from you ties in with a lecture by Schumann[2] that I heard eight days earlier here in Münster, and also with the basically uncongenial article on anthropology by Gogarten,[3] and finally with Brunner's eristics, to form a pattern which I might have spotted earlier, but which has only just struck me, slow as I am with concepts. From my standpoint all of you, though your concern differs from mine in different ways, represent a large scale return to the fleshpots of Egypt. I mean that if I am not deceived, all of you—in a new way different from that of the nineteenth century—are trying to understand faith as a human possibility, or, if you will, as grounded in a human possibility, and therefore you are once again surrendering theology to philosophy. I cannot as yet envisage what this formal and fundamental return to old paths, the forsaking of which is one of my most pressing concerns, means for the material content of theology. To see it clearly I should have to know your dogmatic and ethical principles, both in detail and as a whole, far better than I do. I know only one thing that I can name as the visible fruit of the tree that is planted here: the ethical items that Gogarten sets forth in his work on the guilt of the church,[4] which are then unambiguously developed by Frau von Tilling in her essays in *Schule und Evangelium*.[5] Of this ethics I can only say that I very definitely reject it in content. I see in it a simplification, coarsening, and confusion of the problems that seem to be posed by the Bible and theological tradition on the one side and life on the other, and in view of this I should regard it as a disaster if this teaching were to become dominant in the church. For me there can be no question but that I can only oppose it in the future. And the connection between these unhappy results and the formal presuppositions that more or less all of you have introduced or reintroduced seems to me to be only too plain. Where people play around with a natural theology and are so eager to pursue theology within the framework of a preunderstanding that has not been attained theologically, the inevitable result is that they end up in rigidities and reactionary corners which are no better than the liberalisms of others; on the contrary, where this happens, I would rather be in hell with the Religious Socialists than land up in the heaven in which it will be one's lot to be condemned to a "state of life" for all eternity, to have to gaze at a "Thou" that is foreordained by creation, and to have to maintain this condition for redemption. I wish personally that I could see things differently and be more at one with you. But in my lectures on modern Protestant theology it is now clear to me what has been undertaken and achieved for the last hundred years in every theological camp that has followed considerations similar to those by which you are led, and I cannot avoid the impression that the dialectical theology as a whole is on the point of bringing about a great restoration of all these things; if so, I can only regard the whole thing as simply much ado about nothing. It would be fine if you could console me and tell me that all this is not so dangerous and that we are still allies as before, but I very much fear that you cannot tell me this. It might well be that what I understand by the "Word of God" has never been a concern of yours in this way and that you have developed much more directly than I thought from Herrmann and Otto to the place where you now are, so that our ships were merely ships that passed in the night.

Enough for now! I am returning your draft with sincere thanks.[6] Greetings to your dear wife and children, and in spite of my anxieties, sincerest greetings to yourself,

Yours,
KARL BARTH

[1]To G. Kuhlmann's essay, "Zum theologischen Problem der Existenz. Fragen an Rudolf Bultmann," *ZThK*, 10 (1929), 28–57 (reprinted in *Heidegger und die Theologie* [op. cit., No. 16, n. 3], pp. 33–58), Bultmann had written a reply which he had read to Barth, "Die Geschichtlichkeit des Daseins und der Glaube. Antwort an Gerhardt Kuhlmann," *ZThK*, 11 (1920), 339–364 (*Heidegger und die Theologie*, pp. 72–94).

[2]Unpublished.

[3]F. Gogarten, "Das Problem einer theologischen Anthropologie," *ZZ,* 7 (1929), 493–511; cf. *CD* I, 1, pp. 125ff., 170ff.

[4]F. Gogarten, *Die Schuld der Kirche gegen die Welt* (Jena, 1928).

[5]*Schule und Evangelium. Zeitschrift für Erziehung und Unterricht,* ed. M. von Tiling (Stuttgart).

[6]See No. 56, n. 1.

59

Marburg, 16 February 1930

Dear Mr. Barth,

I am most grateful for your letter and hope it is the beginning of the serious debate that we have unfortunately avoided thus far. I do not view such a debate as pessimistically as you do; i.e., I judge the differences that have appeared between your work and mine differently. For, to begin with the main point, our understanding of faith as a human possibility, or as grounded in such, is true at most only inasmuch as possibility here is understood as *ontological* possibility. In this sense even you cannot, in my view, dispute the thesis if you maintain that the miracle of faith happens to *man*—and to dispute this would be to relapse into the catholic doctrine of grace. Will you accept an analogy? The experience of love (I mean marital love) is simply an experience and cannot be known academically, yet love is still an ontological possibility of existence.

Regarding Gogarten's ethics, I do not really see where he is going, but merely think I see that in his concept of "state" he is trying to do justice to the same concern as that of Kierkegaard with his concept of the "moment." If this is so, the concept seems to me to be legitimate, though I do not for this reason accept the deductions drawn by Frau von Tiling.[1] For my part I believed that I should warn Gogarten here against a relapse to which I, too, am not blind, precisely by pressing him to undertake formal-ontological investigations.

Unfortunately there is no time just now to write explicitly about these matters. I will send you my reply to Kuhlmann when it is printed if it does not come out in *Zwischen den Zeiten,* where you would see it anyway.[2] I merely ask you to do me the favor of real criticism (either in writing or orally). But above all I have a very urgent request. You know perhaps that for some years at the end of October there has been a closed gathering of former Marburg theological students.[3] Herr Hess,[4] who usually participates, wanted to invite you next time to give a lecture. We plan this next time to deal with the question of "natural theology"; Dr. Krüger[5] is to speak first on the idea of natural theology in the theological and philosophical tradition, and a systematic address will follow for which you are to be asked. I beg you very earnestly to come to us. If a lecture is too big an imposition, this need not be an obstacle; the main thing is that you should come. I would almost say that it is your duty to do so, the more so if you believe that we are on the wrong track. Please believe me that there is among us a real earnestness to discuss this question with you!

I would like to connect another proposal with this. Gogarten and especially Brunner have often suggested that we should come together in a very small circle for a discussion. This might be linked to this conference if four of us, or five or six if Thurneysen and perhaps another could join us, were to meet either before or perhaps better after it for a "religious colloquy." Please say yes. If you do, the best Oldenburg tobacco will be at your disposal.

With sincere greetings to you and your family from my wife and me,

Yours,
RUDOLF BULTMANN

[1]See No. 58, n. 5.

[2]Bultmann's reply was not printed in *ZZ* but in *ZThK*; see No. 58, n. 1.

[3]On Bultmann's initiative former students and graduating seniors met each autumn (beginning 24–26 Oct. 1927) for a conference (with invited speakers) to discuss theological problems of the day. After the Second World War, E. Fuchs and G. Bornkamm revived the gatherings, the present leader being Erich Dinkler of Heidelberg.

[4]See No. 25, n. 3.

[5]Gerhard Krüger, Marburg. When Barth refused the invitation, the conference was postponed to October 1931. The papers by Bultmann and Krüger and the ensuing discussion may be found in *Protokoll der Tagung des "Kreises ehem. Marburger Theologen" im Oktober 1931 in Marburg über "Die Frage der natürlichen Theologie"* (Marburg, 1932). Bultmann's essay may also be found in revised form as "Das Problem der 'natürlichen' Theologie," *GuV*, I, 294–312.

60

Münster, 17 February 1930

Dear Mr. Bultmann,

Thanks for your letter of yesterday. You have "caught me in a swordknot" in Bismarck fashion and I have no other choice but to say that, if I live, I will take part in your conference and give the desired lecture, unfavorable though my position will be from the very outset in a gathering made up purely of students of yours. But the most important thing can and should be the discussion in a *very limited* circle. I simply ask you to fix the date as early as possible so that all can come. I will do everything I can to get Thurneysen to be there, and Georg Merz ought to be present on account of *ZZ.* How it will all turn out is a mystery to me, because the possibility of speaking with Gogarten as with other rational beings is for me one of the ontological possibilities which I view with so much disbelief. In the meantime fate has sought to increase my "pessimism" considerably. On Friday eight days ago we had an address from the Frau von Tiling who, according to Gorgarten's own statements, is in theological solidarity with him. She is a Baltic baroness who lacks only a riding whip to make it clear how matters will stand with neighbor, love, and states of life. Face to face with her I can see very clearly the profound justification of *mulier taceat in ecclesia* ["a woman should be silent in the church"] and also a possible reason for the supposed Christian persecutions in the Baltic. It was such a revelation of intellectual brutality that I am still shaken today when I recall the discussion. Gogarten must not come with this type of teaching in October if the second Marburg colloquy is not to be as unfruitful as the first.[1]

You will be glad to see the semester slowly nearing its end. For us there will be many farewells, departure, and a new beginning.[2] During the winter I have come into such good and close accord with Heinrich Scholz[3] that I do not know whether, if I had the choice, I might not give up Bonn for his sake. I shall certainly not find such fellowship with a philosopher again.

May all go well with you,

Yours very sincerely,
KARL BARTH

[1]The Marburg Colloquy of October 1929.

[2]Barth had accepted a call to Bonn for the summer semester of 1930.

[3]Barth's friendship with Scholz (1884–1956), with whom Bultmann was also in contact, survived his departure for Bonn.

61

Marburg, 14 July 1930

[Bultmann has been delayed by overwork and his wife's sickness and he wonders about the date for their little summit. The main conference has to be at the end of October to suit religious leaders, returning seniors, and Bultmann himself.[1] He asks about Thurneysen and Brunner and suggests September as a possible alternative for the "pillars."[2] But this will mean splitting off the "pillars" from the "church" and will necessitate two journeys for Barth, though Bultmann hopes the "church" will pay for one of them.[3]]

[1]Bultmann had arranged to go with his wife Helene (née Feldman, b. 1894) to the Third German Evangelical Theological Conference at Breslau from 5 to 8 Oct. There on the sixth he gave the address "Der Begriff des Wortes Gottes im NT" which was later printed in *GuV*, I, 268–293; cf. *Deutsche Theologie*, III . . . , ed. E. Lohmeyer (Göttingen, 1931), 14–23. From Breslau he went on to give lectures in Scandinavian universities from 10 to 21 Oct. He repeated the Breslau lecture in Uppsala, Oslo, and Copenhagen, and in the first two cities lectured also on "Die Christologie des NT" (*GuV*, I, 245–267) and "Das Urchristentum und die Religionsgeschichte" (unpublished), a lecture which he also gave in Stockholm and Lund. On his return from this journey Bultmann expressed his gratitude to the various colleges and pastors, to archbishop Söderblom, and to the rectors of the universities of Uppsala and Oslo, where he took part in the doctoral disputation of Dr. Asting and the celebration of the fiftieth birthday of the classical philologist G. Rudberg, in an article in *ThBl*, 9 (1930), 308.

[2]The reference is to Barth, Brunner, Thurneysen, and Gogarten.

[3]He has the alumni in mind.

62

Marburg, 9 August 1930

[Bultmann thanks Barth for his card.[1] The Marburg conference will be from the morning of 27 Oct. to midday on the twenty-ninth. There is great rejoicing that Barth is coming. Natural theology will be the subject.[2] If Barth has a title in view he would like to have it as soon as possible so it can go on the invitations. Barth will be staying with him. His wife has had to have two operations recently, but he hopes the problem is now solved. He has not yet been able to read Gogarten's work.[3] The last week in October is the only possible time for the Marburg people.]

[1]This has not yet been found.

[2]See No. 59, n. 5.

[3]F. Gogarten, *Wider die Ächtung der Autorität* (Jena, 1930).

63

Marburg, 27 September 1930

[Neither Barth nor Thurneysen has yet said whether a discussion is possible on 25 and 26 Oct.[1] Brunner is ready to come.[2] Bultmann asks Barth to tell him as soon as possible whether he can come. He is about to set off with his wife for Breslau and Scandinavia[3] and asks Barth to reply to an address in Breslau (c/o Pastor Gottschick).[4]

[1]Bultmann had not asked Barth directly for these dates in his previous letter but seems to have assumed that he had; see Barth's reply, No. 64.

[2]See Appendix, No. 13.

[3]See No. 61, n. 1.

[4]Wilhelm Gottschick (1881–1957) was the minister at St. Salvator, Breslau, and was a friend of Bultmann from the time when the latter was Professor of NT at Breslau (1916–1920). The two kept in touch until Gottschick's death.

64

Bonn, 30 September 1930[1]

[Barth says that it is news to him that he is expected in Marburg on 25 and 26 Oct. He is just expecting to give the lecture on the twenty-seventh and cannot spare three days. He suggests a session on the evening of the twenty-sixth, since Brunner has told him he cannot be there on the Monday and Thurneysen is in a hurry. Barth has expected to discuss his lecture, which he does not think it worthwhile merely to give to the main conference.[2] He suggests it would be better to put off the whole thing until 1931 when there will be time to arrange it properly. He has not yet prepared his address and has many other things to do. So perhaps it is the will of providence that the whole affair should be dropped for the time being. He asks Bultmann to turn the page[3] and has another note on the other side, saying that he has been invited to stay with Frau Schlier[4] but noting that, since Gogarten is *not* coming, and Brunner and probably Thurneysen are leaving before he gives his lecture, there is no point in his spending so much time in preparing it when his hands are already full. He begs Bultmann to consider that the dissatisfaction he has expressed is directed mainly against Gogarten, so that if he is not coming there is no real reason for the summit meeting, and the direction of providence definitely seems to be that it should be postponed for a year.]

[1]See No. 60, n. 2.

[2]This statement is doubly underlined.

[3]This is at the end of the first side.

[4]See Appendix, No. 14.

65

Breslau, 2 October 1930

[Bultmann is sorry to receive Barth's letter.[1] He has arranged that the private discussions should come first simply because Brunner, the only one to answer,[2] can be in Marburg only for the twenty-fifth and twenty-sixth and the main conference has to begin on the twenty-seventh. The meeting of the "pillars"[3] will now have to be dropped or postponed and Gogarten is mainly to blame because he has suddenly and unexpectedly withdrawn even from the meeting *kat' idian.*[4] But the main conference will have to go on, since the invitations (of which one is enclosed)[5] are already out and Bultmann cannot take action while he is away. He pleads with Barth not to disappoint those who attend by backing out at this late date. He is sorry if he has given the impression that the summit was the main thing; discussion with the alumni is equally important. Barth need not put in all that much preparation. Everything is very informal and Barth need only formulate some theses based on his *Dogmatics* and then expand on them. With a last plea to Barth not to leave them in the lurch he sends greetings from his wife and himself to the Barth family.]

[1]Cf. also the letter of Heinrich Schlier to Barth (3 Oct. 1930, Appendix, No. 15), which refers to Barth's letter of 30 September 1930 to Bultmann.

[2]See Appendix, No. 13.

[3]See No. 61, n. 2.

[4]I.e., the private conference. Gogarten's letter has not been found.

[5]This has not been preserved.

66

Bonn, 3 October 1930

[Barth understands and shares Bultmann's disappointment and feels the reproach of the printed program. But after ripe consideration he cannot come under these altered circumstances. He does not like to give outside lectures and the main impulse—the chance of a discussion with Brunner and Gogarten—has now gone. If he comes he will have to work out the questions properly, and without the additional spur he does not think he can set aside his other main work to do this.[1] If he is to meet the alumni and Krüger[2] he must come properly prepared, either doing things right or not at all. As things are, better not at all! He asks Bultmann to explain matters to the conference.]

[1]He is referring to work on his book *Fides quaerens intellectum,* which appeared the following year (Munich, 1931).

[2]After Barth withdrew Krüger wrote to him independently on 7 Oct. 1930; see Appendix, No. 16.

67

Bonn, 27 May 1931

Dear Mr. Bultmann:

Today I met Mr. Fuchs[1] on his return from Marburg, who told me or passed on the message from you that you are very cross with me on two counts: 1) that I never wrote you about the church concordat but let myself be informed and influenced onesidedly by Mr. Schmidt[2] in the matter; and 2) that I would not engage in discussion with you and the others at Marburg last October.

I do not want you to be cross with me and will try to offer the following by way of explanation.

As regards 1), the concordat does not affect me closely. I have indeed let myself be instructed by Schmidt[3] with the attention due to a specialist. But I do not think I was swayed by him when I thought it right to accept the section about professors.[4] I have no zeal for it. At your position,[5] at your reasoning as it was conveyed to me through your letter to Schmidt, and especially at the company in which I found you, I shook my head, but with so little excitement that I never thought for a moment of getting in touch with you. My only more lively action in the matter was when the faculty voted on the special conference desired by your faculty.[6] Perhaps you know about this from Mr. Hölscher, who took your side, and this may be the reason why you are cross with me on the first count. I came out against the conference because I did not regard it as possible to treat honorably with you people under the threat that you solemnly made of leaving the church and vacating your office.[7] This threat displeased me, not in itself, but in relation to what you wanted from us; I thought, and still think, that if you wanted serious discussion with others it would have to take place before the utterance of such a threat. If we are already at the last resort, what other recourse is there? You could not put us in front of this loaded cannon and ask us to be interested in your theological arguments in this situation which for you was obviously decided. At some stage of the proceedings I also prepared a letter which was sent somewhere as a communication from the faculty, but I really do not recall when that was or what it was about. My small participation in the affair was for me in some way very secondary compared to the matters in which I am really involved, and again it never entered my head to indicate my dissent to you in writing. If I thought of you at all it was simply and by no means hastily that we could talk it all over sometime later with a beer and a pipe and discuss the points for and against. The matter never really affected me.

As regards 2)—my failure to come to Marburg last fall—I only need to remind you of the reason I then had for my withdrawal. A discussion with you, Gogarten, Brunner, and Thurneysen had been proposed. The conference of your students and their wish to hear or examine me was never for me a compelling summons. I must admit, however, that my unwillingness to come was connected with the fact that last fall I was still much less clear about your own position in a discussion of natural theology in this circle. From your answer to Kuhlmann[8] I think I now finally understand you to some extent, including what was so strange to me in your book on Jesus, including that which did not seem good or necessary to me in the first part of your essays, including that which unites you with Gogarten in opposition to me, including that which gives to your Marburg students their particular self-consciousness; in short, that in which our paths part company. I did not know then that the matter is as bad as I now, better instructed, see it to be. I believe that with your relating of anthropology and theology you are so little free of the eighteenth and nineteenth centuries, that you so little perceive and reject the old and shameless dictatorship of modern philosophy under the new banner of that of Heidegger, that with you I simply feel myself finally replaced under the same bondage in Egypt that, as I see it, we are supposed to have left with the rejection of Schleiermacher and the new allegiance to the theology of the reformers. For many years when people asked me about you I answered that I found in you some remnants of liberalism but I could not take these seriously. Only with the Kuhlmann essay was the insight forced upon me that things were not as I thought and that the new Marburg was only too closely related to the old. But even now I am in no hurry for a discussion with this Marburg. Perhaps I have not yet understood you properly and I must be sure of this before a debate in front of witnesses would be worthwhile. Or perhaps I have understood you only too well and a debate in front of witnesses would only bring to light the very painful fact how very far apart we are and how little, at root, we ever were together. And perhaps, after Gogarten's discovery of the doctrine of the states of life and Brunner's discovery of eristics, something decisive has been lost between us which can hardly be discussed. This being so, Messrs. Schlier,[9] etc., seem to me to be simply naive with their cheerful request for explanatory debates. A fundamental meeting under four eyes might be a good thing and we should aim at this, but a battle of words with a Marburg that thinks it is only a matter of a few favorite "concepts" does not appear to me today to be a very pressing concern.

In both points then, the harmless first one and the dangerous second, I do not think that being cross meets the real situation, and it is certainly not impossible for you to tell me, after these explanations, that in both matters you at least understand me a little better.

I am engaged in altering and if possible improving the *Prolegomena*[10] for a second edition. Your comments are before me, even though at the decisive point I cannot alter the things you criticize. In the seminar and the society I am also much occupied again with Schleiermacher, whom it is certainly not our destiny to be able to drop.

Please give greetings to your wife and my warmest greetings to yourself,

Yours,

KARL BARTH

[1]Ernst Fuchs (b. 1903), a student and friend of Bultmann, assisted K. L. Schmidt in Bonn, then served as a pastor for many years, taught at Marburg in 1946/47, and then at Tübingen, Berlin, and Marburg (1961), retiring in 1970.

[2]The concordat between the Prussian state and the Evangelical Churches (11 May 1931) was drafted by Prof. Johannes Heckel; the text may be found in *Preussiche Gesetzsammlung 1931,* pp. 107–110. The Marburg professors Frick, Hermelink, and von Soden came out with a statement (16 Nov. 1930, see Appendix, No. 17) in opposition to Art. 11, sec. 2 relating to professorial appointments in the faculties of theology at Göttingen, Kiel, and Marburg. K. L. Schmidt took the lead in opposing their view. For the concordat, which was to be important later, cf. *KJ*, 58 (1931), 49ff.; J. Kübel, *Der Vertrag der Evangelischen Landeskirchen mit dem Freistaat Preussen* (Berlin-Steglitz, 1931); also "Das Evangelische Preussenkonkordat," *CW*, 45 (1931), 477–486; K. L. Schmidt, *Kirchenleitung und Kirchenlehre im NT im Hinblick auf den Vertrag des Freistaates Preussen mit den evangelischen Landeskirchen* (Essen, 1931); A. M. Koeniger, ed., *Die neuen Konkordate und Kirchenverträge mit der preussischen Zirkumskriptionsbulle* (Bonn-Cologne, 1932), pp. 58ff., 185ff.; J. Heckel, "Der Vertrag des Freistaates Preussen mit den evangelischen Landeskirchen vom 11. Mai 1931," *ThBl*, 11 (1932), 193–204; P. Schoen, "Die Rechtsgrundlagen der Verträge zwischen Staat und Kirche untereinander," *Archiv d. offentl. Rechts*, NS 15 (1932), 317ff.; J. Duske, "Zum evangelischen Kirchenvertrage mit dem preussischen Staate," *Preuss. Pfarrarchiv*, 20 (1932), 1–13; A. Sondermann, "Der Vertrag des Freistaates Preussen mit den Evangelischen Landeskirchen, vom 11. Mai 1931" (diss., Hamburg, 1933); U. Haude, "Die Fortgeltung des preussischen Konkordats vom 14.6.1929 und der preussischen evangelischen Kirchenverträge vom 11.5.1931 in den Ländern Hessen, Niedersachsen, Nordrhein-Westfalen und Rheinland-Pfalz" (diss., Bonn, 1955); H.-U. Klose, *Die Rechtsbeziehungen*

zwischen dem Staat und den Evangelischen Landeskirchen in Hessen unter besonderer Berücksichtigung des Hessischen Kirchenvertrags vom 18.2.1960 (Berlin, 1966). For the Marburg opposition cf. M. Rade, "Der Marburger Vorschlag," *CW*, 45 (1931), 231–234; H. Frick, "Die Marburger Opposition. . . ," ibid., cols. 650–662; H. von Soden, "Noch einmal: Evangelische Bedenken zum Staatsvertrag zwischen Preussen und der preussischen Landeskirchen," ibid., cols. 1104–1114. For Schmidt's view cf. K. L. Schmidt, "Evangelisch-Theologische Fakultät und Evangelische Kirche," *ThBl*, 9 (1930), 235–240; also "Evangelisch-Theologische Fakultät und Evangelische Kirche: Grundsätzliches und Geschichtliches," *ThBl*, 10 (1931), 74–80.

[3]Karl Ludwig Schmidt of Bonn.

[4]Art. 11, Sect. 2. Marburg was able to work out a compromise which enabled them finally to accept this paragraph (3 June 1931; cf. *CW*, 45 [1931], 651f.).

[5]The reference is to Bultmann's approval of the statement referred to in n. 2.

[6]The minutes of the Faculty of Theology at Marburg show that as a result of a discussion at Göttingen (17 Jan. 1931) between Wobbermin of Göttingen, Frick of Marburg, and Hans Schmidt of Halle, an invitation was issued to a special conference at Halle to deal with the Church Concordat and its effect on the older Prussian faculties. Most of the faculties refused to come and therefore the conference was never held. This led Marburg to send a protest to Schmidt and to the faculties of Berlin, Bonn, Breslau, Greifswald, Königsberg, and Münster (see Appendix, No. 19). The Bonn faculty, of which Barth had been a member since the summer of 1930, decisively rejected this (see Appendix, No. 20). So did the other faculties and Schmidt himself.

[7]See Appendix, No. 17 and n. 5 above.

[8]See No. 58, n. 1.

[9]Heinrich Schlier.

[10]See Nos. 44ff.

68

Marburg, 14 June 1931

Dear Mr. Barth,

I thank you sincerely for writing me so explicitly. The contents of your letter, of course, were painful to me.

1. What offended me about your conduct in the matter of the church concordat is precisely that you did not see it as closely affecting you. If your Münster colleague Schmidt[1] has informed us correctly, you as dean at Münster[2] did not even tell your faculty about the correspondence and the situation, so that Schmidt came to Breslau[3] in complete ignorance of what was going on.[4] That you yourself did not know the true state of affairs is shown to me again in your letter by what you write about the special faculty conference proposed by us. Though we would naturally have had to give theological reasons there for our position at Marburg,[5] the point of the meeting was not at all to engage in theological discussion. We wanted to assert again the decisions of the Marburg Conference (of 1929, if I am not mistaken)[6] which had been wrongly ignored or violated at the Breslau Conference of 1930, and we also

wanted to pass on information to the other faculties, who had little knowledge of the ecclesiastical situation in the province of Hesse, and to show what was the point of our decisions. You see our decision to leave the church as a threat; it is clear that it might seem to be this, and will so seem to outsiders. It was not meant as such, and the authorities to whom it was imparted were left in no doubt on this score. You also do not know what was meant by it, and I do not propose just now to enlighten you. If K. L. Schmidt[7] has shown you our correspondence you will know that even he was not aware of some important developments (important to us at least) and in certain letters[8] raises objections to things we did or left undone which he could make only as a result of ignorance. We wanted to give precise information to all our colleagues, and rejection of the faculty conference has made this impossible. (The meeting later convened at Berlin by the minister[9] was for a totally different purpose laid down by the minister himself.)

It was painful to us, and especially to me, that you should treat lightly a matter that was so serious to us, and I cannot understand that you who had written the "Quousque tandem"[10] took no notice of how the church leaders were acting in the matter of the concordat—well, that was your affair. What I really cannot understand (and this is why I asked with astonishment why you never once put any questions to me) is that you were the one, as I learned from K. L. Schmidt,[11] who spoke the most sharply against us on the Bonn faculty and who wrote the letter rejecting our wishes in a sharp form, which K. L. Schmidt (according to his communication) softened.[12]

2. As regards the October conference at Marburg, I thought I left no doubt but that you were invited first for discussion with our Marburg group, and I thought that you understood this when you replied on 17 Feb. 1930 that I had "caught you in a sword-knot in Bismarck fashion" and that you had no option but to consent. Since Gogarten had intimated that he would be coming too, I thought the opportunity was favorable to set up a meeting of the "pillars"[13] at the same time. That this was for you the main thing I naturally do not take amiss; that you left us in the lurch in Marburg (when what was for you the most important thing fell through) I do not understand. Or rather I have thought I must understand it as due to the mistrust and apathy that you have for us and our work. Unfortunately this is confirmed by your present letter. I do not know how we aroused this mistrust, as though we wished to "examine" you, and I find it unfriendly that you should describe in this way our desire to engage in serious discussion with you. Do you not think that I seriously want to hear finally what you really have against my work? where the real point is that divergence takes place and where I am possibly wrong? what is the basis of the objections that

come to expression in your present letter? And do you not think that my students and friends are equally serious? My "distinctive Marburg self-consciousness" tells me that scholastic orthodoxy is of very little account in our Marburg group. And I am led to think that our self-consciousness, which you censure, rests on our sense of openness and on the investigative character of theological work. Hence we do not understand why you must be certain you have understood me before coming to discuss with us. Is it impossible that mutual understanding should arise in the course of discussion? We at least asked you in order that we might learn to understand you (and ourselves as well) better in the debate. Now perhaps this view of theological dialogue falls under your material condemnation because you think that such discussion is from the very outset untheological. I do not know. In rejecting a "battle of words" we agree with you, but we do not see that concern for authentic theological concepts cannot be a relevant theological concern but has to lead to a "battle of words."

In short, what saddens us, and saddens us doubly after your letter, is that you did not come to us. I can only hope that you will make *public* your criticism of us and your conviction that I am betraying theology. I believe that this would be a service to the present theological debate. For people who would rejoice at domestic conflict in dialectical theology I have no time anyway. But everything, it seems to me, depends upon settling the difference. Now perhaps you think that I take Marburg too seriously. So be it! We must in any case go our own way and we shall not stop taking you seriously.

With sincere family greetings,

Yours,
RUDOLF BULTMANN

In our Whitsuntide excursion with the children in the Lahn valley and by the Rhine we have been thinking with gratitude of your wife, who last year so kindly took along our Antje and Gesine.

[1]Friedrich Wilhelm Schmidt.

[2]In the winter semester of 1929/30 Barth was dean of the Evangelical Faculty of Theology at Münster and officially handed over this office to F. W. Schmidt on 15 Apr. 1930.

[3]For the Conference of the Evangelical Faculties of Theology on 9 Oct. 1930.

[4]Barth put a mark and a ? in the margin by this sentence.

[5]See No. 67, n. 5.

[6]16 Sept. 1929.

[7]Karl Ludwig Schmidt of Bonn.

[8]These letters have not been found.

[9]It is not clear what conference is meant here, since two discussions between the ministry and Marburg professors took place, 12 Jan. and 27 Jan. 1931.

[10]See No. 57, n. 1.
[11]Barth underlined the words "as I learned from K. L. Schmidt."
[12]Letter dated 28 Jan. 1931; see No. 67, n. 6. The words "which K. L. Schmidt . . . softened" are underlined by Barth and the whole section beginning "as I learned from K. L. Schmidt" is marked by him in the margin.
[13]See No. 61, n. 2.

69

Bonn, 20 June 1931

Dear Mr. Bultmann,

I will try to do what I can to make the situation between us not only tolerable but friendly.

As concerns 1): 1. I was dean at Münster in the winter semester of 1929/30; in the first days of March I handed over this office to F. W. Schmidt[1] and left soon after for Bonn. The Breslau Conference took place on 9 October 1930. I do not recall clearly that anything concerning the question of the concordat had passed though my hands at Münster that I could have withheld from my colleagues. What you write on this must rest on a total misunderstanding which will I hope be removed by the accompanying letter from F. W. Schmidt.[2]

2. I do not believe (having read your correspondence with K. L. Schmidt[3]) that in my position last winter important facts in this complex of questions were hidden from me. If I am rightly informed that you would "only" leave the Hessian church, the point of this step, about which you will not enlighten me, was not unknown to me. Why should there not honestly have been on both sides a different viewing and judging of the same facts known as a whole to everybody? The whole matter of the concordat came to my attention in June of 1930 through a letter from Foerster of Frankfurt to former Marburg students.[4] Here opposition to the faculty paragraphs met me as an unequivocally liberal affair, and all that I have read about it from your pen has not caused me to change my mind. I may not have known this or that detail of the conflict, and I may not do so today—but I do not think that knowing these details would have forced upon me a different picture of the whole.

3. Why should my rejection of the opposition have brought me into contradiction with my Quousque tandem? On the contrary, how can I ask Dibelius[5] and company finally to begin to make theologically responsible statements if at the same time, along the lines of the Marburg thesis, I want the functions of administration and teaching to be so mechanically divided between church leaders and faculties?

4. You complain that I spoke out the most sharply in the Bonn faculty against the Marburgers. I have already written that this sharpness was due to the pressure under which you wanted to make us deal with you. I see from K. L. Schmidt's letter to you on 22 January 1931[6] that he did not tell you anything different about me. Materially I can only say that if you did not want to bring pressure to bear on us, as I will gladly believe, then you should have dealt with us before making, or making public, your decision to leave the church and lay down your offices. Afterwards a discussion with us, no matter how you might have meant it subjectively, could no longer have any honorable basis for us objectively.

5. You say that I "wrote the letter rejecting our wishes in a sharp form which K. L. Schmidt (according to his communication) softened." The passage from K. L. Schmidt's letter to you which you obviously have in mind (the middle of page 5 of the letter of 17 February 31[7]) actually says that "Karl Barth shortened a longer text composed by me and thereby made it sharper rather than milder." You must have quoted from memory and will have to admit that something has been transposed by you here. The simplest thing will be to send you two documents:[8] 1) the letter as it looked *before*, and 2) the letter as it looked *after* I took a hand, so that you can judge for yourself how the words "sharp" and "mild" are to be interpreted in K. L. Schmidt's letter.

As regards 2): 1. You object that in my last letter I relate the terms "hear" and "examine" so closely with reference to your students. In answer I can only say that on a series of occasions I have in fact felt myself treated by your students with a mixture of fatherly kindness and policelike acuteness which does not suit me and which I can only describe as "examining." I also know how Althaus and Brunner were questioned closely at Marburg, and I hear (although not directly) that recently things were not much better for Thurneysen at Giessen. Dear Mr. Bultmann, there among your loyal supporters you do not realize what effect this style has on others, such that one would rather avoid it if possible. I must admit that when I spoke for you in Marburg the previous year I had no complaints along these lines. But I have taken away with me the general impression that one is addressing an invisible wall at Marburg. Even so, I would have come in October if the collapse of the summit discussion, which was the only thing that really interested me, had not caused me to give priority in those weeks to the other work which was more than enough to occupy me. Do at least believe that there is no question of "mistrust and antipathy" in relation to you (it is another matter that I reject your theological starting point as I understand it). I have always felt at home with you, but I cannot abide the mixture of the fatherly and the policelike in your students, and this was why coming to Marburg had no attractions for me at that time of uncertainty. That something of this kind is possible you must in all friendship understand.

2. Do not regard it as a disparagement of your work if I tell you that my material antithesis to you is not at the forefront of my thoughts, as you think, and that I do not feel any summons to speak about it publicly. If Eva Krafft,[9] to whose correspondence with me you obviously allude, harasses me with the stupid student question whether I find in your work a legitimate "continuation" of my own, for good or evil the only answer that I can give is that it is impossible for me to do so. But why should I have to say this publicly? Implicitly, your association with Hans v. Soden in the reconstitution of the *Theologische Rundschau*[10] is a repudiation of me for which I have not demanded and do not demand either a personal or a public explanation from you—especially since it has become clear from your last publication[11] that in substance, at the decisive point, you really go along with Hans v. Soden and not with me and that what unites you to H. v.S.[12] is what you call the "openness" of Marburg theology and its "investigative character." I myself call it a new form of the old neo-Protestantism from which I am separated not only by a different theology but, as in the case of Catholicism, a different faith, or, in humanistic terms, a different feeling for life. But why should I fight against this form of this opponent when over the years it causes me less anxiety and mental exertion than my opponent on the right, Catholicism? That this is how things are in relation to you, that I do not see myself to be one with you in principle, can hardly surprise you, knowing yourself and me as you do, and what can you hope for if I explicitly oppose my principially different starting point to yours? I can only repeat that with your well-known attachment to Heidegger (not because he is Heidegger but because he is a philosopher, who as such has nothing to say to and in theology) you have done something that one ought not to do as an evangelical theologian. And if you ask: Why not? I can only answer you, not with an argument, but with a recitation of the creed. Which will certainly not be compatible with the openness of Marburg theology or its investigative character. Why, then, open up a conflict of this kind? Have we not more pressing things to do? Let us allow a few years to pass, and above all let us allow time for some good personal talks. I still believe that through such—apart from the continuation of our work on both sides—many things might be clarified which cannot be clarified now,

With sincere family greetings,

Yours,
KARL BARTH

[1]Friedrich Wilhelm Schmidt; see No. 68, n. 2.

[2]See Appendix, No. 21.

[3]This correspondence is no longer extant.

[4]This has not been found either in Barth's papers or Bultmann's.

[5]Otto Dibelius (1880–1967) became General Superintendent of the Kurmark in 1925 with a seat and voice in the church council in Berlin. See O. Dibelius, *Das Jahrhundert der Kirche* (Berlin, 1927), and on this, Barth's "Quousque tanden . . . ? ", see No. 57, n. 1.

[6]No longer extant.

[7]No longer extant.

[8]No longer extant.

[9]A former student of Bultmann's.

[10]The new series of *Theologische Rundschau* was started in 1929 and edited by R. Bultmann and H. von Soden, assisted by W. Baumgartner, H. Faber, F. Gogarten, M. Heidegger, and F. K. Schumann.

[11]R. Bultmann, "Die Krisis des Glaubens," in R. Bultmann, H. v. Soden, H. Frick, *Krisis des Glaubens, Krisis der Kirche, Krisis der Religion. Drei Marburger Vorträge* (Marburg, 1931), pp. 5–21 (*GuV*, II, 1–19).

[12]Hans von Soden.

70

Bonn, 18 October 1931[1]

[Barth asks Bultmann for help on Dehn's behalf at Halle.[2] He encloses a declaration that he and K. L. Schmidt have sent to the Rector and the Dean of the Faculty of Theology;[3] he would like Bultmann to sign it too. Similar requests have been sent to Deissmann at Berlin, Dibelius at Heidelberg, Gogarten at Breslau, Heim at Tübingen, Koepp at Greifswald, Macholz at Jena, Piper at Münster, A. D. Müller at Leipzig, Schmitz at Münster, Staerk at Jena, and Wünsch at Marburg, all people who will be ready to support Dehn personally and materially. A quick reply is requested.]

[1]The original of this letter has not been found. Bultmann's reply carries the same date, so one of them obviously made a mistake.

[2]Various student groups were opposing the appointment of Günther Dehn as the Professor of Practical Theology at Halle. The German Students' Union there had made a statement on 17 Oct. 1931 calling on students to leave rather than be taught by one for whom they could feel only "fierce hatred and profound contempt." This hostility arose on account of an address by Dehn on "Kirche und Völkerversöhnung" on 6 Nov. 1928 in Magdeburg. On the Dehn case cf. G. Dehn, *Kirche und Völkerversöhnung. Dokumente zum Halleschen Universitätskonflikt* (Berlin, 1931), pp. 49ff.; K. L. Schmidt in *ThBl*, 10 (1931) and 11 (1932); H. Sasse in *KJ*, 59 (1932), 77ff.; E. Bizer, "Der 'Fall Dehn,' " *Festschrift f. Günther Dehn zum 75. Geburtstag*, ed. W. Schneemelcher (Neukirchen, 1957), pp. 239–261; G. Dehn, *Die alte Zeit, die vorigen Jahren. Lebenserinnerungen* (Munich, 1962), pp. 247–285 (with documentary sources).

[3]In the declaration the signatories state that they are in "personal and material solidarity with Dr. Dehn" and they think it would be appropriate to draw the attention

of the Halle students to the "grotesque situation" that might arise for those who leave on this account. With Barth and Schmidt, Martin Dibelius of Heidelberg, Otto Piper of Münster, and Georg Wünsch of Marburg signed the declaration (*ThBl*, 10 [1931], 332), though Wünsch stated that he was only in personal solidarity with Dehn (*ThBl*, 10 [1931], 360f.).

71

Marburg, 18 October 1931

[Bultmann explains that he cannot sign the declaration as requested 1) because he knows too little about the matter, and 2) because the statement of solidarity is too broad; he cannot endorse Dehn's theological position. He also has doubts as to whether Dehn should be called to this professorship. He thinks his appointment to Heidelberg was a mistake[1] and an appointment to Halle would be folly. He agrees with Barth in opposing the politically motivated demonstration at Halle and thinks something should be done. If Barth and Schmidt would change the declaration he would be ready to sign it and thinks he could persuade others at Marburg to do so. A simple expression of solidarity with Dehn in this issue would be enough. Or perhaps a negative condemnation of the attitude of the students would be better. While haste is necessary, a later declaration by many would be better than a quick one by a few, at least so far as impressing the students goes.[2]]

[1]For details cf. the bibliography in No. 70, n. 2.

[2]Shortly afterwards, Bultmann signed a declaration drafted by Otto Schmitz and Wilhelm Stählin of Münster, and signed by over thirty professors of theology, which was sent to the Rector of Halle University in condemnation of "the attempt of student circles to debar Dr. Günther Dehn from academic teaching." For the declaration, which was also signed by E. Balla, K. Bornhäuser, K. Budde, H. Frick, F. Heiler, H. Hermelink, A. Jülicher, F. Niebergall, R. Otto, M. Rade, and H. v. Soden of Marburg, cf. *ThBl*, 10 (1931), 361. Barth wrote about the Dehn case in his "Warum führt man den Kampf nicht auf der ganzen Linie? Der Fall Dehn und die 'dialektische' Theologie," *Hochschulblatt der Frankfurter Zeitung*, 15 Feb. 1932, and *Neuwerk* (1932), pp. 366–372.

72

Marburg, 25 October 1931

Dear Mr. Barth,

Finally I am getting round to answering your letter of 20 June. I should like to let the first point rest just now. I shall be expressing myself publicly again on the concordat question and this will also be a reply to your letter. I am very sorry that there were some misunderstandings in my criticisms of you—partly not my fault, as in the question of the report of K. L. Schmidt, whose letter I am sending back to you—and I am grateful for your explanation.

More important to me is the second point. Naturally I am sorry if the Marburg students have behaved in a fatherly, policelike way toward you and even more so that you take it so tragically. Is this really the *Marburg* style, and not the style of a certain stage in student life? You are mistaken if you think that I have not experienced something of the same kind from your students. I have tried to take it humorously. You obviously have a wrong idea of my friends Schlier and Krüger. I am very glad to be in dialogue with you again, but if you really refuse in a given case to meet with Schlier and Krüger too, I must declare myself to be in solidarity with them. I hope this eventuality will not arise. Eva Krafft's question whether you see in my work a legitimate "continuation" of your own may have been "stupid" in form. But do you not see that behind it there stands a question which agitates her and many others and which you yourself have put to Heim in *ZZ*:[1] how these young people are to find their way between you, me, and others? On behalf of Eva Krafft I should also like to note that she never passed on to me any communications from you or told me of her correspondence with you. Any reference to her in my letter to you has come from a friend of hers.

I am naturally sorry that you do not feel any need for debate with my work. We did not mean to take ourselves too seriously, of course, when we asked you to come last year, for we at Marburg felt a need to discuss with you for our own sakes. Whether it really is, as you say, that we are only a form of the older neo-Protestantism is something we would like to know. For the time being I cannot believe it. That I edit the *Theologische Rundschau* with v. Soden is not a sign of it, and I really do not understand why it should be a repudiation of you. The liberals who complain to v. Soden about the influence of the dialectical theology in the *Rundschau* do not see it in this light. I for my part have seen my partnership with v. Soden in editing the *Rundschau* just as little a confession of this theology as you supposedly regard your joining Althaus and Heim in the *Forschungen zur Geschichte und Lehre des Protestantismus*[2] as a confession of the theology of these colleagues.

At any rate, what is certain to you—that our starting points are basically different in principle—is not at all certain to me. I for my part think I see you artificially suppressing questions which are posed by your starting point and which I am trying to settle. But I will indicate this today only by referring to Thurneysen's essay on Christ and his future.[3] When Thurneysen thinks that the concept of the future is changed by Christ and that the continuum of time is broken by him, this may be right. But when (in unfortunate association with Heim) he understands future and time only in terms of the concept of the impending time, and when he can represent as the Christian concept of time and future only what a philosophical analysis of historicity might also reveal, I maintain that a problem arises here which he does not perceive but which he ought to perceive in the light of his question. It does not do so to ignore philosophical work that one does not know that one has said something philosophical when something theological was intended. Whether *I* do this correctly is a very different question, but it is no question at all to me that you in your work are suppressing a complex of problems which will one day give vent to itself. That you are in the right in relation to G. Kuhlmann is not in question for me, but neither is it in question that you ought to reply to his statements in *Theologia naturalis bei Philon und Paulus.*[4]

With sincere family greetings,

Yours,
RUDOLF BULTMANN

[1]"Karl Barth an Karl Heim," letter, 27 Apr. 1931, *ZZ*, 9 (1931), 451–453.

[2]Edited from 1927 on by Paul Althaus, Karl Barth, and Karl Heim.

[3]E. Thurneysen, "Christus und seine Zukunft. Ein Beitrag zur Eschatologie," *ZZ*, 9 (1931), 187–211.

[4]G. Kuhlmann, *Theologie naturalis bei Philon und Paulus. Eine Studie zur Grundlegung der paulinischen Anthropologie* (Gütersloh, 1930).

73

Marburg, 13 July 1933

[Bultmann wants to know whether it is true that *Theologische Existenz heute* has been confiscated, and if so by whom and where;[1] and if it is true that Barth "must go" in eight days whether this means his dismissal.[2] He will try to reach him on the telephone but if he fails would like a quick reply in view of what is at issue. While he does not agree with Barth's assessment of the early Reformation period he will stand by his work.[3]]

[1]Barth's *Theologische Existenz heute* (Munich, 1933; ET *Theological Existence Today* [London, 1933]) sold 37,000 copies before being confiscated on 28 July 1934. On 10 Oct. 1936 Barth was forbidden to issue the journal of the same name, on 11 Feb. 1937 he was prevented from any further association with the Kaiser Verlag of Mu-

nich, and on 23 Oct. 1937 any works of his on the premises of Kaiser Verlag were confiscated. There is no monograph on the role of either Barth or Bultmann in the church conflict, but cf. K. Barth, *Eine Schweizer Stimme, 1938–1945* (Zollikon, 1945); W. Niemöller, "Karl Barths Mitwirkung im deutschen Kirchenkampf," *EvTh*, 14 (1954), 50–70; *Karl Barth zum Kirchenkampf. Beteiligung, Mahnung, Zuspruch, ThEx*, 49 (Munich, 1956); E. Wolf, *Karl Barth im Kirchenkampf* (Stuttgart, 1970), pp. 71–92.

[2]Barth was not dismissed.

[3]K. Barth, *Theologische Existenz heute*, pp. 30ff.

74

Bonn, 13 November 1933

[Barth thanks Bultmann and his wife for a night's hospitality in Marburg[1] and for their discussion over beer and a pipe. To his surprise he was also favorably impressed by v. Soden and would like further discussion with him. It is a real gift from heaven to be able to speak freely and rationally these days. He would like Bultmann's daughter,[2] if she would, to send him some typewritten copies of the Latin version of the H. W. song[3] to pass on to his sons. He has just read with dismay the latest from Tübingen: Heim, Kittel, and the faculty letter to theologians abroad.[4]]

[1] On 11 and 12 Nov. 1933 Barth, G. Hölscher, F. Lieb, and E. Wolf of Bonn were in Marburg to discuss the church situation with Bultmann, H. v. Soden, and H. Schlier.

[2]Heilke Bultmann.

[3]The Horst Wessel Song.

[4]Cf. *ThBl*, 12 (1933), 374f. On 30 Oct. 1933 Heim, along with A. Juncker and J. Schniewind, withdrew his signature from the declaration of "The NT and the Race Question" of 23 Sept. 1933, which had been widely distributed and signed, among others, by Bultmann (cf. *Junge Kirche*, 1 [1933], 201–204; *ThBl*, 12 [1933], 294–296; *Bekenntnisse 1933*, pp. 189–191; and for the related Marburg resolution of 20 Sept. 1933, cf. *Junge Kirche*, 1 [1933], 166–171; *ThBl*, 12 [1933], 289–294; *Bekenntnisse 1933*, pp. 178–182).

75

Marburg, 14 November 1933

[Bultmann also looks back with pleasure on Barth's visit and hopes there can be more such meetings. Heilke has typed out the H. W. song. He has not heard the latest news from Tübingen. Not all his colleagues are inclined to sign the letter drafted on Sunday but some will. He is planning an essay against the "existential religious psychologist" of Göttingen for *Theol. Blätter.*[1]]

[1]R. Bultmann, "Der Arier-Paragraph im Raume der Kirche," *ThBl,* 12 (1933), 359–370, directed against G. Wobbermin, "Zum theologische Gutachten in Sachen des Arier-Paragraphen—kritisch beleuchtet," *ThBl,* 12 (1933), 356–359. Wobbermin replied with "Nochmals die Arierfrage in der Kirche," *DtPfrBl,* 38 (1934), 9f., and Bultmann counterreplied with "Zur Antwort auf Herrn Professor D. Wobbermins Artikel: 'Nochmals die Arierfrage in der Kirche,' " *DtPfrBl,* 38 (1934), 87f.

76

Bonn, 17 November 1933

[Barth thanks Bultmann for the H. W. song. He has really no firsthand news from Tübingen, but he has in mind Kittel's little work on the Aryan Paragraph and Dean Wehrung's commendation of this as an expression of the convictions of the faculty. He has been summoned by Pastor Jacobi[1] of Berlin to a discussion of the new situation created by the Sports Palace scandal.[2] He asks Bultmann to suggest to v. Soden that their declaration should come out as soon as possible now that the church authorities have donned the toga of orthodoxy. He has at the moment no great confidence in the committee of the Pastors' Emergency League, especially Niemöller; if the present D.C.[3] leaders fall, and these people replace them as bishops, little will be gained.[4] He hopes Wünsch at Marburg will not be one of the signatories, as he would rather not be publicly associated with him.[5]]

[1]Gerhard Jacobi, pastor of the Kaiser-Wilhelm Memorial Church, later General Superintendent in Berlin and Bishop of Oldenburg, was a member of the Fraternal Council of the Pastors' Emergency League from 20 Oct. 1933, along with M. Niemöller, H. Hahn of Dresden, L. Heitmann of Hamburg, E. Klügel of Hanover, K. Lücking of Dortmund, L. Müller of Heiligenstadt, and G. Schulz of Barmen.

[2]On the Sports Palace statement of the German Christians (13 Nov. 1933) cf. H. Buchheim, *Glaubenskrise im Dritten Reich. Drei Kapitel nationalsozialistischer Religionspolitik* (Stuttgart, 1953), pp. 124ff. (reprint of the resolution, p. 130); G. von Norden, *Kirche in der Krise. Die Stellung der Evangelischen Kirche zum nationalsozialistischen Staat im Jahre 1933* (Düsseldorf, 1963), pp. 129ff.; K. Meier, *Die Deutschen Christen. Das Bild einer Bewegung im Kirchenkampf des Dritten Reiches* (Göttingen, 1964), pp. 32ff.

[3]Deutsche Christen (the German Christians).

[4]For a short account of Barth's controversy with Niemöller cf. K. Kupisch, "Zur Genesis des Pfarrernotbundes," *ThLZ,* 91 (1966), 730.

[5]Georg Wünsch. Barth, Bultmann, Hölscher, Lieb, Schlier, v. Soden, and Wolf had drawn up a declaration on the Aryan question in Marburg on 12 Nov. 1933, but it was never published; cf. Nos. 74 and 75.

77

Marburg, 24 February 1934

[Bultmann suggests another meeting at Bonn or Marburg or midway between early in March—he will be in Wiesbaden from mid-March to mid-April.[1] He also wonders if Barth can help to get published an exclosed essay on "Christliche Verkündigung und politische Existenz" by a Pastor Jacob.[2] The Furche Verlag has rejected it as too relevant! and now that Wolf has written for *Theologische Existenz heute*[3] Barth might have it printed there. He may perhaps know Jacob as the author of "Gewissensbegriff in der Theologie Luthers" (Mohr-Siebeck, 1929).[4] He will not like this because it betrays Heidegger's influence, but Barth will admit that this does not lead into the ranks of the German Christians, and the present manuscript is not Heideggerian. Its style differs from that of *Theol. Ex.*, but Bultmann thinks it says something that needs to be said, though it needs to be supplemented by the essay on Luther's relation to the state which Jacob has also written and which Bultmann will send if Barth wants to pursue the matter. In a postscript he asks if Lieb is still in Bonn.[5]]

[1]He was at a spa in Wiesbaden from 17 Mar. to 16 Apr. 1934.

[2]G. Jacob, "Christliche Verkündigung und politische Existenz," *Junge Kirche*, 2 (1934), 309–321. When Barth rejected the essay (see No. 78) E. Wolf published it in the new journal *Junge Kirche*, which favored the Confessing Church. It was reprinted in G. Jacob, *Die Versuchung der Kirche. Theologische Vorträge der Jahre 1933–1944* (Göttingen, 1946), pp. 7–21. The essay on Luther was never published.

[3]E. Wolf, *Martin Luther, das Evangelium und die Religion*, *ThEx*, 6 (Munich, 1934).

[4]G. Jacob, *Der Gewissensbegriff in der Theologie Luthers* (Tübingen, 1929).

[5]Fritz Lieb was forbidden to teach on 21 Nov. 1933 and emigrated to Paris in March 1934.

78

Bonn, 27 February 1934

[Unfortunately Barth is leaving at once for Switzerland for the vacation and will then be in Paris 8 to 15 April for some lectures,[1] sermons, and seminars. Since he cannot postpone this he suggests a meeting in Switzerland. Lieb will be leaving on 20 March for Paris. Jacob has already sent his work and Barth is impressed by its qualities, but after reading it twice and Bultmann's letter three times he has two reasons for rejecting it. First, he does not like the position of "Christian proclamation—which has been worked out in a philosophically very sober, but more philosophically sober than theologically pure way—as the center of a system of coordinates in which it . . . again lacks any theme. Where is 'scripture' in Jacob's construction? Where is the 'community'? . . . I am now unable to rid myself of the impression that in what he calls Christian proclamation we really have to do with a specter." Second, in the section on the preacher's political task he does not like the playing off of the category of "enthusiastic fervor" against that of "exasperated criticism." Behind the characterizing of these errors he finds the typical presupposition of the Emergency League "that in National Socialism we have to do with a 'turning to the future' or an earthquake affecting 'the deepest zones of being,' etc.[2] How does Jacob know this truth beyond the two errors? In virtue of what theological insight does he demand that we confront the National Socialist revolution neither fervently nor—how does he arrive at this antithesis?—critically? Is National Socialism problematical only the moment it manifestly becomes a 'political religion' and not already *in principle* as a 'political order'? Also as seen from the standpoint of the watchman office of Chr. preaching? If not, this standpoint, too, is to be sought somewhere within those 'deepest zones of being' in which Nat. Soc. is, according to Jacob, a nonproblematical affair. I must contest whether in these circumstances it is really the standpoint of that watchman office. At the point where Jacob wants to put the preacher he can be genuinely open to neither scripture nor the community." Barth is pleased that Jacob rejects the fervor of the German Christians but not so pleased that he rejects the criticism that scripture and the community might demand, attributing it to middle-class resentment, and seeing it as the opposite extreme of the fervor. At the decisive point, then, "the Word of God has *no* freedom." Barth admits that he himself has not yet dealt with the problem, but he cannot accept any distinction in principle between political religion and political order and he cannot grant any immunity to National Socialism in the triangle of scripture, preaching, and community. He is sending a copy of the letter to Jacob and returning the manuscript to Bultmann.]

[1]These lectures (at the Sorbonne) were published as *Offenbarung, Kirche, Theologie, ThEx*, 9 (Munich, 1934; Ges. Vorträge, III, 158–184).

[2]For Barth's criticisms of the Pastors' Emergency League, in the formation of which Jacob played a decisive part, cf. K. Kupisch, "Zur Genesis des Pfarrernotbundes," *ThLZ*, 91 (1966), 721–730, esp. 730.

[3]Cf. G. Jacob, *Christliche Verkündigung und politische Existenz*, p. 317.

[4]Ibid., p. 321.

79

Wiesbaden, 4 April 1934

[Bultmann suggests Wiesbaden as a possible meeting place if Barth gets back in time. There are good amenities and he is enjoying the cure.]

80

Marburg, 6 May 1934[1]

[Bultmann thanks Barth and his wife for their hospitality at Bonn.[2] He acknowledges what a gift Barth is for the age and asks him not to wear himself out, since he is indispensable. On the evening of their return Hermelink received a letter from Berlin.[3] He asks Barth to have Miss v. K.[4] send him the address of a lady with whom a young Strassburger[5] might stay—best on a separate sheet that he can pass on directly to Strassburg.]

[1]The manuscript has 6 Apr. 1934 but the postmark (7 May 1934) indicates that it was written on 6 May 1934.

[2]At the beginning of May Bultmann and v. Soden had visited Barth in Bonn to discuss the church situation. Shortly after (23 May 1934) the pamphlet *Bekenntnis und Verfassung in den evangelischen Kirchen* was conceived (*Bekenntnisse 1934*, pp. 81–83, but without the thirty-five signatories). Among the signatories were Barth, Hölscher, Horst, Weber, and Wolf of Bonn and Bornhäuser, Bultmann, Günther, Jülicher, Maurer, Schlier, Sippell, and v. Soden of Marburg.

[3]By § 5 of a law of 7 Apr. 1933 Heinrich Hermelink, Professor of Church History at Marburg, was transferred to another university on 4 May 1934. By the same law Friedrich Heiler was transferred from the theology faculty at Marburg to the philosophy faculty at Greifswald and then at Marburg. Just before this Barth's colleague Gustav Hölscher had also been transferred.

[4]Charlotte von Kirschbaum, for many years Barth's secretary and helper.

[5]Bultmann was unable to recall who this was.

81

Marburg, 7 July 1934

Dear Mr. Barth,

With sincere thanks I am returning the copy of your letter to Kittel,[1] which v. Soden and I read with glad agreement. I am sending on a copy of v. Soden's answer to Kittel, which I would ask you to pass on to Wolf too.[2] Kittel has not replied, and I willingly leave it up to you whether you let us know of any further letters from him and your answers. Instructive as your letters are to me, Kittel's letters hold little interest. In them, so far, fervor has to make up for the feeling of embarrassment.

Today I have a very different concern. We are arranging (probably on 22–24 Oct.) our traditional Marburg conference,[3] the Lord willing. We, i.e., Schlier, Krüger, and I, are venturing to ask you to take part in this conference, and we know that this request is made in the name of all the participants. The theme is ecclesiastical office. Schlier has proposed to ask H. Vogel for a paper. With this request, then, we do not need to bombard you—which I naturally say only with respect to your time; for if you feel the urge to do a paper, we shall be delighted.

It will be a difficult question for you whether you have time to stay two and one-half days with us. But perhaps the fundamental question is even more important. You had some distrust of our circle earlier; rightly to the extent that we then thought we should criticize some of your theol. formulations, but wrongly to the extent that we did not know, and wanted to learn in discussion with you, how far our criticism should go, and whether mutual criticism did not indeed rest partly or totally on misunderstanding. At any rate we have never regarded ourselves as a forum before which you are to be invited to answer; and I almost have the feeling that you credit us with something of this sort. I hope that the distrust has disappeared. You will find us repenting of the sins that you have had to charge us with and which you openly allege against us. That you for your part admit some misunderstanding I may assume after you conceded on the important night of 11/12 Nov. 1933[4] that you had expected me to go over to the D.C. This admission, which struck me hard at the time, has grieved me since and been a spur to me to examine myself; but it has also helped by seeming to show that you really did misunderstand me.

How do things stand then? Is the hatchet buried between us and are you ready to come? A secondary aim is that your visit (and Wolf is naturally welcome too) might provide an occasion for a conference with v. Soden and other like-minded colleagues. Please give our invitation friendly consideration.

My wife and I send sincere greetings to you and yours,

Yours,
RUDOLF BULTMANN

P.S. I am simply sending on v. Soden's letter and keeping yours for a few days as I want to make a copy.

R.B.

[1]The correspondence between Kittel and Barth was published at Kittel's request: K. Barth and G. Kittel, *Ein theologischer Briefwechsel* (Stuttgart, 1934). Cf. G. Niemöller, *Die erste Bekenntnissynode der Deutschen Evangelischen Kirche zu Barmen I. Geschichte, Kritik und Bedeutung der Synode und ihrer Theologischen Erklärung* (Göttingen, 1959), pp. 156ff., and cf. Appendix, Nos. 22–24.

[2]Bultmann and v. Soden were in constant contact with Ernst Wolf of Bonn and received regular news from him about what went on in the faculty there. Wolf replied to Kittel's *Offene Frage* with "Eine Antwort," *Ref. Kirchenzeitung*, No. 25 (24 June 1934), p. 207.

[3]Alumni Conference on State and Church with Heinrich Vogel and Ernst Wolf as the speakers.

[4]See Nos. 74 and 75.

82

Bonn, 10 July 1934

Dear Mr. Bultmann,

Well, if you wish, I will be in Marburg 22–24 Oct. with complete openness and interest, and without the pressure of preparing a paper, since a month ago in Neuenburg canton I had to speak in French on the same theme, and also because I am now able to think of your Marburg circle without distrust.

Do not be upset any more that I was in fact filled with distrust to the extent that I had expected to see you turn up among the D.C. It has been proved by facts that I made a mistake in this case and therefore that something may have been wrong in my basic suspicions as well. You must grant me not only the general truth that it was possible to suspect anyone of anything this crazy year but also the particular truth that you did not make it easy for me to see clearly in advance that you would not do what Heidegger has done with drums and trumpets and also Gogarten, whom I had to regard as the normative theologian in your eyes. According to my observations it was a fact that all those who worked positively with a natural theology or the like *could* become D.C. and that most of them incidentally or definitively *did* so. One may validly infer reality from possibility. It is plain that in your case I was wrong about the reality. But you will need to explain to me how far the possiblity did *not* reside in *your* fundamental theology. Perhaps on this occasion I will be able to find out what I have thus far misunderstood about *your* fundamental theology and how far I was wrong even before 1933 in lumping you together with Gogarten.

We have read v. Soden's letter to Kittel with pleasure here. He[1] has sent a second long letter to me, to which I have sent only a short answer. I have also received from him a proposal to publish this whole correspondence. I had no desire for this, but obviously Kittel finds what he has written to me so important and so right that he wants to spread it abroad *urbi et orbi* against the dark relief of my replies. Let it be so then.[2]

With sincere greetings to you and yours,

Yours,
KARL BARTH

[1]Kittel.
[2]See No. 81, n. 1.

83

Marburg, 13 July 1934

Dear Mr. Barth,

Sincere thanks for your letter and promise. I am very glad and hope our meeting will prove fruitful. Perhaps you will have some time to read my article on Paul[1] in *RGG*[2] or one of my articles in *Theol. Wört.* (e.g., γνῶσις),[2] for I think that what you call my fundamental theology must be clear in these. And then you can show me in specific detail where I go astray. But there is no hurry; for in these days there are more urgent, if not more important, things to do than to engage in intramural discussion. You will have read Stauffer's incredible article against "molelike theology" in the *Westdeutsche Akadem. Rundschau.*[3] I am glad that I did not spare this grandiloquent colleague recently in the *Theol. Lit. Ztg.*[4]

I gratefully return your excellent reply to Kittel. That K.[5] is going to publish the correspondence is amusing. But I am glad that these documents are going to be made generally accessible.

With sincere family greetings,

Yours,
RUDOLF BULTMANN

[1]R. Bultmann, "Paulus," *RGG*², IV, 1019–1045.
[2]R. Bultmann, "γινώσκω, γνῶσις . . . ," *TDNT*, I, 689–719.
[3]E. Stauffer, "Liberalistisches und mythisches Denken im Kampf um die Bibel," *Westdeutsche Akadem. Rundschau*, 4 (1934), No. 17, 1–2.
[4]R. Bultmann, "Grundbegriffe einer Morphologie des neutestamentlichen Denkens," *BFChTh*, 33 (Gütersloh, 1929); *ThLZ*, 59 (1934), 211–215.
[5]Kittel.

84

Bonn, 27 November 1934

Dear Mr. Bultmann,

Today the press will make public my suspension on the ground of having "refused" to take the prescribed oath. This reason is not in keeping with the facts.[1] I am sending you the formula with the addition (underlined in red) which I proposed in order to make it possible for me to take the oath. I would ask you to share this with Mr. v. Soden,

With sincere greetings,

Yours,
KARL BARTH

I swear that I will be loyal and obedient to the leader of the German Empire and people, Adolf Hitler, so far as I can do so responsibly as an Evangelical Christian, and keep the laws, and conscientiously discharge the duties of my office, so help me God.

[1]By order of the ministry Barth was suspended by Wildt, the university curator, on 26 Nov. 1934 (see Appendix, Nos. 25 and 26). He protested (Appendix, No. 27) but was dismissed on 20 Dec. 1934. An appeal went in his favor (14 June 1935), simply reducing his salary for a year, but on the basis of §6 of the civil service law of 7 Apr. 1933, Rust, the Minister of Science, Education and Culture, removed him on 21 June (see Appendix, No. 28). Barth moved to Basel on 25 June 1935. On this whole series of events cf. W. Niemöller, *Karl Barths Mitwirking im deutschen Kirchenkampf* (see No. 73, n. 1); M. Eras, "In Karl Barths Bonner Hörsaal," in *Antwort, Karl Barth zum siebzigsten Geburtstag* (Zollikon-Zurich, 1956), pp. 876ff.; K. Kupisch, "Karl Barths Entlassung," in *Hören und Handeln (Festschrift für Ernst Wolf)* (Munich, 1962), pp. 251–275; A. Gerlach-Praetorius, *Die Kirche vor der Eidesfrage. Die Diskussion um den Pfarrereid im "Dritten Reich"* (*AGK*, 18) (Göttingen, 1967), pp. 68–82 (cf. pp. 69f. for Barth's explanation of his addition). I am grateful to Prof. Ernst Wolf for letting me see a copy of his unpublished address at Bonn (16 July 1965) on Barth's dismissal ("Karl Barths Entlassung—Die Tragödie einer Fakultät").

85

Marburg, 3 December 1934

Dear Mr. Barth,

My thanks for letting me know the facts about your suspension. Your request to be allowed to put that clause in the oath did, of course, amount to the refusal of the oath reported in the papers. For I cannot think that the state would permit the clause nor in my view *should* it do so. It cannot allow—and this is how it must look from its standpoint—that officials who are commanded to take the oath should safeguard themselves by this or that clause (for other reservations are possible and the state cannot enter into a discussion of them) and thus be relieved of the obligation should the occasion arise. As I see it, the reservation requested by you is self-evident for every Christian, yet the Christian cannot bind the state to it, but in case of conflict must give up the office that he has assumed. In such a case he can naturally ask the state: Will you let me remain in spite of my disobedience at this point? But he cannot guarantee an affirmative answer in advance when he takes the oath—which is the point of inserting a clause in taking the oath. The state for its part recognizes this situation by not punishing an official who at some point refuses obedience for breaking his oath or for perjury, but simply dismissing him.

You can imagine, then, that the news of your case was for us a great shock which was hardly lessened by your justification. And the longer I think about the matter the more I regret the step you took—for all my respect for the truthfulness which ruled it and the real courage which it showed, as I hardly need to say. Materially I agree with what v. Soden has written to you[1] and share his concern at the consequences your step will have for the confessing front. Indeed I fear that a discussion between state and church on the legitimate or illegitimate significance of the state's totalitarian claim, which will have to take place some day, will be made more difficult or wrecked in advance by steps such as yours.

Can the matter be remedied? Even if you are ready to revise your position? I want nothing more urgently, but have little hope.[2]

Please tell Mr. Wolf, who will as a friend inform me as to the future course of events, about this letter. Because of lack of time I will simply send him a card.[3]

With sincere greetings,

Yours,
RUDOLF BULTMANN

[1]See Appendix, No. 29 (and Appendix, No. 30 for Barth's reply).

[2]When church leaders publicly argued that taking the oath to Hitler in God's name excluded any act contrary to the command of God as attested in holy scripture, Barth in a letter to the rector of Bonn University stated that he was ready to take the oath in the prescribed form; see *Bekenntnisse 1934*, pp. 177f.; also *ThBl*, 14 (1935), 27ff.

[3]Wolf no longer has this.

86

Marburg, 26 December 1934

Dear Mr. Barth,

Mr. Wolf has kept us informed about your case, as you know.[1] That our thoughts are often with you these days—in concern about the matter as well as faithful remembrance of your person—I need hardly say. At this time you will also have received so many letters that I will be as brief as possible. Quickly, then, to the most important point at the moment. Mr. v. Soden and I would like to know whether you have appealed your sentence to the next court. If not—and we hope you have—we urgently ask you to do so at once. From the news sent us by Mr. Wolf it seems probable that the president shared your view of the oath and the decision was due to the assessors who overruled him. These are not jurists, whereas the president is. The next court consists wholly of jurists and it is not unlikely (or so thinks Mr. v. S.)[2] that the verdict will be different there. It is thus of decisive importance in the interest of the cause. And our urgent request (in case you have not already reached a decision) is that you should bring the matter to the second court even though—as I can well imagine—you might scorn to do so on personal grounds. We shall be very grateful to you or Mr. Wolf for prompt news.

With sincere greetings and true wishes for you and yours,

Yours,
R. BULTMANN

[1]Bultmann sent a copy of this letter to Ernst Wolf with the addition: "Dear Mr. Wolf, Sincere thanks for your news. You will shortly receive from Mr. v. Soden and Beyer an invitation to a conference (on 5/6 Jan., place not yet fixed) which we hope you will accept. The basis of the judgment against Barth will then, we hope, be available and the appeal submitted to the superior court. Every good wish for the New Year and sincere greetings, Yours, R. Bultmann." (E. Wolf of Göttingen has the letter.) The decisive move against Barth took place on 20 Dec. 1934. Wolf told Bultmann about this, and Bultmann informed von Soden.

[2]von Soden.

87

Marburg, 29 March 1935

Dear Mr. Barth,

May I ask you for some information? The university of St. Andrews[1] is conferring a D.D. on me and has invited me to come for the diploma on 28 June. You have already received a similar honor.[2] And I am asking you for hints as to the right procedure. Does one have to make a speech in reply? The question of clothes is especially difficult. Is formal dress worn? Do I need to buy doctoral robes, either in part or whole? (I have already received an offer from a shop in Edinburgh.) I should be very grateful for your advice in these matters and for anything else worth noting. Do you expect to be in Bonn in June? I could visit you there and get help when passing through.

How are things with you and your family? We are well here. Sincere family greetings,

Yours,
R. BULTMANN

[1]In Scotland.

[2]Barth had received a D.D. from Glasgow on 18 June 1930, but did not do so from St. Andrews until 1937. Bultmann was confusing Glasgow and St. Andrews.

88

Bonn, 31 March 1935

Dear Mr. B.

No, you do not have to make a speech. This will be done, probably by prior arrangement, by one of the Anglo-Saxons among the graduands. On the other hand the rector will speak at the dinner and you should pay attention so that you may smile nicely at the right moment when you are mentioned. Formal dress is not necessary. The university will certainly lend you the robes; so it was at least in Glasgow.[1] Later they will offer to sell you the hood, which is the real mark of distinction. I rashly purchased it, although it cost four pounds, and have since worn it at all university functions here. In for a penny, in for a pound, I thought, and I have told the astonished medical faculty and others here that I am the papal legate. The conferring of the doctorate itself is very solemn; I had to kneel, as at confirmation, and something was muttered over me in unintelligible Latin. The students, however, make a din according to ancient custom. St. Andrews is a quaint and finely situated miniature university. See to it that you adopt in good time the hypothesis of the Ephesian imprisonment, for your amiable colleague Duncan is very keen on this. A former student of mine, Porteous, teaches OT. The whole thing will be a joke to you, which we really need nowadays.

I congratulate you and wish you all the best. Where I shall be June cannot be foreseen.[2]

With sincere greetings,

Yours,
KARL BARTH

[1]See No. 87, n. 2.
[2]Barth was dismissed on 21 June 1935 and left for Basel a few days later for his professorship there.

89

Marburg, 10 December 1935

Dear Mr. Barth,

I am enclosing two sermons with the question whether you will put them in an issue of *Theologische Existenz.* Since you are abroad I regret that I cannot send return postage.

The first sermon on "true confession"[1] has the character of a homily, the second on "advent readiness"[2] is a topical sermon, though it does not, I think, use the text only as a motto. For some time I have been telling the students that they should avoid topical preaching as much as possible and give exegetical sermons. I cannot, of course, reject topical preaching as radically as you do. Indeed, I would say on the contrary that it is just as valid as exegetical preaching. As conformity to scripture is not guaranteed by the homily form, the authority of scripture is not abandoned by that of topical preaching. Nevertheless, in the face of the corruption of topical preaching, and for pedagogical reasons, I emphatically advocate today the homily form.

All this is not an apology for the second sermon but for the sake of understanding. And this is the reason why I am sending the sermons to *you*. I know that you follow *my* work with more or less distrust. And it will be no secret to you that I for my part shake my head sadly at much of what *you* say. Yet *I* am convinced that we are fighting together for the same cause; and my sending them might cause you to ask whether you are of the same conviction. It will be a proof of comradeship if you accept the sermons for *Theol. Existenz.* Naturally it will be painful for me if you say No, but I will not take it personally.

For the sake of understanding I would rather make it harder than easier for you by making some critical observations on some issues of *Theol. Existenz.* The issues "The Church and the Churches,"[3] "The

Theological Presupposition of Church Constitution,"[4] "The Confession of the Reformation and our Confessing,"[5] and "Law and Gospel"[6] I read with full agreement, except for some exegetical wrestings (No. 32, p. 6: Ἰησοῦ in πίστις Ἰησοῦ at Rom. 3:22 and Gal. 2:16, etc., is certainly *not* to be taken as a subj. genitive. P. 10: the ἔσεσθε of Mt. 5:48 is not "more precisely and accurately" you *shall* be but you *should* be. P. 12: the fulfilment of the law in Rom. 3:21 is certainly not the same as in Mt. 5:17f. P. 18: the τέλος of Rom. 10:4, in spite of Lohmeyer,[7] is not the "goal" but the "end," etc.). But what I find hard to take are, as I openly admit, your sermons and Bible hours. The text is investigated by you according to the formula of dogmatics and does not speak with its own voice. After a few sentences one knows all that will be said and simply asks occasionally how it will be produced out of the words of the text that follow. Obviously things may be different for other hearers and readers, but for myself I can only say that I am not reached by this kind of exegesis; the text does not speak to me, but the lid of dogmatics is placed over it. —It will also serve to clarify matters if I say that I laid aside the last issue, Thurneysen's "Fulness in Christ,"[8] with painful horror at this arid dogmatics. —You will scent heresy in my *Faith and Understanding.* But I am of the opinion that Paul spoke to the existence of his hearers very differently from the way you and Thurneysen do, namely, by lighting up their existence under the Word in such a manner that God "per sui cognitionem infert nobis et nostri cognitionem" (Luther, *Schol. zu Rom., 3:5).* —I might also say that the Kierkegaardian element that once influenced you and Thurneysen so strongly has now disappeared. And Kierkegaard did indeed understand exegesis. And *you*? Well, you preach more clearly and powerfully in your systematic essays than in your sermons; *there* I hear the word of scripture as well through your words.

Perhaps I have spoiled everything; but I had to chance this test.

Sincere greetings from my wife and myself to you and your wife.

Yours,
RUDOLF BULTMANN

[1]This sermon of 7 June 1935, on Acts 17:22–32, was later published in *Bekenntnis-Predigten*, 21 (Munich, 1936), 14–26 (cf. Bultmann's *Marburger Predigten* [Tübingen, 1968[2]], pp. 1–13; it is here erroneously dated back to 1936).

[2]Not published.

[3]*ThEx*, 27 (1935); this and the other writings are Barth's.

[4]*ThEx*, 28 (1935).

[5]*ThEx*, 29 (1935).

[6]*ThEx*, 32 (1935).

[7]E. Lohmeyer, *Grundlagen paulinischer Theologie* (Tübingen, 1929), pp. 63ff.

[8]*ThEx*, 33 (1935).

90

Basel, 22 December 1935[1]

Dear Mr. Bultmann,

I count on your friendly goodwill if I do in fact return your sermons. Thurneysen has also read your letter and the sermons, and you should consider merely that your criticism of ours does not really seem to be occasional or due to some avoidable errors. For with the same definiteness we have to say to you that we cannot find your sermons "good" (along the lines of what we regard as good preaching). It corresponds to your criticism of the "arid dogmatics" of our productions if we for our part do not find Christ truly proclaimed in yours but instead we see something that ought not to happen in a "good" sermon, namely, the explicating of believers. We thus find that as sermons—I must use this dreadful word to clarify our objections in terms of practical theology—they are tedious, not going beyond what one hears from, e.g., "positive Ritschlians" (a breed that is widespread hereabouts). Behind our mutual criticisms there naturally lurks a material difference. Mistrust is not really a good word for what I experience in relation to you. In face of your circling around the existence of believers—as I find this again in these sermons—I do not see how far, when the smoke has cleared, you have really broken through the schema of eighteenth- and nineteenth-century theology. Was it not a painful confirmation that we are not together at the decisive point that no unity could be reached between Marburg and Bonn in the church conflict, that you quietly took the oath over which I "stumbled," and that not without your consent your friend von Soden (whom I have learned sincerely to value personally) set up the church government of Marahrens, to which I for my part attribute all the mischief of the past year, after having protested against it from the very outset.[2] I believe that all this has a great deal to do with our difference on the relation between christology and anthropology. And I would thus regard it as misleading to our readers smoothly to publish you, in spite of all of this, in *Theol. Ex.*, where thus far with more or less good success we have tried to follow a different track.

May it be our lot in some foreseeable time to have another personal meeting. I have here a student called Schweizer[3] who was and is a student of yours and who quotes you industriously in seminars and open evenings. Provision is thus made that you are constantly with me *kata pneuma.*

And now sincerest greetings and good wishes to all of you for the Christmas season,

Yours,
KARL BARTH

[1]Barth put January by mistake.

[2]On the setting up of the provisional government of the German Evangelical Church, which included Marahrens, and on Barth's subsequent resignation from the Fraternal Council of the Confessing Church, see W. Niemöller, "Von der Dahlemer Synode bis zur Gründung der ersten Vorläufigen Kirchenleitung," *EvTh*, 21 (1961), 82ff. (*Wort und Tat im Kirchenkampf*, pp. 135ff.); E. Klügel, *Die lutherische Landeskirche Hannovers und ihr Bischof 1933–1945* (Berlin-Hamburg, 1964), pp. 175ff.; Klügel's evaluation differs from that of Niemöller. That Bultmann consented to the establishment of the provisional government under Marahrens cannot be documented. On v. Soden's role cf. G. Niemöller, op. cit. (No. 81, n. 1), pp. 139f.; W. Niemöller, op. cit.

[3]Eduard Schweizer.

91

St. Andrews, 14 March 1937

Dear Mr. Bultmann,

As I tread here blushingly in your steps (between my Gifford lectures in Aberdeen),[1] I cannot help thinking about you. Really *blushing*—for you have left behind a terrible mess here through your teaching that X[2] might finally never have lived at all. All St. Andrews is still speaking about this, and I have the greatest difficulty explaining in German and English what you might have meant critically by this. But so far all in vain, and this whole business is blandly chalked up to my account. For the rest it is very beautiful here and the thought of the continental kingdom of darkness terrifies us only from a remote distance.

With very sincere greetings,

Yours,
KARL BARTH

[Underneath]
You must not believe everything that Mr. Barth says! Warmest greetings to yourself and to Mrs. Bultmann,

Yours,
D. M. BAILLIE[3]

[1]Cf. Karl Barth, *Syllabus of Gifford Lectures, 1937*, Part I (Aberdeen, 1937); also *The Knowledge of God and the Service of God*, The Gifford Lectures 1937-38 (London, 1938; German, Zollikon, 1938). Bultmann had been in St. Andrews on 28 June 1935 to receive an honorary doctorate.

[2]Χριστός.

[3]Donald M. Baillie.

92

Marburg, 9 November 1950

Dear Mr. Barth,

By the same post I am sending on as printed matter an essay by Ebbinghaus on the idea of tolerance[1] which he has asked me to pass on to you so that you will not lay it aside unread. He lays great store—and in my view rightly so—by your reading it (Appendix 4 is especially important to him)[2] and giving your opinion of it. He is not thinking, or thinking primarily, of a written statement, but of the adoption of a position in some context. For my part I can only support this request and I believe that the essay will please you even if you oppose it at points.

With sincere greetings and good wishes for the semester,

Yours,
RUDOLF BULTMANN

[1] J. Ebbinghaus, "Über die Idee der Toleranz. Eine staatsrechtliche und religionsphilosophische Untersuchung," *Archiv für Philosophie,* 4 (1950), 1, 1–34.
[2] Ibid., pp. 31–34.

93

Marburg, 25 April 1952

Dear Mr. Barth,

It was a great and very delightful surprise, when I returned to Marburg, to discover your dedication in the second edition of your *Prot. Theol.*[1] Receive my sincere thanks and pardon me that for the moment they can only be brief. I have to go to Wiesbaden, where unfortunately I must take another cure; and the days from my return to now have been packed full of tasks both great and small that could not be put off.

With happy memories of our meeting at the Charon[2] I send sincere greetings,

Yours,
RUDOLF BULTMANN

[1]K. Barth, *Die protestantische Theologie im 19. Jahrhundert. Ihre Vorgeschichte und Geschichte,* 2nd ed. (Zollikon-Zurich, 1952; ET *Protestant Theology* [Valley Forge, 1973]). Bultmann visited Barth in Basel 17–18 Apr. 1952. Shortly before, he had taken part in the General Meeting of the Studiorum Novi Testamenti Societas in Bern (10–15 Apr.).

[2]A hotel in Basel near Barth's home (Pilgerstrasse 25).

94

Marburg, 11–15 November 1952

Dear Mr. Barth,

At first I was tempted to cap your quotation from *Figaro*[1] with one from the end of *Don Giovanni*: Komthur (K.B.): "Pentiti!" Don Giovanni (R.B.): "No!" But I resisted this so as not to lead you into the temptation of answering me as Komthur: "Ah, tempo più non v'è!" I thus decided to reply to you directly, though with some doubt whether I would succeed in making myself understood, since I believe that the answers to your questions are basically already given in my contribution to *Ker. u. Myth.*, II.[2]

To your assertion (or objection) that it is so hard to understand me[3] I might first reply: "Do I understand myself?" For at least when I took the path of demythologizing I did not realize where it would lead, even though I thought I was certain as to its direction.[4]

But I think I always saw one thing clearly, namely, that the decisive thing is to make it clear with what concept of reality, of being and events, we really operate in theology, and how this relates to the concepts in which not only other people think and speak of reality, being, and events, but in which we theologians also think and speak in our everyday lives. Ontological reflection is thus needed, and I think that this may be seen in my essay on the christological confession of the World Council[5] and the so-called "Abschliessende Stellungnahme" ["definitive position"] (the title is not mine) in *Ker. u. Myth.*, II.[6]

If such ontological reflection is part of the business of theology—and your questions have not made me doubtful but simply confirmed me in the belief that it is so—it follows that theology must concern itself with philosophy, and today with the philosophy which has posed the ontological question afresh; it must clarify its relationship to this.

If you think you do not understand me, is it not partly because you do not perceive this task, which is in my view posed for theology, and consequently have not wrestled seriously with existential philosophy?[7] So many of your misunderstandings would not, in my view, otherwise be possible, e.g., your constant discrimination against existential analysis as anthropology (in the traditional sense), or your trivializing of the distinction between "existential" and "existentiell" in the amusing note on p. 35 [42]. But I will say more about these things in what follows.

Another reason for your failure to understand seems to me to lie in the fact that you do not see the problem of "translation," or do not see it as I think it ought to be seen. This problem—and naturally you fail to see this—entails the task of making Christian proclamation intelligible to modern man in such a way that he achieves the awareness that *tua res agitur* ["your own cause is at stake"]. I am convinced that this is possible only when the link between proclamation (in the Bible as well as the traditional preaching of the church) and a dated view of the world is radically severed. Ultimately we need to be rid of any link to a world-view of objectifying thinking (cf. *K. u. M.*, II, 187f., 207);[8] but first we need liberation from the mythological world-view of the Bible, because this has become totally alien to people today, and because the link with it constitutes an offense—a false one—and closes the door to understanding. Liberation from it cannot, in my view, be trivialized as an incidental or secondary matter; it must rather be achieved with full and open criticism.

The situation today seems to me to be this: Man lives with the world-view which is projected by objectifying science; but he is increasingly aware (or beginning to be aware) that he cannot understand his own existence in terms of this world-view. The Russian attempt to do this with radical consistency shows "Western" man by its results the absurdity of this enterprise. Modern man, who needs the world-view of science for his work, feels with increasing strength the character of his being that existential philosophy calls "historicity." And therein lies the extraordinary significance which this philosophy has acquired today. Man is in fact open to this philosophy because it opens up to him an understanding of himself. Self-evidently, that understanding does not have to come from Heidegger or even the discipline of philosophy. It may equally well be poetry, in which the quest and discovery of existential philosophy is existentially vital.

It is a mystery to me how you can deal with this so lightly on pp. 38f. [45f.]. There can be no contesting the fact that the influence of Heidegger and Jaspers in Germany extends far beyond technical philosophy. And how are we to explain the success in Germany of the novels of Camus and Sartre (the latter unfortunately most unappetizing), and especially of the plays of Sartre, and also of Anouilh and Giraudoux? Also the poems and writings of T. S. Eliot? Is the question of the understanding of existence a less vital one in English and American novels? In Thornton Wilder, Graham Greene, Hemingway, Faulkner?

Your cautious statement on p. 39 [46] that American philosophy has not yet become existentialist is, of course, true. But the price paid for this is that philosophy plays no role in American life. I naturally do not know how much emphasis is to be placed on the "yet." But I think I perceive that existentialism is gaining significance in it, which is certainly due, at least in part, to the influence of German philosophers who have emigrated there. It is also of interest that Erich Frank's *Philosophical Understanding and Religious Truth*[9] is one of the books at Union Theological Seminary[10] which is required reading for theological students during some semesters. Reinh. Niebuhr and Tillich both teach at Union and seem to have considerable influence. In Chicago and Emory (Atlanta) as well I have found people, and not just theologians, agitated by existential questions. At Drew some young teachers wanted to found a new journal to be devoted particularly to the theme of theology and existential philosophy, and I was asked to contribute. Almost all the theological seminaries at which I was a guest in 1951[11] wanted to hear about demythologization, and it is perhaps a symptom of American interest in this theme that three houses approached me about publishing my lectures.[12] For me, of course, it was more significant to notice the openness of the students and the way they were agitated by the question of existence.[13]

Your observations on pp. 38f. [45f.] provided me with the occasion for this excursus. At root nothing matters more than that the situation of modern man demands an existential interpretation of proclamation. But you do not seem to see this problem as I do, and therefore you obviously cannot understand me. Not to mention H. Traub, who does not see the problem at all! I am horrified at his work.[14] In what world, or, better, in what remoteness from the world, does this man really live?

I must now go into your detailed questions, and since it is not possible to write a systematic treatise I ask your permission to make some running comments on your work.

I.

I can agree with what you say on pp. 4–6 [10–12]—with one reservation. For my part I would say on pp. 4/5 [11]: "Only when the person who seeks understanding takes its message (that of the NT) as a question that is directed to himself,[15] and only when, as its expositor, he *either* becomes its bearer or rejects it in protest."[16] Primarily, understanding can be only understanding of the question of decision that is put to me, the expositor. The "Yes," in virtue of which understanding becomes faith and exposition becomes preaching, can be understood only as the gift of the Holy Spirit. But I have not to reflect about this methodically. I cannot enter upon my exegetical lectures with a sense or feeling of obligation that I have to make myself a believer. Nor can I offer my exposition as *direct* preaching. But I can exert myself to show that the question of decision which is put in the text is put to me and my hearers, and in this way my exposition (if it succeeds to some extent) becomes *indirect* preaching.

Your objection (p. 6 [12]) against the idea that an understanding of the NT is an understanding of the self obviously rests on a misunderstanding of the concept of self-understanding (cf. *Ker.u.Myth.*, II, 201f.). If this concept is properly understood, it should be clear that becoming incomprehensible to oneself is in fact a mode of existential self-understanding. It is not part of this, of course, that one can "tell" something about oneself. One can tell about oneself only indirectly through decisions taken in faith, i.e., through love, or joy,—or humor. Hence your question whether this is what Bultmann means [12] is to be answered in the affirmative.

The question on pp. 7f. [13f.] whether this is an accurate presentation of Bultmann's concern is to be answered in the affirmative—with the reservation that I cannot accept *in this form* the preceding "first . . . then." For if knowledge (of the NT message) is really *historical* knowledge in its union with that first historical form, there already takes place *in it* "translation" into the language and conceptuality of the expositor. I thought I had shown this in "Zum Problem der Hermeneutik."[17] The "first . . . or not yet first" (p. 7 [14]) is for me an impossible antithesis. Hence I reject the "first" and "then" (p. 8 [14]), the "work of translation" being understood as practical application, whereas, as I understand it, it takes place along with the grasping of the message. Translation does not answer the question: "What shall I say to my children?" but consists of the question: "How shall I say it to myself?" or rather: "How shall I hear it myself?" I can understand the NT as a word that encounters me only if I take it to be spoken to my existence, and in understanding it thus I already translate it. Thus to your protest (p. 8 [15]) against the equation of understanding (encounter) and translation I can either say: *oleum et operam perdidi* ["I have lost my time and trouble"], or I can take it to mean that *believing* understanding and translation are not identical. For an understanding of the question of existence that is put to me in the text is identical with translation. The believing "Yes," however, is, as I have already said, the gift of the Holy Spirit.

II.

On p. 10 [15]: The question of translation has grown out of form-critical work because such work has given rise to the unavoidable difficulty of saying what the kerygma really is. It does not lie plainly before us in certain statements. (In this regard I may recall my contribution to the Goguel Festschrift.)[18]

On p. 11 [17f.]: Can the great and true theme of theology, the message of the Bible, ever be put in any other way (and can the message of the NT itself ever be presented in any other way) than in *controversy*, in a specific antithesis? You once said that (definitively formulated) dogma is an eschatological quantity. This means that there are only temporary and provisional formulations. That the message must be constantly reformulated ("translated") in accordance with the current understanding of being and that it can never be formulated except in controversy—these two concepts belong together.

Is it really correct that the Reformation did not find its theme in "controversy" with an authority "*of this character*" (namely, with the modern understanding of the world and man)? I believe that it did. At root, the controversy is always with a specific human self-understanding. For the Reformation it was that which underlay Roman Catholic teaching and practice; for modern theology it is that which underlies the modern view of the world and man. The mistake of theology for more than two centuries is really that it did understand the theme correctly, but it did not wrestle with the *self-understanding* of modern man, but with its *scientific objectifications*—which is why it also did not question the NT in the matter of self-understanding.

III.

(Page 13, line 8 [19, line 14]): Is this a printer's error? Should it not read "erheben" instead of "ergeben?"[19]

On p. 13 [19]: Certainly the NT message does not begin with an explication of man experiencing himself as a hearer of the message, the reason being that it speaks about God's action in the objectifying language of myth. But the question is precisely whether this objectifying way of speaking is legitimate, i.e., in this case, appropriate to the message of the NT itself![20] Can the reality of which the NT seeks to speak be grasped by objectifying thought? (We cannot evade the ontological question.)

"Should a faithful translation of the NT conceal from modern man the hard fact that the thrust of NT thinking is different from that which is familiar to him and even opposed to it?" Certainly not! But here again everything depends upon what is understood by the "hard fact" of offense. The offense that NT thinking is mythological is one that I do not merely fail to conceal but openly proclaim in order to show modern man that the offense that it causes is a false one. The thrust of NT thinking (insofar as it is mythological) is indeed *different* from the thinking of modern man, but (insofar as it is mythological and therefore *objectifying*) it is not *opposed* to this thinking. Modern man, too, tries to understand his existence by means of objectifying thinking (to the extent that he has not overcome it as an "existentialist"). For him the genuine offense is that he is not expected to conceive of himself in terms of objectifying thinking, which is always a striving after certainty.[21] The thrust of NT thinking, to the degree that it is opposed to modern man, lies precisely in its shattering of man's certainty and its showing him that he can exist authentically only in the surrender of certainty and by the grace of God. The true offense is at root one that is posed for the *will*; it is posed for thinking only insofar as the will explicates itself in thought! (The offense is naturally the same for the existentialist insofar as he secures himself, not by objectifying thinking, but by his free resolve.) Everything depends on interpreting the NT "existentially" in order that the thrust of its thinking may be shown to be in opposition to modern man. "Translation," then, has to show what it means that "God has acted to thee and for thee," because modern man cannot regard the mythologically formulated expressions of God's action as relevant to his existence, which is, of course, the NT's own intention.[22]

On p. 14 [20]: Here I should like it to be stated precisely in what way God's Word to man about the "old man," about sin, is something completely new. For my part I might say that what is new is the perception that the perverted human decision (for self-certainty) is the perverted (existential) self-understanding, *sin*. But I am concerned, of course, to show that a phenomenon is recognized as sin, which existential analysis as such can demonstrate. Otherwise all talk about sin remains completely unintelligible or is (usually) misunderstood moralistically.[23]

If the older orthodoxy did nothing else but bring to light phenomenologically the phenomenon known to faith as sin (I cannot tell about this for lack of knowledge), I should think that it acted legitimately.

On p. 15 [21]: Yes, I do indeed believe that what is said in the NT about the life of faith as the life of the new man can be denoted by the concept of desecularization.[24] Possibly through incautious formulations I have given rise to the impression that I am abstracting away from the abiding orientation of the new life to the Lord. But I have at any rate 1) left no doubt that desecularization is not to be understood in the sense of mysticism, and 2) sufficiently stressed that desecularization is not a status or quality which is in my possession, but that desecularizing faith is vital only as it is constantly renewed, i.e., as it ("constantly") stands in living orientation to its counterpart.[25]

On p. 16 [22]: I would not maintain that in the exposition of the NT the saving act of God which is the ground of Christian existence *must* be put second (and I would not take this course in *direct* preaching), but it is my conviction[26] that one can do this without harm and that it must be done today.

On pp. 17ff. [23ff.]: Yes, I purport to say that Christ (insofar as he is relevant to us) is the kerygma, because he is Christ only as Christ for me, and as such he meets me only in the kerygma. If he were not present in the event (of the kerygma and faith) he would be a mythical figure. And for this reason I regard christology and soteriology as a unity. Certainly Christ as God's act precedes my faith. The kerygma is *address* (*verbum externum*, external word, *Ker. u. Myth.*, II, 204). But it does not follow from this that christology must precede soteriology in theological explication.

Naturally it is easy to argue against me from the statements of the NT, but only because the christological statements of the NT are clothed in the language of mythology which I want to strip off. Hence such arguments do not affect me at the basic level.

Is my doctrine of the Christ event really only a doctrine of the "event of transition"? Is it not rather the doctrine of the Word of God in which Christ is present? If that is so, the I can only reply to the question of (p. 19 [25]) how far the kerygma (in my view) really speaks about God's act by saying that it is *itself* God's act.[27]

On p. 20 [26f.]: I see well enough that in the NT the cross of Christ is described as an *intrinsically* significant event which *then* may and can become significant for faith too. But I cannot follow this sequence, which is possible in mythological thinking, because I cannot understand the phrase "intrinsically significant"; I can understand significance only as a relation.[28] I must repeat that I do not feel affected in any basic way by arguments that simply play off the statements of the NT against me. The question is always that of their interpretation.

As I see it, the repetition of the suffering and death of Jesus Christ in the life of those who believe in him must be regarded, if not as the *consequence*, then at least as the constantly new *concretization* of faith. Faith is in itself already the (believing) repetition of the suffering and death (and therewith the resurrection) of Jesus Christ. What else can it be?[29]

On p. 21 [27f.]: The formulations ". . . to see in the crucified Jesus Christ . . . the subject which has *already* suffered the . . . sentence of death, which has *already* accomplished the transition, which has *already* brought about the transposition into eschatological existence, which has not merely inaugurated, then, but completed this process," seem to me to need interpretation if they are to be understood.[30] I have attempted, in *Ker.u.Myth.* II, 204ff., to give my interpretation[31] in what is said there about ἅπαξ and the *verbum externum.* In your interpretation it seems to me that you intend to interpret the Christ event as an *eschatological* happening but have not expressed this clearly. For I constantly find in the "already" a reference back to a past date, whereas my own concern is to understand the eschatological event as one that cannot be given a fixed date in this world but is always present (in proclamation). In a certain way one might speak of it as an event that is outside time (though naturally not timeless in a Platonic sense), namely, to the extent that the eschatological event puts an end to secular time. Hence one can equally well speak of it as an omnitemporal event which can always be present—so long as we do not abandon the paradox that 1) the eschatological event[32] as the one that puts an end to time begins at a point of time—from the standpoint of secular time; and that 2) it continues in time. To me the paradox seems to be that for our vision, for which time is the setting of the eschatological event, this event seems to be temporal although it puts an end to time. Might one say, perhaps, that the paradox is that God's "time" comes into our (secular) time?

My "famous-infamous" statement (p. 21 [28]) simply means that it is not possible to establish *first* that Christ's crucifixion is the saving event and *then* to believe (for that would mean seeing Jesus as Christ *before* believing him to be so), but that the crucifixion can be seen as the saving event (and Jesus as Christ) only *in* faith;[33] though naturally in such a way that I first believe and then confirm that the crucified one is Christ. To believe in Christ and to understand the crucifixion as the saving event are one and the same thing.

On pp. 22f. [28ff.]: From what has been said it should be clear why I reject speaking about the risen Christ "in himself and as such." This kind of talk seems to me to be necessarily mythological. Indeed, it is only in the kerygma about him and in faith in him, not in historical processes seen in space and time, that the glory of Christ is beheld or believed. This does not mean that the kerygma says that "Jesus Christ moves toward his resurrection in us" (p. 23 [30])—unless this statement be understood in terms of the eschatological event to which proclamation and faith belong.[34] Even then, of course, I would not say "moves toward," but that the resurrection of Jesus Christ realizes itself "in us." If Paul sees the resurrection as a cosmic event, this means that it is not an event which can be viewed as an isolated past event in (secular) time but that it is what it is only "in connection" with the resurrection of believers—true though the "each in his own order" may be in secular time (cf. Rom. 5:12ff.; I Cor. 15:12ff., esp. 20ff.; not, of course, I Cor. 15:5–8, but cf. Col. 2:12; Eph. 2:6).

IV.

On p. 27 [33f.]: I am not aware of having put those "elements" at the "center" of my exegetical attention. I have certainly taken them as the starting-point of my hermeneutical efforts, or my efforts to deal with the problem of translation. For those elements form an offense, a false offense, for modern man. How else can the context in which they occur in the NT, and their "estimation" in this context, claim my attention but in attempts to interpret the understanding of existence in the NT? Their "common denominator" is the objectifying thinking of myth which obtains in them and which contradicts the real understanding of existence in the NT (the understanding of existence as "historical" and therefore nonobjectifiable).

V.

On p. 29 [35f.]: You rightly say that my demythologizing has its source in the insight that the mythological view of the world and man is now outdated. But should it not be clear in the course of demythologizing that the decisive point is not the fact that it is outdated but the fact that the thinking of myth (contrary to its true intention) is objectifying?[35] I do not replace mythical thinking with the thinking of an objectifying science.

On p. 30 [37]: You ask whether one can understand any text if, instead of openly looking for and patiently following its self-disclosure, one approaches it with a prior decision as to the measure and limits of intelligibility and nonintelligibility. This seems to be enlightening and yet it veils or ignores the problem of understanding.

I ask the counterquestion: How does the NT disclose itself to thinking that is no longer mythological? That the text of the NT is and remains closed to such thinking is what gives the spur to my hermeneutical efforts, and these are meant only to lead to the point where the text discloses itself to the hearer. For this reason I must also ask what is meant by "openly looking for" and "patiently following." My own efforts are not meant to lead to anything different. But what can it mean for you when you reject hermeneutical effort, i.e., the effort to achieve valid presuppositions with which to question a text and hear it? What does "openly looking for" mean for you and how do you attain it? For you can approach the text as little as any others without presuppositions and questions. And even if you were to maintain that the only legitimate "presupposition" is the absence of presuppositions, I should have to ask what this means in a historically existent individual. If you reply: a willingness to listen, I say that this is an answer which talks past the problem. Naturally I, too, presuppose this willingness; the problem lies in the "listening."

On pp. 30f. [37f.]: I do not make a prior decision as to the measure and limits of intelligibility, but I do try to recognize the factual measure and the factual limits. The "prior decision" is made concerning me, for I am a man, and a man of a particular age. Hence also I have no "canon."[36]

My efforts (presupposing that they are to the point, and I am ready to be taught here) do not lead in any sense to a provisional "working hypothesis" (which is something quite different) but to a *questioning* of the text. If I try to achieve this in the form of the question of what the text says about existence and the understanding of existence, then so far as I am concerned you might call the concept of existence my canon, but not the concept of myth. (So as not to become too long, may I refer at this point to my essay on the problem of hermeneutics?[37] I should like you to tell me what your canon is, i.e., what other canon you think the NT offers us.

On pp. 31f. [38f.]: I am sorry that you force me to go into the concept of myth, as though I had to choose among the various productions that call themselves myths, as is so common today. The "myth of the twentieth century" is a perverted myth. For if true myth is putting the other world in terms of this world, the twentieth-century myth is the putting of this world in terms of the other world (i.e., its absolutizing).

Now you have not convinced me that my formal view of myth is wrong. For my part I regard your material view as much too narrow. For myth lives not only in stories of the gods but also in the world-view presupposed by them. The NT authors did not, of course, present "general" cosmic relations and connections in the form of a story of the gods. But sharing the mythical world-view of their age, they tell the story of the Christ event as a story of the gods, as a myth. The gnostic parallels, e.g., to Phil. 2:6ff.; Col. 1:15ff., anyone will (rightly) describe as myth. Is what is said in these NT passages any the less myth (in terms of its material presentation)?

On p. 32 [39]: Your "I do not understand" rests, I think, simply on the fact that you leave undiscussed the concept of reality. And your asking what causes me to choose the concept of myth to describe these problematical elements is easily answered: for one thing, because these elements are to be called mythological in the language of scholarship; and for another because the concept of myth denotes a mode of objectifying thinking, and this characterizes the NT.[38]

Certainly what I call mythological in the NT may coincide materially with what used to be called "supernaturalism." But I avoid this term because I want to make it clear that the salvation event is "supernatural" in a radical sense. My "canon," the concept of existence, serves precisely this purpose.

On pp. 32f. [39f.]: The question whether the demythologized kerygma can speak of the otherworldly God becoming thisworldly is one that I think I have answered already in *Ker.u.Myth.*, II, 196, namely, by trying to show in what sense one can speak of God's action non-mythologically. It seems to me that your doubting questions have their basis in your failure to see the meaning of the historicity of existence.

On p. 33 [40]: The statement that the first disciples beheld the "glory" of the incarnate Word in a resurrection from the dead in time and space, that they saw this with their eyes, heard it with their ears, and touched it with their hands, I regard as sheer mythology;[39] nor does it seem to me to catch the real meaning of I John 1:1. And your "*so* human, *so* worldly . . . ," while it may not contradict Luke, certainly contradicts John (cf., e.g., John 14:18ff.).

Naturally there is not only a "Nevertheless" of faith but also a "That"—presupposing that this "That" is not understood as a fact guaranteeing the certainty of faith, which would then have to be thought of as one that is established prior to faith (but how? by another kind of faith?).[40] I would rather not say, then, that there is a "Therefore" but instead a "Therein."

The same is to be said about the "first" and "then and therefore," and it should also be pointed out that the eschatological character of faith is missed in such a formulation.

On pp. 33f. [40f.]: As you see it, the intention of the (in my view not merely allegedly) mythological elements of the NT is naturally "to show that we . . . are not alone precisely in this human . . . existence of ours, but. . . ." Yet I think this can be said in other terms than those that I call mythological; cf. *Ker.u.M.*, II, 185ff.; 204ff. Does what I said there smack of docetism?

On p. 34 [41]: Is it true that I know "painfully little" how to deal with the OT? I might refer to my essay "Weissagung und Erfüllung."[41] But I cannot suppress the counterquestion: What do you (and your followers) really make of the OT, the OT that is "so unmistakably earthly and historical"? Well, I might have missed much that you have said, and if so I can be grateful for specific references. What I have seen[42] awakens the suspicion that you do not relate to the OT in its earthly and historical form but use a Christianized OT as an instrument.[43]

On the other hand you are right that I have not thus far explicitly elucidated the significance of the historical Jesus for the kerygma.[44] I do not see, of course, that I can understand the preaching of Jesus otherwise than as the preaching of the law, as Luther also did—with the radicalness, of course, that drives the hearer to cry for the grace of God, so that—from the standpoint of faith—it must itself be understood as a summons to grace.

VI.

On p. 35 [42]: The rendering of my view by your combination is correct.

To be noted: Is not the confusing of *existential* and *existentiell* really a fundamental misunderstanding and the source of further misunderstandings?

On p. 37 [44]: Can one really say, or in what sense can one say, that theology (specifically here the exposition of the NT), if it adopts the inquiry of existential philosophy and uses its conceptuality and terminology, has therewith found a "philosophical key" which it uses in exegesis? Are you not confusing existential philosophy with philosophies which make the NT their own theme? In other words, with philosophies which take man's responsiblity for his existence from him even as they think they can impart an existential self-understanding to him? This would be the case with existential philosophy if it disclosed the meaning of my existence to me as my own. But the direct opposite is the truth, in support of which I may refer to *Ker.u.M.*, II, 191ff. and 202f. If theology learns from existential philosophy how existence is to be explicated conceptually, I do not see how this dependence does violence to theology. Conversely, existential philosophy has learned from theology or the NT to perceive the phenomenon of existence, as may be seen from the significance that Paul, Augustine, Luther, and Kierkegaard have had for Heidegger and Jaspers (and already indeed for Graf Yorck).

If you insist on your contention that theology, if it falls into that learning dependence on philosophy, blocks its own access to the NT, I must reply with Hartlich and Sachs that the battle will have to be fought on the field of exegesis[45] (and since this will have to involve a discussion of hermeneutical principles, I do not believe that in the case of Hartlich and Sachs "the serpent is biting its tail").

On the concept of "preunderstanding": Preunderstanding is not an invention of Heidegger's but a phenomenon discovered by him. I do not see that a text can be understood unless there is already some preunderstanding of that which is at issue in it.

On pp. 38f. [45ff.]: That the playing down of the significance of existential philosophy seems to me to be inappropriate, I have said already.[46]

On p. 39 [47]: The reference to C. Wolff seems to me to show particularly well how complete is the misunderstanding of the concept of self-understanding. For the existential interpretation of human existence says precisely that the human subject (or human being, I might also say) is not without his world, nor even without God insofar as the philosopher regards it as legitimate to speak about God, so that self-understanding is *also* understanding of (God and) the world. How, then, can you constantly discriminate against the existential interpretation of human being as "anthropology?" (For the rest, Heidegger has said expressly that his analysis of human being is not anthropology.)[47]

On p. 40 [47]: What the Christ event means as the *Christ* event I have tried at least to show in *Ker.u.M.*, II, 204ff.[48] I do not deny that it might be done better. But that I have "broken out of the existentialist schema" can be said only by someone who has not seen that existential analysis leaves us free for concrete encounters (and therefore also for those with God's Word) and does not seek to control them. If one wants to say that existential analysis leads to an ideal of existence, one would have to oppose to it a different (and better) analysis.

VII.

On p. 42 [49]: Have I not expressed in *Ker.u.M.*, II, p. 207, my conviction as to the relativity of the modern view of the world?

On p. 43 [50f.]: It is true that I exegete the NT as a historian. But the distinction between the historical motif (No. 3, pp. 43f. [50ff.]) and the philosophical (No. 4, pp. 44f. [52f.]) no longer seems to be a valid one now that Dilthey, Graf Yorck, Heidegger, and others have come to see that genuine historical research goes hand in hand with philosophical reflection; i.e., genuine historical research investigates history in terms of the possibilities of existence and its understanding that are displayed in history (which naturally does not have to be explicit nor to apply in every individual investigation).

On p. 45 [53]: That "philosophical fragments" float in the soup of all theologians—this is the very thing that forces me to ascribe to philosophical work its fundamental importance for theology. For I regard it as impermissible to be uncritically satisfied with a few "philosophical fragments."[49]

On p. 46 [53]: That the question of the application of salvation was the real one for Luther shows that the question of the understanding of existence was the decisive question for him. Those who regard the understanding of existence as the decisive question will be delighted at this.

On p. 47 [55]: That W. Herrmann anthropologized the Christian message seems to me to be contradicted already by the role that the concept of trust plays for him. Certainly his conceptuality was inadequate in relation to what he was trying to say. But it was because I learned from Herrmann that I was ready for Heidegger. Heidegger, too, learned from Herrmann and rated him highly (esp., e.g., his essay on the penitence of the evangelical Christian).[50]

VIII.

On p. 48 [55f.]: It is misleading to equate the NT and the Word of

God when discussing the methodological problem of NT hermeneutics. The Word of God is spoken in the human word and the NT stands before us as a literary record of history. Can it be interpreted otherwise than according to general hermeneutical rules? That it is God's Word cannot be made a presupposition from which to deduce hermeneutical rules of a different kind. It can show itself to be God's Word, and therefore validate itself, only in the event of believing understanding.

I know of no "canonized" preunderstanding, nor do I know what this might mean. I know only that everyone comes to the NT (as to any other text) with some preunderstanding (however it may be formed). This is posited by the very fact that everybody stands in some concrete history in which he himself takes part. Reflection on the preunderstanding seeks to clarify the true question to be put to the text. When I say that the true question to be put to the NT as a text which is first offered to me as a historical document is to ask what it says about human being as my being, and that the question of human being is always derived from a preunderstanding of this being, I am not hereby canonizing any preunderstanding but simply attaining to the true question.[51]

It is a misunderstanding that this procedure does not correspond to the fact that God's Word encounters man as an "alien truth and reality that runs counter to his own ability to understand." The opposite is the case. Existential analysis can only clarify in what sense God's Word can be called an alien one that runs counter to my own ability to understand. This clarification has to take place if "alien" is not to be taken in a trivial sense and "counter to my own ability to understand" is not to be misunderstood along the lines of sheer absurdity.

On p. 49 [56f.]: Existential interpretation seeks precisely to give force to the true offense, to bring to awareness the real contradiction of the natural man. Reflection on the modern view of the world serves the same end.

On p. 50 [57]: For this reason you miss the point with your statement that instead of trying to understand the text in the framework of our supposedly normative (!) self-understanding we should seek to understand ourselves as we find ourselves understood in the text. For understanding the text in the framework (or, better, under the question) of our self-understanding is precisely the way toward understanding ourselves as we find ourselves understood in the text. Methodologically I can seek, of course, only an existential [*existential*] interpretation; what the *Divinus Spiritus* effects is an existential [*existentiell*] self-understanding.[52]

On pp. 50f. [57ff.]: It seems to me that preunderstanding and prejudgment are confused. For have I ever denied, or not indeed emphasized, that an understanding is not possible without the greatest possible openness? (e.g. "Zum Problem der Hermeneutik," p. 63 and esp. p. 64). But I cannot understand without a particular line of questioning, and achieving this is the issue,[53] not a "definition" of preunderstanding that has anything whatever to do with "limitation." That I cannot understand someone else without a readiness for openness is self-evident. Is not (pp. 51f. [59f.]) existential (*existential*) analysis confused with existential (*existentiell*) understanding? To the extent that the latter presupposes, or is, a distinctive movement of the will, it can be received—if it is radically meant as self-surrender—only as the gift of the Holy Spirit.

On p. 52 [60]: The concept of understanding the NT (and OT) current before your eruption did indeed presuppose that the interpreter basically knew already what can be imparted in the text and needed only to be "reminded" of it by the text. In this case the text does not "encounter"; it is not part of an address, and therefore the interpreter does not achieve an awareness of becoming and being known from the object of his knowledge. Do you not understand that my point is to show how the text must achieve validity as a word of address? what genuine hearing means?[54] The decisive impulse for me was what you once described in the preface to the second edition of your *Romans* (1921);[55] I have reflected on this, and existential philosophy has helped to clarify things for me. I do not intend to reverse the revolution achieved by you some thirty years ago but to solidify the new path methodologically. (Cf. for the rest what I wrote in my "Kirche und Lehre im NT" in 1929; then in *Glauben und Verstehen*, pp. 154–162.)[56]

I can now close for today—though naturally not without the feeling of doubt that I expressed at the start. I cannot do so, however, without saying that I find your "epilogue"[57] painful because it was obviously written in irritation.[58]

In clarification I must at least say that I dislike the title "Abschliessende Stellungnahme" ["definitive position"] that the editor has given to my contribution.[59] It was far from my intention to write anything conclusive. "Stellungnahme" is also incorrect, for it awakens the impression that I want to take up a position in relation to all the preceding contributions. This was not so, for I did not know the essays of Prenter and Oepke until the publication of *K.u.M.*, II, and I became acquainted with that of Buri in manuscript only when my own essay was ready for the press.[60] To lengthen it, or add a postscript, was something I had no wish to do, for I believed my contribution already contained indirectly my answer to Buri.[61] That I had to reject Kümmel's effort[62] as absurd would be, I thought, understandable to anyone who has grasped the point of "demythologizing" as a hermeneutical method.

How I earned the reproaches you make against me on p. 56 [64f.] I really do not know. I thought I had sought a discussion, especially with you, by putting to you some concrete questions; and I have not seen any answer from you to the questions that were put in, e.g., "Zum Problem der Hermeneutik," pp. 68f. (I am anxious to see whether you will answer equally concretely the concrete criticisms of Hartlich and Sachs.)[63] I did not realize that my discussion of Schniewind (*K.u.M.*, I, 122–138) or Schumann (*K.u.M.*, II, 193f.) would have to be described as "dismissal."[64]

To the question: "What is finally and ultimately the theme of this debate?" I can only reply: The theme is the question of hermeneutical method in the service of exposition of the NT.

And now let me close by continuing your quotation from Figaro:

"How can I be angry?
My heart speaks for thee!"—and adding the last line of Figaro:
"Sorrow be for ever banned!"

With sincere greetings,

Yours,
RUDOLF BULTMANN

[1]" 'O Angel, pardon me!' (*The Marriage of Figaro,* 2nd Finale), from the author," was Barth's longhand dedication to Bultmann in his work *Rudolf Bultmann. Ein Versuch ihn zu verstehen* (Zollikon-Zurich, 1952; ET "Rudolf Bultmann: An Attempt to Understand Him" in *Kerygma and Myth,* Vol. II [London, 1962]). This was reprinted several times along with Barth's *Christus und Adam nach Rom. 5* (Zollikon-Zurich, 1952; ET *Christ and Adam* [New York, 1957]). The references in Bultmann's letter are to the first edition of 1952 and those in square brackets to the third edition of 1964 (Zurich). In connection with Barth's attempt to understand Bultmann cf. his letter of 29 May 1947 to Bishop Wurm of Stuttgart, Appendix, No. 34. Cf. also Appendix, Nos. 31–33 and 35.

[2]R. Bultmann, "Zum Problem der Entmythologisierung," *KuM,* II (1952), 179–208.

[3]K. Barth, *Rudolf Bultmann, Ein Versuch ihn zu verstehen,* pp. 3f. [9f.].

[4]Cf. Bultmann's "Neues Testament und Mythologie" (1941) in *Offenbarung und Heilsgeschehen* (Munich, 1941), pp. 27–69 *(KuM,* I [1948], 15–53). On demythologization cf. *KuM,* II (1952) and G. Bornkamm, "Die Theologie Bultmanns in der neueren Diskussion . . . ," *ThR,* NF 29 (1963), 33–141 (G. Bornkamm, *Geschichte und Glaube, l. Teil. Gesammelte Aufsätze,* III [Munich, 1968], 173–275). On Barth's role cf. E. Hübner, "Entmythologisierung als theologische Aufgabe," ΠΑΡΡΗΣΙΑ (Zurich, 1966), pp. 238–260; F.-W. Marquardt, "Religionskritik und Entmythologisierung . . . ," in *Theologie zwischen gestern und morgen. Interpretationen und Anfragen zum Werk Karl Barths,* ed. W. Dantine and K. Lüthi (Munich, 1968), pp. 88–123.

[5]R. Bultmann, "Das christologische Bekenntnis des Ökumenischen Rates," *Schweizer. Theol. Umschau,* 21 (1951), 25–36; also *EvTh,* 11 (1951/52), 1–13 (*GuV,* II, 246–261).

[6]R. Bultmann, "Zum Problem der Entmythologisierung," *KuM,* II (1952), 179–208.

[7]This sentence and the previous paragraph are marked by Barth in the margin.

[8]R. Bultmann, "Zum Problem der Entmythologisierung." Barth marked this sentence in the margin.

[9]London, 1945.

[10]New York.

[11]On Bultmann's American tour (2 Oct.–20 Dec. 1951) cf. Appendix, Nos. 36, 37, and 39.

[12]Cf. R. Bultmann, *Jesus Christ and Mythology* (New York, 1958).

[13]The whole section beginning "Modern man . . ." is marked by Barth in the margin.

[14]H. Traub, *Anmerkungen und Fragen zur nt. lichen Hermeneutik und zum Problem der Entmythologisierung* (Neukirchen, 1952).

[15]Underlined by Barth.

[16]Underlined by Barth.

[17]R. Bultmann, "Zum Problem der Hermeneutik," *ZThK*, 47 (1950), 47–69 (*GuV*, II, 211–235).

[18]R. Bultmann, "Zum Problem des Verhältnisses von Theologie und Verkündigung im NT," *Aux sources de la tradition Chrétienne* (Neuchâtel-Paris, 1950), pp. 32–42.

[19]Barth wrote "no" in the margin here.

[20]This sentence and the previous one are marked by Barth in the margin.

[21]This sentence is marked in the margin.

[22]This sentence is marked in the margin.

[23]The section from "that the perverted human decision . . ." is marked by Barth in the margin.

[24]This sentence is marked by Barth in the margin.

[25]The section from "but . . ." is marked by Barth in the margin.

[26]Bultmann crossed out "opinion" here and substituted "conviction."

[27]This sentence is marked by Barth in the margin.

[28]This sentence is marked in the margin.

[29]This sentence is marked in the margin.

[30]This sentence is marked in the margin.

[31]The MS has "gegeben zu haben" ("to have given").

[32]This sentence is marked by Barth in the margin.

[33]Marginal note by Barth: "p. 40?"

[34]This sentence is marked by Barth in the margin.

[35]The section from "the fact that . . ." is marked by Barth in the margin.

[36]This paragraph is marked by Barth in the margin.

[37]See n. 17.

[38]This paragraph is marked by Barth in the margin.

[39]This sentence is marked by Barth in the margin.

[40]This sentence is marked in the margin.

[41]In *Studia Theologica*, 2 (1949), 21–44; *ZThK*, 47 (1950), 360–383 (*GuV*, II, 162–186).

[42]MS: "bekam" for "kam" ("mir zu Gesicht kam").

[43]This sentence is marked by Barth in the margin.

[44]This sentence is marked in the margin.

[45]See n. 63.

[46]This sentence is marked by Barth in the margin.

[47]The two previous sentences are marked by Barth in the margin.

[48]Barth marked this sentence with a cross in the margin.

[49]This paragraph is marked by Barth in the margin.

[50]W. Herrmann, "Die Busse des evangelischen Christen," *ZThK*, 1 (1891), 28–81 (W. Herrmann, *Gesammelte Aufsätze*, ed. F. W. Schmidt [Tübingen, 1923], pp. 33–85).

[51]This paragraph is marked by Barth in the margin.

[52]This paragraph is marked in the margin.

[53]The sentence to this point is marked by Barth in the margin.

[54]Barth marked this sentence with a cross in the margin.

[55]K. Barth, *Der Römerbrief* (Zurich, 1967), pp. vi–xviii: Preface to the Second Edition (Safenwil, Sept. 1921). Cf. Bultmann's review in *CW*, 36 (1922), 320–323, 330–334, 358–361, 369–373, and Barth's reply in the Preface to the 3rd edition (1922), pp. xixff.

[56]R. Bultmann, "Kirche und Lehre im NT," *ZZ*, 7 (1929), 9–43 (*GuV*, I, 153–187). The last two sentences are marked by Barth in the margin.

[57]Pp. 54–56 [62–65].

[58]This sentence is marked by Barth in the margin.

[59]*KuM*, II (1952), 179–208.

[60]R. Prenter, "Mythos und Evangelium," *KuM*, II (1952), 69–84 (previously in *Rev. de Théol. et de Phil.*, 35 [1947], 49ff.); A. Oepke, "Entmythologisierung des Christentums?", *KuM*, II (1952), 170–175 (previously in *Geschichtliche und übergeschichtliche Schriftauslegung* [3rd ed., Gütersloh, 1947], pp. 56ff.); F. Buri, "Entmythologisierung oder Entkerygmatisierung der Theologie," *KuM*, II (1952), 85–101.

[61]Barth marked the last two sentences with a cross in the margin.

[62]W. G. Kümmel, "Mythische Rede und Heilsgeschehen im NT," *KuM*, II (1952), 153–169 (previously in *Coniectanea Neotestamentica*, 11 [1947], 109–131); cf. Kümmel's *Gesammelte Aufsätze*, ed. E. Grässer, O. Merk, A. Fritz [Marburg, 1965], pp. 153–168); also W. G. Kümmel, "Mythos im NT," *ThZ*, 6 (1950), 321–337 (*Ges. Aufs.*, pp. 218–229).

[63]The paragraph is marked to this point by Barth in the margin. C. Hartlich and W. Sachs, "Kritische Prüfung der Haupteinwände Barths gegen Bultmann," *KuM*, II (1952), 113–125 (previously in *Für Arbeit und Besinnung*, 4 [1950], 15–19, 21, 22, 24; 5 [1951], 15, 16; 6 [1952], 4, 13. Hartlich and Sachs criticized Barth's discussion of Bultmann in *CD* III, 2, pp. 443ff. [*KuM*, II (1952), 102–109]). Barth took up the issue again in *CD* III, 3 and IV, 1. In June 1953 he wrote in the Foreword to *CD* IV, 1: "The present situation in theology and also the peculiar themes of this book mean that throughout I have found myself in an intensive, although for the most part quiet, debate with Rudolf Bultmann. His name is not mentioned often. But his subject is always present, even in those places where with its methods and results before me I have consciously ignored him. I respect the man, his mind and aim and achievements and the zeal of his following. I only wish that I could do him greater justice. But if I have to choose between, on the one hand, accepting the rule which he has proclaimed and thus not being able to say certain things which I perceive and which I believe ought to be said, or having to say them very differently from how I perceive them, and on the other hand saying them quite freely, but making myself guilty of what he regards as an 'obscure conceptuality,' then I have no option but to choose the second. His hermeneutical suggestions can become binding on me only when I am convinced that by following them I would say the same things better and more freely. For the time being, I am not so convinced."

[64]R. Bultmann, "Zu J. Schniewinds Thesen, das Problem der Entmythologisierung betreffend," *KuM*, I (1948), 135–153; also "Zum Problem der Entmythologisierung," *KuM*, II (1952), 179–208; cf. J. Schniewind, "Antwort an R. Bultmann. Thesen zum Problem der Entmythologisierung," *KuM*, I (1948), 85–134.

95

Basel, 24 December 1952

Dear Mr. Bultmann,

I ought to have written you long ago and thanked you for your very thorough answer to my book.[1] And now you have been kind enough to send me the second volume of your *Glauben und Verstehen*, of which I have attentively applied to myself the two new pieces at the end.[2] For this gift, too, I thank you, and ask you to forgive my long silence. I am not yet in the honorable state of retirement that you have now attained but have to tread the winepress day by day and week by week, so that many other good works get left undone for a long time and sometimes for ever.[3] But today seems to have been made just to write you a few lines.

Where shall I begin? I have read your notes again and again. And provision has been made in another way that keeps you constantly present with your drilling mechanism: not only because our common and very promising student H. Ott keeps giving me installments of his dissertation on your "twofold concept of history"[4] but also because I am constantly listening to you in my ongoing work as you try to stop me doing the things that I then obstinately do all the same. I, too, am a Don Juan who certainly hears the powerful bass of Komtur, but does not repent as demanded.

Is it clear to you how things are with us—you and me? It seems to me that we are like a whale (do you know Melville's remarkable book *Moby Dick?* You ought to have a high regard for it because of its animal mythology!) and an elephant meeting with boundless astonishment on some oceanic shore. It is all for nothing that the one sends his spout of water high in the air. It is all for nothing that the other moves its trunk now in friendship and now in threat. They do not have a common key to what each would obviously like to say to the other in its own speech and in terms of its own element. A riddle of creation whose solution in the eschaton I like to depict as Bonhoeffer does by pointing toward the "I restore all things" of the Christmas hymn.

The continuous offense that you take at me—I must have been prepared for it, but I was surprised that it came out so pointedly in your comments—is obviously due to the fact that I do not adequately understand, and take seriously, existential philosophy, or its binding character as an axiom of all possible theological thought and utterance today. I have to admit the charge. I cannot change in this matter—as you on your side obviously cannot change either—and the most triumphant expansion of that philosophy over the whole earth could not make the slightest impression on me. Look, after being a Kantian up to my ears in my young days, after having been tempted no less fully by Schleiermacher's romanticism, after being given later (when studying nineteenth-century theology) an unforgettable impression—I got a sharp taste of this in a seminar on Biedermann—of the radiant certainty with which it was once thought that the first and last word about each and all "understanding" had been heard in Hegel—I am not an enemy of philosophy as such, but I have hopeless reservations about the claim to absoluteness of any philosophy, epistemology, or methodology. Occasionally I may cheerfully make use of existential categories—not without going back again sometimes to father Plato and others—but I simply do not summon up the ethical zeal to feel any consequent obligation to that philosophical approach. What do you want? Obviously I am no longer "existentially" (*existentiell*) captivated by it—as I was only too often earlier, but am now finally frightened off—just as I can no longer join any political party—I was once a Social Democrat. And just because I could make myself heard quite well (communication!) among my contemporaries (and not just the theologians among them), not even on this score, apart from all else, have I found occasion for repentance and conversion. I see and understand that all this must be an "abomination" to you—almost like the Blumhardt stories.[5] But this is how I am. You want to explain to me that what you are doing to the NT with existentialism is not measuring it by an alien canon, not putting it in a strait-jacket, etc., but engaging in *the* relevant exegesis. And that is what is not clear to me when I think about it. In your exposition I find the textual element concealed which, I believe, should not merely be brought to light, but brought to light first and decisively. And because this is connected with your principial philosophical presupposition, this becomes really frightening to me as you apply it. At which you will be vexed again and demand either directly or through the little schoolmasters in Tübingen[6] that I should answer your questions without being able to understand that these are of any particular importance for me. Hence a new shaking of the head on your part. Etc.!

It was materially impressive to me in your comments that for you the really irksome thing about "mythological thinking" turns out to be its "*objectifying.*" The situation between us could be made clearer by this, but not easier. And is it really made clearer? For how you will complain if I argue in opposition that you are obviously favoring a consistent "subjectivizing." I always thought I should lay emphasis on what might emerge as the objective content of your demythologized statements. For the thing that puts me off in your translating of the NT was and is that your statements seem to point to a kind of vacuum and claim to have content precisely in saying nothing beyond the existence of the believing "subject." I would not press my basic uneasiness more sharply in this regard than I did on pp. 32f. and 38f. of my booklet.[7] You have certainly said it often enough but this time it has come home to me: The bad thing about myth is "objectifying." And now my perplexity is really great, especially when I see at the same time how actively you protest against the equation of existentialism and anthropologism (but what do I read in *Glauben und Verstehen*, II, 262, right at the beginning?).[8] What is beyond question is that what you say about "objectifying" (insofar as it obviously has for you a pejorative sense, seeking certainty and the like) falls on deaf ears with me, for I have learned precisely from the NT, and will not merely continue but will do so by preference, to objectify first and only long after to "subjectify." What a dreadful contrast; my interest in NT "mythology" is precisely that it "objectifies" the statements of the NT in such unheard of fashion. And at that you see red! How can we come to terms with one another when you obviously can do no other than finish the ride you have begun? The only thing is that you cannot ask me to do a 180° turn and follow you in this direction—not even if it is true that you did in fact (even though I was not aware of it) break off in this direction as a result of my 1921 preface.[9]

But now you seem to be asking me to go where I cannot—or will not—follow you. Dear Mr. Bultmann, how can I explain this to you when I see from what you write, and hear it confirmed on every hand, that you for your part do not read me in context but at best seek to listen to me only in relation to your own special concern? Far, far be it from me to take that amiss! In the eschaton I hope to be able to find and read very different and much better books than my own. But understanding in the temporal present is made a little difficult if I read you but you do not know where my special interest—for my part with some persistence—lies. At the risk of more headshaking and displeasure I will at any rate venture to whisper one thing to you, namely, that I have become increasingly a Zinzendorfian to the extent that in the NT only the one central figure as such has begun to occupy me—or each and everything else only in the light and under the sign of this central figure. As I see it, one can and should read all theology in some sense backwards from it: down to anthropology, ethics, and then methodology. This is what I have attempted and am still attempting. I have not become "orthodox" for this reason; I could list for you the points at which I have diverged a good deal from the paths of what can be meaningfully called "orthodoxy" and at which I shall continue to diverge on the stretches that are before me. Nor have I attained to "certainty" and the like. These last weeks have I not been certified in a Dutch book and a French book[10]—and not for the first time—as being fundamentally an "existentialist"? But in this light theology has become for me a very positive business. You must understand—if you can—why for this reason I cannot do justice to your postulates and on the other hand take pleasure in the "objectifying" that you forbid. I will not expand on this either polemically or otherwise. One cannot discuss the fact that "Jesus lives," as we are both convinced. But one can, as a theologian, either refrain or not refrain from thinking to and from this "objective" reality. I myself cannot refrain from doing so, but do it. Hence I have different concerns from yours. The whole kerygma-myth problem is for me a question of second rank. I can even become annoyed (as obviously happened in relation to *Kerygma und Mythos*, II) when I see you and your friends acting as though the priority of your concerns were written in the stars. You will understand from this that for me the illuminating points in your comments may be found on pp. 10 and 11 [above, p. 99] (and on p. 13 in connection with Buri's unsettled question [above, p.101]), where you seem to contemplate a further return to the complex of the "Christ event."

Dear Mr. Bultmann, my best and most peaceful thoughts about you are when I try to think of you with the hypothesis with which I seek to bring the great Schleiermacher before myself and my students, namely, that what you are after is to be regarded as an attempt at a theology of the "third article" and therefore of the Holy Spirit. I could view this as a fundamentally legitimate and even fruitful undertaking. But then the relation between the third and the second article must be clarified, i.e., the latter must not be dissolved in the former but set forth in its own dignity over against it. This is where I balk at you as I do at Schleiermacher (and often also at the younger Luther). If you could make a move in this direction, we would be able to talk easily about many things. I should no longer view your statements as being in a vacuum, I would not need to oppose you so defiantly that I intentionally "objectify," and I might even, as you desire, "heidegger" a little with you. You for your part . . . but I will not depict this millennial possibility further, simply saying that the whale and the elephant would then at least find their common theme.

But now the Christmas bells are already ringing outside and I will break off. There are hints that the Christ child has ready for me a whole set of Mozart records. When you visit Basel again it may be that we can listen to some of them together before or after a session in that small inn.[11] I sincerely hope that when this letter reaches you, you and yours will have had a good Christmas and will have ahead a good transition into the New Year,

With best wishes,

Yours,
KARL BARTH

[1]See No. 94, n. 1.

[2]R. Bultmann, *Glauben und Verstehen. Gesammelte Aufsätze*, II (Tübingen, 1952; 5th enlarged ed., 1968). The two essays at the end of the 1952 ed. are "Formen menschlicher Gemeinschaft," pp. 262–273, and "Die Bedeutung des Gedankens der Freiheit für die abendländische Kultur," pp. 274–293.

[3]Bultmann retired in 1951, Barth not until 1962.

[4]Heinrich Ott later succeeded Barth at Basel. His dissertation, dedicated "with gratitude and respect to his esteemed teachers Karl Barth and Rudolf Bultmann," was published under the title *Geschichte und Heilsgeschichte in der Theologie Rudolf Bultmanns* (Tübingen, 1955).

[5]This is an allusion to Barth's attachment to the Württemberg pietists Johann Christoph Blumhardt (1805–1880) and his son Christoph (1842–1919). Bultmann had said in *KuM*, I (p. 150), that stories about the Blumhardts were an abomination to him.

[6]Gerhard Ebeling and Ernst Fuchs.

[7]*Rudolf Bultmann. Ein Versuch ihn zu verstehen*, pp. 39f., 45f.

[8]R. Bultmann, "Formen menschlicher Gemeinschaft," *GuV*, II, 262: "The concern that induces the following discussion is not sociological but anthropological—anthropology understood as reflection on human being—and therefore, so far as I am concerned, existential."

[9]See No. 94, n. 55.

[10]M. P. van Dijk, *Existentie en genade* (Franeker, 1952); M. Neeser, *Karl Barth, l'homme de l'arête* (Neuchâtel, 1952).

[11]See No. 93, n. 2.

96

Basel, 18 December 1959

Dear Mr. Bultmann,

I was glad to hear from you again (for I have had constant occasion to think about you) and to receive such an important greeting as your essay on Rom. 5:12f.[1]

You will recall that my own modest effort on this theme[2] was published along with my notorious attempt "to understand you." I originally meant to have stated expressly that this was a specimen of my exegesis of a NT text, but then preferred to leave it to readers who were so inclined to figure out the coincidence. You as the chief person concerned did at least get the point.

I am grateful to you for taking the time to discuss and debate with me, and I will sit down and try to follow you point by point. My first impression is that in the difference in our expositions we have perhaps a reflection of our approaches to the NT, the difference in which we shall never overcome in this life. In heaven (as the top floor of the mythological world-structure) we may perhaps seek out the apostle Paul together—in my case, of course, only after a longer excursion to W. A. Mozart—and ask him to explain to us what he himself ultimately had in mind. But this happy prospect should not be an excuse for not letting myself be better informed by you, if possible, at least in details.

I should very much like to see you again face to face, to hear from you, for example, what you think about your followers engaging both individually and together, as it seems, in a new search for the "historical Jesus."[3] Also what you think about the book on Heidegger by our Mr. Ott[4] and his other developments. Also whether and how far you have been influenced, and eventually carried to new shores, by the new Tillich wave that has come to us across the Atlantic.

Our common friend Baumgartner[5] is now in happy retirement, but

I am still at the plow and am constantly pushing a little ahead with the *Church Dogmatics*[6] (which you, you naughty man, are known not to read).

However that may be, I wish you and yours a happy Christmas and New Year.

Again with sincere thanks and friendly greetings,

Yours,
KARL BARTH[7]

[1]R. Bultmann, "Adam und Christus nach Römer 5," *ZNW*, 50 (1959), 145–165, reprinted in *Der alte und der neue Mensch in der Theologie des Paulus* (Darmstadt, 1964), pp. 41–66 (*Exegetica*, pp. 424–444).

[2]K. Barth, *Christus und Adam nach Röm. 5* (Zollikon-Zurich, 1952; reprinted along with the essay on Bultmann, Zurich, 1964). In a preceding note to the second edition (Jan. 1964) Barth says that he is associating the two works because he thinks it will be a good thing to supplement his attack with an example of his own NT exegesis. Reviewers have not to his knowledge noticed the connection. Perhaps Bultmann did when he wrote his own work on Romans 5 in 1959 and in it made his reply to the attempt to understand him. Barth admits that he does not understand Bultmann, and it is plain that Bultmann for his part does not understand Barth. And after reading Bultmann's mild approval of the "flatfooted theology" of the Bishop of Woolwich (J.A.T. Robinson, *Honest to God*, reviewed by Bultmann in *Die Zeit* [10 May 1963], p. 18 [*GuV*, IV, 107–112], and also *ZThK*, 60 [1963], 335–348 [*GuV*, IV, 113–127]) Barth wonders whether any agreement between them is even conceivable, let alone possible, in this world. In other words, younger scholars, instead of seeking common ground beyond Barth and Bultmann, might be better advised to follow one or the other consistently. Neither he and Bultmann, nor he and Tillich, nor he and the posthumously trimmed Bonhoeffer can coexist as heraldic lions on the entrance gate to the paradise of a better future theology. Decisions are needed similar to those made forty years earlier "in place of further stumbling about in a deadend."

[3]Ernst Käsemann announced the new quest of the historical Jesus in his lecture "Das Problem des historischen Jesus" at the meeting of Marburg alumni at Jugenheim on 20 Oct. 1953. This lecture was printed in *ZThK*, 51 (1954), 125–153 (E. Käsemann, *Exegetische Versuche und Besinnungen*, I [Göttingen, 1960], pp. 187–214). It initiated an intensive discussion: "Die Frage nach dem historischen Jesus . . . ," *ZThK* Occasional Paper 1 (Tübingen, 1959); R. Bultmann, "Das Verhältnis der nt. lichen Christusbotschaft zum historischen Jesus," *Exegetica*, pp. 445–469; E. Käsemann, "Sackgassen im Streit um den historischen Jesus," *Exegetische Versuche und Besinnungen*, II (Göttingen, 1964), pp. 31–68; R. Bultmann, "Antwort an Ernst Käsemann," *GuV*, II, 190–198.

[4]H. Ott, *Denken und Sein. Der Weg Martin Heideggers und der Weg der Theologie* (Zollikon, 1959).

[5]Walter Baumgartner; see No. 24, n. 7.

[6]*KD (CD)* IV, 3, Second Half, came out in 1959 (ET 1962).

[7]The original has not been found and the copy was not signed.

97

Basel, 28 December 1963

Dear Mr. Bultmann,

It was very kind of you to send me an offprint of your last essay in *ZThK.*[1] I had already read it there but have now considered it once again. If only we agreed in our evaluation of these works and[2] especially that of the Bishop of Woolwich![3] Ponder this, I usually reject this book with Schiller as a "document of the scandal of our times" and compare its origin to the act of a man who went and drew off the froth from three full glasses of beer (with the inscriptions R.B., P.T., and D.B.),[4] and made out that the resultant mixture was the finally discovered theological elixir, as which it was merrily consumed by thousands and thousands of buyers. But (with Fontane): "Let us leave, this, Luise, it is too big a field." I have recently seen a nativity by Botticelli that was previously unknown to me. Up above in a very lively dance are the angels ("Glory to God . . ."), in the middle are Joseph, Mary, the child, the oxen, and the asses, and down below are three couples embracing one another, one of the couples consisting of two really old gentlemen who are joyously smiling at one another ("Peace on earth . . ."). In spite of Woolwich, etc., let us be like these two!

I am sorry to hear that you have not been too well. Is this true? For in this respect, as in all others, I send my sincerest wishes for the coming year and in recollection of the "beginnings of the dialectical theology" my friendliest greetings.

Yours,
Karl Barth

[1]R. Bultmann, "Der Gottesgedanke und der moderne Mensch," *ZThK*, 60 (1963), 335–348 (*GuV*, IV, 113–127). Bultmann wrote in this copy the dedication: "Sincere Christmas greetings, Rudolf Bultmann."

[2]The MS has *uns* here for *und.*

[3]J.A.T. Robinson, whose *Honest to God* is reviewed by Bultmann.

[4]Rudolf Bultmann, Paul Tillich, and Dietrich Bonhoeffer.

98

Marburg, 9 May 1966

Dear Mr. Barth,

From ancient Marburg, too, there has to be a greeting for your eightieth birthday.[1] From the depths of his heart your old friend wishes you good health and good courage for the new year of your life.

Yours,
RUDOLF BULTMANN

[1]10 May 1966.

APPENDIX

1

[A letter from Dr. Friedrich Siegmund-Schultze of Berlin to Karl Barth]

Berlin, 5 January 1924

[In this letter, Siegmund-Schultze expresses his concern that, with an appeal to Barth, opposition has arisen to his society on the ground that one ought to preach waiting rather than working. He does not think that Barth himself really supports this but wants reassurance on the point.]

2

[A dispute arose on the Göttingen faculty as to whether Barth should entitle his 1924 lectures "Dogmatics" or "Reformed Dogmatics." This is a letter from Dean Rahlfs to Barth on the subject, and Barth replies in App., No. 3.]

Göttingen, 22 December 1923

Highly Esteemed Colleague,

At the request of the theological faculty I must ask you to change the title of your main course next semester, in accordance with your teaching assignment, to:

"Prolegomena to *Reformed* Dogmatics."

I am thus returning the schedule of lectures which has already been sent in and would request that you kindly send it back amended as suggested.

With best wishes for the holiday,

Yours truly,
A. Rahlfs, Dean

3

[This is Barth's reply to App., No. 2]

Göttingen, 31 December 1923

[Barth has corresponded with the Reformed Moderator for Germany and the Hanover Superintendent regarding his status as an honorary Reformed professor at Göttingen. He contends that he is a professor *in* the faculty and that the request made through the dean is without precedent. It does not correspond even to the letter of his assignment and would seem to imply that Reformed dogmatics is a sectarian teaching alongside dogmatics proper, i.e., Lutheran dogmatics. While he recognizes that he does not have the freedom to do anything, this request restricts his proper freedom, and even his obligation, to present Reformed dogmatics as *the* dogmatics. It is also superfluous, for everyone knows Barth's confessional stance. He should have been notified of restrictions of this kind, if they existed, when the position was established three years before. He thus asks the dean to request the faculty to reconsider and rescind their decision. If they cannot do so, he asks for advance notice concerning other areas (ethics, symbolics, practical theology) to which a similar restriction might be applied.]

[Editor's note: According to a letter from the Prussian Minister, Barth's assignment was formulated as follows: "Introduction to the Reformed confession, Reformed teaching, and the life of the Reformed community." He was given the title: "Honorary Professor in the Theological Faculty of the University of Göttingen."]

4

[An undated letter (probably July 1924) from O. Urbach to Karl Barth]

[Urbach, who is unknown to Barth, has read his *Romans* (3rd edition) and also Bultmann's article "Die liberale Theologie und die jüngste theologische Bewegung." He has been told that Barth agrees with this article, and if so he is most disappointed, for Bultmann derives Barth's theology from liberalism, whereas Barth himself says he feels closer to positive theology, and this is how the circles in which Urbach moves have understood him. He believes that if their view is right, Barth is really breaking new ground, but not so if Bultmann's interpretation is correct, since what Bultmann has in mind is diametrically opposed to

Barth's thinking. Bultmann is right enough in his criticism of liberalism, but this is agreement only in negation. Bultmann believes in the principle: The more radical, the better! The less there is of history, the greater the venture, the leap! But if there is no historical basis, why trust in Christ rather than Mohammed or Marx or a self-created idea? Abandonment of history means a relativism, not of history, but of ideas. There are two kinds of religion: objectivism and subjectivism. Bultmann rejects both and clings to an idea which is supposedly reached through history. It would be tragic if Barth were to reach a compromise with him. He thus pleads with Barth to avoid this; only then can his theology be and become what it ought to be. He asks him to state clearly that this theology is not a fulfilment of liberalism, the very thought of which would shock his father, the Blumhardts, and his other mentors. A crisis has arisen in the Barth circle and the time has come for Barth to make it plain that he does not share the views of Bultmann. In *Come Holy Spirit* he sees the hope that the theology of *Romans* will truly represent a twilight of the dawn and not of the sunset.]

5

[A letter from Pastor Hermann Kutter of Zurich to Karl Barth]

Zurich, 16 June 1925

[Kutter explains the position relating to the choice of his successor at the Neumünster in Zurich. Barth and Thurneysen are his own preferences—the only ones, in his view, who "can give great, and in our day increasingly important, witness to God in the pulpit—which is, as I see it, the true arena of the kingdom of God. The whole Christian community is waiting for the decisive word, and I note here in my own congregation that something has broken through, a great demand for the 'objectivity' of God, not merely among students, but everywhere." Since he knows that Barth would not be averse to returning to Switzerland and a parish, he hopes that he and Thurneysen will discuss it together and that one of them at least will come. There will be no diffusion of effort here, since he has taught his people to focus on witness itself. An opportunity will thus exist "to prosper mightily the seed that has been sown and perhaps to gather it into the barns; for the time presses and is germinating everywhere."]

6

[A letter from Pastor Rudolf Schlunk of Melsungen to Karl Barth]

Melsungen, 21/22 June 1925

[Schlunk does not think Barth should be tied to Göttingen, since his position rests on the Word. On the other hand, the chair is an extension of the pulpit. He will have to be guided, of course, by God, and it may be that he should go back to Switzerland to renew his strength and contribute what he has learned abroad. Kutter is right to give precedence to the pulpit, though this is not a common view, and a return to it would certainly focus attention in the right place. Perhaps another academic post will open up which will be free of the ambiguity and subversion of the professorship in Göttingen. Better still would be the birth of a free theological faculty, if possible in Prussia, on which Barth could write his dogmatics in peace. This path would have its thorns but Barth would be captain of his own ship. Staying in Göttingen has its thorns too, and is much less stimulating.]

7

[A review of books which R. Bultmann wrote for the evening edition of the Berliner Tageblatt und Handels-Zeitung, *3 August 1925, pp. 2f.]*

Georg Brandes and Johannes Müller on Jesus

Two works have been passed on to me which I should like to compare for the reader.[1] I looked forward to reading them, for when a theme like theirs has been treated so often by specialists, and research is so freighted by tradition, it may be that an uninhibited layman coming to the subject will see things that scholarship does not see because he looks in a surprising new direction. How is it in these cases?

The first work is entitled *The Jesus Saga* and the name of the author is that of the famous Danish literary historian Georg Brandes. It tells us that the Jesus of the Gospels is a legendary figure like William Tell. The picture of Jesus developed out of the centuries old picture of a divine figure which is plainly visible in Revelation, "the foundation of the New Testament." This is the heavenly being whose eyes glow like flames, whose voice is as the sound of many waters, who holds the seven stars in his hand, from whose mouth proceeds a two-edged sword, and whose face is as radiant as the sun. In the "not many genuine parts" of Paul's letters the same figure appears as the firstborn before all creatures by whom heaven and earth were made. Paul, a sick, quarrelsome, and probably hunchbacked Jew, knows nothing about the historical Jesus, as little as the secular writers of the time. Ancient longings and ideals created that picture in Israel as the picture of the Messiah. It merged with the picture of God himself and together with it there grew up the figure of a dying and rising-again divine savior which was widespread in Near Eastern religions. The questioning and curiosity of newly formed believers brought it about that with the help of anecdotes, legends, and the like, a Gospel was compiled ("a brew was concocted," says the tasteful author) in which the grandiose or grotesque imaginary picture became the idyllic one of a young man who went about teaching in Galilee. The Old Testament in particular provided the material; several scenes in the "life of Jesus" hark back to its themes. Yet the picture of Jesus which developed in this way is not uniform; various trends overlap in it. Sometimes Jesus appears as full of the joy of life, sometimes as a gloomy Puritan; here as a Jew who is faithful to the law, there as a revolutionary. In his alleged sayings less worthy elements mingle with those of higher rank, though these never reach the heights of Greek and Roman morality.

The specialist is not surprised after reading the work, although many lay readers may be. But even the specialist may be surprised as he makes *one* strange discovery, namely, that obviously the author of this book never lived. Like the New Testament according to the way it is seen here, the work is a grotesque compilation of old and new materials; like the supposed "life of Jesus" it is totally composed of themes from earlier works. I have recognized David Friedrich Strauss in it, along with French and Dutch writers (who are sometimes very naively mentioned); there is a trace of the eccentric American W. B. Smith and also of the English ethnologist Frazer. The materialistic or socialistic authors of lives of Jesus, the Assyriologist and interpreter of the Gilgamesh epic P. Jensen, and the philosopher A. Drews, who has joined the astrologers, have all had to contribute. In short, there is nothing to read here that I have not read elsewhere. Is it possible that such a book should have had a real author? Furthermore, the historical picture presented in the book is by no means consistent. Various tendencies intersect. Here the exposition is according to the method of ethnology and religious history; there it is rationalistic or materialistic. Here humanistic enthusiasm prevails for the Greek and Roman ethos; there the reverence of the modern primitive may be felt for ancient rites of purification. Here the results of the most recent historical scholarship are presented; there a naive uncertainty obtains concerning the development of the Mishnah or the ancient Quartodeciman controversy, concerning which the author is all at sea. Here scepticism is not arrested even by well-attested statements; there the personal description of Paul is credulously taken from apocryphal sources.

With this I am to compare the work by Johannes Müller. But how can I compare two writings that are so fundamentally different? For in Müller's there is no doubt as to the existence of the historical Jesus, and the Gospel accounts are very naively evaluated without any consideration of the differences in their historical reliability. Yet at *one* point comparison is possible. For as the one book dresses up again old material, this one, in spite of its qualities, belongs fundamentally to a world that has gone. And, to be frank, it can also compare with the other in tedium. The *one* thought that runs through it is harried to death, and one is finally choked by its "immediacy to and from God," its "creative fermentations" and "developments," and its "unconscious spiritual depths and vital processes." The author writes about "Jesus as I see him." This might sound modest, but the author, who regards "immediacy to and from God" as the constitutive thing in the life of Jesus, assures us: "I understand this because I know the distinctive character of a life of immediacy." Indeed, he thinks: "We can truly follow Jesus, more authentically and genuinely, indeed, better and more easily than his disciples, because we know him more profoundly and essentially than they did. For we know him according to the spirit, according to what inwardly composed and constituted and activated him. We know the peculiar disposition of his soul and the inner law of his life." In this case I must unhappily range myself on the side of the alleged Georg Brandes, who does not know all this; for I know nothing about it either. I must also state candidly that in my view J. Müller also knows nothing, absolutely nothing, about it. In reality his presentation consists of a very naive projection onto the figure of Jesus of the ideal of "a life of immediacy to and from God," whose distinctive character he knows. And this might not be so bad; for if the historian is not satisfied, the naive reader might be when he is led to the sources of a life of immediacy. But what does he find? A possibly naive but schoolmasterly and impotent romanticism distinguished neither by tradition nor imagination. I know that J. Müller has his merits, but to offer this book about Jesus to the modern age one has to be completely blind to the fact that such romanticism belongs to an age that is past. To the past also belongs the battle against subjectivity and reflection that might have been justified once. But this battle is badly fought if one appeals from rationalism to the unconscious spiritual life instead of to the facts with which we have to do; if one appeals for surrender to subconscious impulse instead of to that which encounters us as a demand; if one understands as an objective event the act which does not enter the consciousness as an act of will, but which proceeds unreflectingly from nonknowledge as an inner compulsion and which regards the demonic area "where the conscious is completely excluded by the superior power of the subconscious" as the most objective recipient of the divinely filled nature of Jesus; if one understands the decision in which man is placed as the decision for the elemental thrust and sure taste of an "autonomous feeling for life," and fails to see the decisions in which the reality of life meets us in the concrete relation of I and Thou, in the concrete present with its needs and obligations. I say that the battle is badly fought, for such a one is trying to drive out the devil by Beelzebub and does not realize how deeply he himself is caught in the subjectivism of a reflective culture.

I feel the presumptuousness of this work so strongly that I must say no more. If the author had only had a picture of Jesus in which he never spoke connectedly and he was obviously not concerned about understanding or being understood, he might have acted in the same way and left his 96 pages unwritten. Or has he acted in this way? For there are in fact sentences that do not seem to count on being understood, e.g.: "Only the form of his [Jesus'] spiritual life was subjective; the content was objective. This was the given, the divinely given, that after the manner of genius unconsciously found subjective representations. . . ." I at least can form no conception of a content that is gifted with genius. But seriously, the style itself is a symptom that a theme that is too serious for dilettante efforts is treated here with a minimum of mental labor. Those who believe that only a turning to the subject matter can rescue us from reflection and subjectivism will not approach even history in the way this author does; they will investigate, not the spiritual life of a great person, but what he has to say, the content of his words, the things to which these words point.

[1]Georg Brandes, *Die Jesus-Sage* (Berlin: Erich Reiss, 1925), 155 pp. Johannes Müller, *Jesus wie ich ihn sehe,* Vol. 27, No. 1 of *Grüne Blätter, Zeitschrift für persönliche und völkische Lebensfragen* (Elmau: Verlag der Grünen Blätter, 1925), 96 pp.

8

[Letter from Johannes Müller to R. Bultmann]

Schloss Elmau, 6 August 1925

Reverend Professor,

When I read your review of my *Jesus, wie ich ihn sehe* in the *Berliner Tageblatt,* I found it impossible at first to imagine how you could come to see and evaluate and treat it as you did. Singularly, for the first time in the twenty-seven years of the existence of the *Grüne Blätter* a large number of leading people wrote to me very incisively about this issue, and all of them with a high degree of recognition and agreement in essentials, different though their stance and outlook might be in other matters: Adolf v. Harnack, Karl Barth, Dr. Kattenbusch, Graf Baudissin, Chamberlain, Ricarda Huch, Lehrer Flemming, Roman Woerner, etc. I could finally solve the riddle only by assuming that you had not read the first two pages of the work, the preface. For this in fact invalidates all that you say about and against it, since what I proposed and offered was completely different from what you assumed. I would have to doubt your sincerity, justice, and sense of propriety if you had read the preface and still held up my presentation of how I see Jesus to the scorn of the public as something that it neither is nor seeks to be. I ask, therefore, for the only possible restitution, namely, that you should now read these two pages very carefully and thoughtfully. Then I shall not need to show that all your blows do not in fact touch me.

But your conclusion is still beyond my comprehension. How can you accuse me, and me specifically, of not asking what Jesus has to say, what is the content of his words, what are the things to which they point. You know that for three decades I have wrestled intensively with the sayings of Jesus. You know at least by hearsay my book on the Sermon on the Mount and the three volumes of the sayings of Jesus, though you probably have little acquaintance with the innumerable essays on his sayings in the twenty-six volumes of the *Grüne Blätter.* My whole life's work has been devoted to that of which the sayings of Jesus inform us, to the kingdom of God as divine reality. Only in my sixty-first year have I attempted for the first time to show how Jesus lives directly in my consciousness, and this only at the desire of my hearers and readers, and with express emphasis on the very personal character of this picture, which arose without my cooperation in my contact with Jesus over many decades. I think that hardly anyone is less open to this criticism than I am.

I for my part had sent you this volume as a mark of gratitude for the great help that my eldest son Michel has received from you in the study of theology at Marburg. I am upset, then, that you took it so ungraciously, and I will certainly not burden you with any more of my productions. But I hope that perhaps in time you will come to appreciate the present work.

Yours respectfully,
JOHANNES MÜLLER

9

[A letter from Pastor Schneider of Posen to Karl Barth]

Posen, 1 December 1925

[In this letter Schneider gives Barth a tentative schedule of addresses at the Danzig Seminar. Rendtorff of Leipzig will lecture for three hours on Tuesday, 5 Jan. 1926, and Bultmann and Barth will share the next three days, Bultmann lecturing for three hours on modern eschatology and Barth for three hours on Philippians 3, with perhaps a contribution from Hans Schmidt of Giessen, Blau, or Kalweit. The evenings will be devoted to discussion and fellowship. Travel details will be sent later.]

10

Posen, 2 December 1925

[This is another letter from Schneider sent to Rendtorff and Bultmann as well as Barth, asking if the second week in January might be suitable instead of the first. He wrote again on 13 Dec. 1925 to say that applications were coming in, and they had now fixed definitely on the first week.]

11

[This letter is from Wolfgang Friedrich, a theological student at Marburg, to K. Barth.]

Marburg, 29 November 1927

[Friedrich tries to persuade Barth to change his mind about coming to lecture on the church at Marburg. The interest of the Theological Society is not a sensational one in Barth's person. They want a strong presentation of the theme and feel that Barth is well qualified to give this. The aim is to establish what is at issue when one talks about the church in the modern situation. As has already been suggested, a time at the end of February might be suitable.]

12

[This is a letter from Karl Barth, now at Münster, to Friedrich Gogarten.]

Münster, 16 July 1928

Dear Gogarten,

Could you drop me a line to fill me in on Hans Michael Müller, your colleague at Jena, who has ventured out so mischievously in the *Theologische Blätter.* Previously I have always read with pleasure things by him, but the way he has done this, playing me off against you and then Bultmann against me, the whole business of the Chinese generals, etc., seems to me to be very boorish on the part of a man who has obviously drawn so much from us (not to speak of all that may be said about the subject itself)—unless the importance of what he himself has to say, after he has put us all in his pocket, subsequently justifies him. What I want to know from you, then, before I do anything, or don't do anything, is how significant this man is in your judgment. At a first glance he seems to me to be simply a frivolous destroyer who is unmistakably clever enough to smash very thoroughly the china that comes into his hands. The story of the "fall of Gogarten" on p. 174 is a real bit of devilry. And what is K. L. Schmidt thinking about when first he prints Peterson's lament to Scheler and then this? I know that you do not like writing letters and are even more unwilling to make observations on the intellectual situation. But I would be really glad to learn from you again, or even to get some hints, as to how things look from Jena-Dorndorf.

With sincere greetings,

Yours,
KARL BARTH

13

[A postcard from Emil Brunner to Rudolf Bultmann]

Zurich, 20 August 1930

[Brunner would like to come to the "pillars' " conference but since he lectures the second half of the week he can only come Saturday and Sunday. He could also manage Monday and Tuesday if these are not needed for the Marburg alumni. But this will have to be decided at Marburg.]

14

[A letter from Erna Schlier of Marburg to K. Barth]

Marburg, 29 September 1930

[Mrs. Schlier suggests that, since the Bultmanns have no guest room in their new home, Barth should stay with herself and her husband when he is in Marburg. It is only five minutes from the Bultmanns' residence and will be convenient for private discussions. She would like a brief reply since they will put up someone else if Barth makes other arrangements.]

15

[A letter from Heinrich Schlier to K. Barth]

Marburg, 3 October 1930

[Schlier has learned that Barth may not come to Marburg. He pleads with him not to withdraw, for many will come to hear him and it is too late to change or cancel the conference. He recognizes that the idea of the summit meeting altered the point of coming for Barth, but this is not integrally related to the Alumni Conference. They are not interested in merely getting "personalities" nor do they want a battle, but their aim is to learn and to further discussion. Some may come out of curiosity but most will want to take the chance of learning things they cannot learn in the isolation of parish life. Barth, he hopes, will not allow misunderstanding as to the purpose and forum of his lecture to disappoint those who look forward to hearing him.]

16

[Letter from Dr. Gerhard Krüger of Marburg to K. Barth]

Marburg, 7 October 1930

Reverend Professor,

Now that you have abandoned your lecture at Marburg, you will hardly expect to hear from someone else about the matter. I do not really want you still to decide to come because of our "much importunity" if you can do so only unwillingly. But our situation is more difficult than you perhaps imagine, for the Marburgers cannot do without you; and on the other hand it might serve some purpose for you if you were to give the lecture. Obviously a good deal will be missing if you cannot speak with all those you would like, but there will still be opportunity to do this in the future if you use this preliminary chance to work on the matter: *scriptum est, manet.* And it would save the conference. For otherwise everything would—quite literally—depend on *me.* Bultmann cannot really replace you; the theme is defined in such a way that only a systematic theologian can handle it. Romans without some knowledge of dogmatics is not enough. But I am giving only a historical introduction and am not yet in a position to deal systematically with the philosophical side of the issue, let alone the theological. But this is what counts in this matter and especially for those who are coming to the conference. Plato and Aristotle are of no interest if it is not stated what we are to think dogmatically about them and their incorporation into the older theology. It was because of this that the decision was reached to invite *you.* Obviously it is not possible to change things so soon before the event. In short, I am in great difficulty. Shall I cancel too—which would mean the end of the conference and threaten its continuation, or shall I be satisfied with a half job for which it is not worth people's while coming? Unfortunately I cannot reach Bultmann. So Schlier and I have decided to tell the participants of the threat to the program so that they can make up their own minds whether to come or not. This is the situation that I have to tell you about. You will pardon me, who am particularly involved, for doing so.

I want to convince you and not to force you. You have had a different conception of the matter and not taken these difficulties into account. I need not say more about the way your lecture will help us and me in particular. The theme constantly engages me, and I have no one here who can speak to it adequately at the theological level.

Finally I should like to take this occasion to thank you for the friendly interest you showed in my work on Kant. I still hope that I shall be able to thank you, too, for coming to Marburg.

Yours respectfully,
G. KRÜGER

17

[From a letter sent by Hans von Soden to the authorities of the Evangelical Church of Nassau. This letter was also signed by his two colleagues, Hermelink and Frick. The former sent a copy to the authorities of the Evangelical Church

of Hesse-Kassel, while the latter, the Dean of the Faculty at Marburg, sent a copy to Directors Prof. Richter and Dr. Trendelenburg of the Prussian Ministry of Science, Art, and Culture at Berlin.]

Marburg, 16 November 1930

[While protesting their ongoing loyalty to the church the signatories issue a reminder that "this loyalty, like all true loyalty, is bound to conscience" and that they cannot "violate the core of their theological calling." They thus declare that they cannot accept the concordat proposal relating to the Marburg faculty, which does violence to this faculty and tries to solve a matter of conscience on a purely political basis. If it goes through it will be impossible for them conscientiously to "remain members of a church body that has become unevangelical and to remain the holders of chairs that have been weakened in their essential responsibility." They thus ask for reconsideration of the proposal.]

18

[Profs. Balla and Bultmann of Marburg, through Dean Frick, had made it known to the minister at Berlin (Grimme), in a letter dated 22 December 1930, that if the proposed reorganization went through they would leave the Kassel church and take the consequences. Several conferences followed and various memoranda were composed, including this one by Bultmann.]

Marburg, 18 January 1931

[Bultmann finds in the proposal a claim on the part of the church authorities that they should control the work of theological scholarship. Behind this claim lie two valid motifs: 1) the view that the doctrine which is proclaimed in the churches by preaching, and in which future pastors are instructed by the theological faculties, is not a matter of opinion but has a *definite content* and *definite* limits, so that the possibility of error arises; 2) the view that this doctrine is offered only in connection with the *church* and its *tradition,* so that *theology is a function of the church* and the church is therefore the court which distinguishes between correct doctrine and heresy.

One can thus understand the demand of the rulers of the church that they should watch over the purity of teaching by authoritative pronouncements. And yet *the deduction made from this by the church's rulers is quite untenable.*

1. *In the Protestant church no court can exist which fixes the norm*

of doctrine and distinguishes authoritatively between correct doctrine and heresy.

The point is that the subject of the church's teaching and theology is the revelation of God in history. Hence *theology* stands always in a distinctive analogy to the *discipline of history.* The subject of this discipline, history and its phenomena, is not offered to the historian as a simple object in the way that natural objects are present to natural science. They are seen and understood in their specifically *historical* significance only by *those* who are in history and take part in it, so that historical knowledge is always at the same time a position or decision. Similarly theological science can see its object, the revelation of God in history, only on the basis of a position, i.e., in this instance, faith. . . .

As it would be absurd for political or intellectual history to set up a court whose fixed teaching norms should control true and false teachings, so it would be absurd to set up a similar court for theology. Naturally, as history does not abandon the question of objective truth and proclaim relativism, no more does theology. History, like theology, *has a controlling court,* namely, the *object itself* which motivates research. For this reason theology, like history, has to be a *free* science with the possibility of error. For only if it has the possibility of *error* does it also have the possibility of *truth.* A church court that tries to eliminate or reduce the possibility of error for theology reduces or destroys the possibility of truth. The objection is obvious that the church cannot submit to dependence on theology, which as a science is vacillating in its results, constantly opposing, criticizing, and correcting itself. The fact is true, but the objection is false. In fact *the church does not live by theological science but by the object* of this science, the revelation of God. This object is not first discovered, disclosed, and established by theological science, but theology, like the church, lives on the basis of the existing relation to its object, i.e., on the basis of faith. The discipline of theology has the same relation to its object as does history. For this does not begin with its object (whether this be the Renaissance, or Goethe, or the French Revolution, or the unification of Germany, or the World War). It lives by the existing relation of a people to these historical factors. Every nation and age has *the* historical science corresponding to its own relation to its history, and historical science brings awareness of this relation, clarifying and purifying it.

In exactly the same way theology lives by the church's life. And as the political and intellectual life of a people fructifies and controls its historical science, so the life of the church fructifies and criticizes theology. As for historical science the actual political and intellectual life is the only controlling court, because in it the object, history, is present and at work, so the actual life of the church is the only controlling court for theology. As on the other hand history has a clarifying and critical influence on political and intellectual life (yet not because it stands outside it, but because it stands within it as a member), in exactly the same way theology as a member or organ of the life of the church has a clarifying and critical impact on it.

It is thus a complete contradiction to create an administrative agency (however modest in scope) which will control the teaching of theology. Church life itself can be the only control, and as its constituent and instrument the work of the church in which this life achieves conceptual awareness. Certainly there is true teaching and false, but what is true and false can only be continually rediscovered, defended and opposed, destroyed and established. What theology must never lose, and in this the church can and does exercise controlling power, is the awareness that what is at issue is the question of truth, that there is true doctrine and false. But the decision as to what is true and false doctrine can be made only in the work of theology.

2. *The claim of the church authorities to control the theological faculties presupposes a totally false view of the relation between these authorities and the faculties.*

The church can ascribe to itself control over the faculties along the lines set forth above. But the church's agencies, according to the Protestant view, are not the church, and the less so the more they are dependent on synodal majorities according to modern ecclesiastical constitutions. The church can exercise its control through the actual life of the church with its expressions of faith, as also of questioning and doubt. How else can it do so? How can it do so through its governing bodies?

Church agencies can judge theology critically only *by means of* theology. If as a whole or through a commission any agency of the church takes over the control of theology, two theological bodies are set up. And if this agency or a commission takes seriously its theological control of the faculties, it takes over the whole work of theology with its possibility of error and its discussions. And at once a new controlling authority will become necessary—and so ad infinitum. Naturally this will not happen, but the practical consequence will be that *the church agency will build on the theology of the past generation,* on the theology which members of the agency happened to have learned in their student days.

Apart from this absurdity, however, it is presumptuous for the church's agencies, which have the office of administration, to claim the office of teaching. Theology holds the office of teaching in the church, and it is for this reason the court that controls church government. It was a normal situation when in the past church rulers used the faculties as controlling authorities for measures in which doctrinal issues arise. Today, too, the agencies of the church should consult the faculties when it is a matter, e.g., of introducing new liturgical forms, or controlling the preaching of ministers, or in any instance when the question of doctrine is an urgent one in administration.

The freedom that scientific theological work must claim for itself *cannot* be claimed by the minister's preaching in the church. To be sure, preaching cannot be controlled by a set doctrinal norm. On the other hand, it cannot be absolutely free and subject to the individuality of the pastor. This means, however, that it can be under the control only of the theological faculties which handle the concept of correct teaching with the breadth and freedom with which it can be handled only in Protestantism. Instead, the church's agencies want to control the faculties, and they are concerned very little, if at all, about the preaching of ministers, leaving it to the subjectivity of the individual.

With guilt on both sides, things developed in the nineteenth century in such a way that today confusion reigns. From what happened with no responsibility on the part of modern theologians, these must now suffer as they strive for reform. *But what ought to take place today and in the future is something for which they do have responsibility.* For this reason we resist to the very last the claim of the church authorities. If our church officers uphold the right that they claim, we can no longer recognize our church as a Protestant church but shall declare our departure from it and lay down our office as teachers of theology.

PROF. RUDOLF
BULTMANN

19

[This letter from the Faculty of Theology at the University of Marburg was sent to the President of the German Evangelical Theological Conference, Prof. Hans Schmidt of Halle, and to the faculties of theology in Berlin, Bonn, Greifswald, Königsberg, and Münster.]

Marburg, 24 January 1931

[The letter explains why the Marburg faculty wanted an extraordinary meeting of the faculties of theology, namely, to clarify and discuss its position relating to the new system of appointment proposed in the concordat. They regret that their call for personal interaction was not adopted, and object to the failure to carry out the decisions of the Marburg Conference of 1929. They do not think that Schmidt correctly interpreted the Breslau conference to the ministry in Berlin (various points being adduced in evidence). The letter, which goes out above the name of Bornhäuser as Acting Dean, closes with a sharp reprimand for Schmidt, who, it is alleged, "has abandoned objectivity and broken the impartiality of his office."]

20

[A letter from the Faculty of Theology at Bonn to the Faculty of Theology at Marburg]

Bonn, 28 January 1931

To the Faculty of Theology, Marburg/Lahn:

To your communication of the 24 inst. we take the liberty of replying: We cannot regard your serious charges against the President of the Conference of German Evangelical Theological Faculties, Professor Hans Schmidt of Halle/Saale, as sustained either in general or in detail.

We refused the invitation to the conference because we regarded as impossible the basis created for it by the threat of leaving the church and resigning office on the part of five members of your faculty. We must also reject the accusation of uncollegiality that you have brought against us.

We regret that you did not first wait to learn the position of the accused and that of the other faculties but saw fit to bring these internal matters immediately to the notice of an external authority. We are compelled by your procedure to report our statement to the head of the educational administration.

This is the unanimous decision of all members of the faculty apart from Professor Hölscher.

The Evangelical
Faculty of Theology at
Bonn,
DEAN PRO TEM.
GOETERS

21

[A letter from Prof. F. W. Schmidt of Münster to K. Barth]

Münster, 19 June 1931

Dear Mr. Barth,

I have just come from class and found your letter, and for the sake of clarification I am doubly grateful for it. For my astonishment is no less than yours.

Should I be more astonished at Bultmann's doubt whether I gave correct information or at the total misunderstanding of the situation? I never gave the *Marburgers* any specific information. At the Breslau Conference of Deans I addressed a question put by President Hans Schmidt and did not mention your name at all. (I note that Bultmann was not at Breslau but Bornhäuser represented Marburg.) The issue was a communication of *our* faculty through *Stählin** to the church conference last summer which in my time did not go to the faculties. At Breslau I could not give the reason for this unusual communication (did St. simply write to Prussian faculties?). Nor did I have the piece at hand, and while I knew its general drift I did not at the moment know all the details. The question was whether a call could be approved until the ministry stepped in and the church was consulted and expressed itself.

This is the actual course of events. I repeat that I did not mention your name at all in this connection, nor refer to you in a single syllable at Breslau. Hence your suggestion that there has been a *complete misunderstanding* is an apt one.

I hope that all is going well with you, as it is with us (except that the children have colds). I have regular students at my lectures and seminars, can get around without help, and am venturing many fine bicycle rides around Münster.

I am sending you an essay on "the Theological Basis of Ethics" which may interest you.

With sincere family greetings,

Yours,
F. W. SCHMIDT

*Stählin was asked to do this because he had taken part in a corresponding meeting in Berlin (May, 1930).

22

[A letter from Prof. D. E. Wolf of Bonn to R. Bultmann]

Bonn, 21 June 1934

[Wolf is sending on the latest from Kittel and his reply, which is to be printed in *RKZ*. He thinks it might be worth saying something about the hopeless misuse of I Cor. 9:20, since the judgment of a NT scholar would be helpful. He will publish it in the July issue. In a lengthy correspondence with Barth, in which he argues that the Confessing Synod will have to choose between them, Kittel "persistently evades Barth's question as to the correctness of his 'exegesis' and insists instead that he has every right to give thanks continually for wife, children, vocation, people, country, etc. as 'erga theou.' In Bonn they presumably do not do this, as he told his audience at the beginning of this semester."]

23

[A letter from Hans von Soden of Marburg to Prof. Gerhard Kittel of Tübingen, a copy sent to K. Barth and E. Wolf with the handwritten note: "To my honored colleagues Wolf and Barth, for information only; need not be returned. Sincere greetings, v. Soden"]

Marburg, 25 June 1934

Honored Colleague,

You were good enough to have sent to me a copy of your open question to the Fraternal Council of the Confessing Synod and of your correspondence about this with our colleague Karl Barth. I have naturally studied these with particular interest. As a member of the Barmen Synod I cannot avoid answering your question. You will understand that I am doing so as briefly as possible. We have both been adequately informed about the state of the controversy and have both been heavily burdened by theological and ecclesiastical correspondence.

The situation is made easier for me by two factors. First, I had no hand in drawing up the Barmen theses. I accepted them with the wish that is natural in any independent theologian in such a case, namely, that this or that might have been stated differently, but with full and conscientious agreement and coresponsibility for their adoption by the synod. If I might have put many things differently, this does not mean that I did not espouse the theses (as one can meaningfully do in such situations) or make them my own in all essential matters. The second alleviating factor is that I have often enough borne witness to my critical attitude to dialectical theology and specifically to K. Barth. This has not changed. I have consistently recognized that dialectical theology, along the lines of the famous corrective, has performed a great and genuine service to the development of theology and particularly to that of the church crisis into which we have been led. Like all earlier theological fronts this, too, has been split by the crisis, and the only normative thing for me in church questions is what a person says about it and not who that person is or what he might say about other questions than that which demands an answer today.

I think I should also say that I have given testimony prior to the present crisis that I recognize the theological concern of your question and have acknowledged it as my own, e.g., in my Helsingfors lecture on Christianity and culture and elsewhere. I am of the opinion that this concern is by no means neglected in the Barmen theses either. The state of No. 5 is the specific state, the state of the historical hour. But what it demands is definitely limited in No. 5 and No. 1. My decisive objection to your amendment (I ask permission to state this plainly) is its ambiguity. What you express in your "we reject, etc.," is incontestable and in my view is not contested either formally or in principle, but it is of no help if it is not applied concretely to the historical moment and if it does not state plainly what is the relation between Hitler's hour and the proclamation of the gospel. I do not know who first used the phrase: "as though nothing had happened." If it was Barth, his struggle shows very plainly how it was not meant. If you noticed the two academic sermons that Bultmann and I preached in the summer of 1933 and that were printed together in *Neuwerk* (XV, 2), you cannot say that they were preached as though nothing had happened, and the same applies to responsible utterances in many places. The condemned formula can mean only that what has happened, and cannot and should not be ignored, ought not to be set aside but should alter the gospel in both its message and its demand, and that is your view as well as ours. But unfortunately we do not agree on what is altered and what is not. This seems to be stated clearly in the Barmen theses but is not obvious in yours. Someone once said, very well in my view, of certain proposals for action that they were "fundamentally an evasion." It would have been this if I had voted for your amendment, knowing very well that it covered over the conflict that we have to endure.

You will graciously permit me not to go into other matters, especially the application and exposition of I Cor. 9, which seem to me to be questionable, and your attacks on Barth, in which you seem to me to lay on him the burden of proof which as I see it really lies on you. It will not be profitable to go into this more closely. I can only hope that your question will help to clarify the antitheses; for in my view the only way to real peace can be via plain and fearless clarification. It is certainly our common view that this clarification may and can be achieved with mutual respect by people who agree that their concern is for the church.

With collegial greetings,

Yours truly,
VON SODEN

[For the Helsingfors address (21 Sept. 1932) on "Christentum und Kultur in der geschichtlichen Entwicklung ihrer Beziehungen," cf. H. v. Soden, *Urchristentum und Geschichte. Gesammelte Aufsätze,* ed. H. v. Campenhausen, Vol. 1: *Grundsätzliches und Neutestamentliches,* with a preface by R. Bultmann (Tübingen, 1951), pp. 56–89.]

24

[A postcard from E. Wolf to R. Bultmann]

Bonn, 29 June 1934

[Barth will be sending Bultmann a copy of his answer to Kittel's "lengthy effusion," which left Wolf with an impression of sophistry. Perhaps Kittel will send a copy too. He accuses Barth of a "docetic ecclesiology." Wolf hopes to visit Marburg briefly on the fourteenth after lecturing at Giessen.]

25

[A letter from the ministry at Berlin to the curator of the University of Bonn]

Berlin, 26 November 1934

[This letter refers to the action against Barth for failing to fulfil the obligations of his office by attempting to add to the oath of loyalty the phrase: "so far as I can responsibly do so as an Evangelical Christian."]

26

[A letter from Ernst Wolf to Rudolf Bultmann]

Bonn, 26 November 1934

[Wolf writes in haste to say that Barth has been suspended and that the Gestapo has ordered that his lectures be discontinued. Barth had told the rector that he could take the oath of loyalty only with an explicit proviso, and this was passed on to Berlin. He is taking the matter calmly and Wolf hopes it will be resolved. He wonders, however, whether some statement should not be considered on the limits of the oath. He regrets the appointment of Marahrens, but reserves final judgment. Marahrens is weak and privately regards Barth as the church's greatest threat.]

27

[This is Barth's judicial statement of 27 November 1934.]

[I. Barth protests against the irregularities 1) of being suspended without the statutory opportunity to reply; 2) of being suspended without even the choice to hear the charges; and 3) of the press announcement that he refused to take the oath.

II. He states that he will take the oath with the addition: "so far as I can responsibly do so as an Evangelical Christian," and argues in favor of this addition: 1) that an oath is possible only if the obligation is known; 2) that it used to be known when the oath was made to the constitution or even to the Kaiser; 3) that it is now made personally to Hitler, and therefore 4) has an infinite and unpredictable scope; and 5) that a conscious limitation is thus required, 6) in terms of the authority which necessarily restricts allegiance and obedience to Hitler.

III. He made this proposal to the rector, who promised to forward it to Berlin, but has received no answer to the proposal as thus forwarded. He cannot agree, therefore, that he has been remiss in his official obligations.]

28

[A letter from the Imperial Prussian Minister of Science, Education, and Culture, Rust, to K. Barth, with an addendum to the Curator of the Rhenish Friedrich Wilhelm University of Bonn]

Berlin, 21 June 1935

[Barth is informed that his professorship will terminate in accordance with § 6 of the law of 7 April 1933. He will be paid up to the end of September 1935]

29

[A letter from Hans v. Soden to K. Barth]

Marburg, 2 December 1934

[von Soden is very upset to learn of Barth's suspension and assures him of warm personal feelings even though he cannot agree with his position. As he sees it, Barth is asking the state "formally and principially to put a reservation of Christian conscience into the oath of office." He is thus anticipating "in an abstract formality the *status confessionis* which can arise only in a concrete, actual struggle." He is asking the state "to recognize an obligation of faith which . . . as such it cannot recognize." The clause Barth wants to insert has serious meaning only for believers; to unbelievers "it seems to be simply a masked evasion of the oath." To believers it is obvious that they must obey God rather than man in case of conflict, and take the consequences. Refusal of the oath is understandable, but "it seems to me to be impossible to accept the oath and add a clause which contests its obligatoriness in advance and sets aside the—earthly!—sovereignty of the state which is acknowledged by taking it." "The state cannot concede such a clause to anyone," since what one person claims for the Christian conscience another might claim for the German conscience, a third for the human, a fourth for the scientific, a fifth for his conscience as a father, etc. "The oath does not in fact demand more of you than has been demanded previously as the presupposition of your official relationship." This relationship may be renounced but it cannot be made conditional. von Soden urges Barth to consider these points (might he not be wrong in his individual stance?) and also to consider how his position reflects on colleagues like Bultmann and himself who have taken the oath without reservation. He further pleads with him to think of the effect on the whole fellowship of the Confessing Church when one of its leading theologians and a leading teacher of theology "will not render to the state what, according to my conviction, and that of many theologians, are the things of the state, thus involuntarily but unavoidably giving rise to the suspicion that the confessing front opposes the legitimate claim of the state and contends for an unevangelical autonomy of the church within the state." There is as yet no need for an independent theological school, as suggested in the *Basler Nachricht* of 29 November 1934, since Christian theology can still be taught by the state faculties. Certainly theology will often have to criticize the institutions of both state and church, but church control will not promote this any more than state control. It will be necessary to abandon the faculties of theology at state schools only when "the state no longer lets the faculties work in accordance with their material commission" and not when "professors of theology cannot meet their obligations to the state in accordance with laws which are binding for all of us." The letter ends with a plea that Barth should consider whether there is not a viable way, that accords with truth and right, to settle the process initiated against him.]

30

[Barth's reply to von Soden's letter]

Bonn, 5 December 1934

Dear Mr. von Soden:

Many thanks for your fine letter, which I will answer point by point to show you how the whole matter looks to me.

From the very first moment that I heard in Switzerland of the requirement of this oath it was very clear to me that insofar as it touched myself I would be placed by it as concretely as possible in the *status confessionis.* In face of the specific content of *this* oath I could not content myself with the position that it is self-evident to an Evangelical Christian that even after swearing an oath, if conflict arises, he will obey God rather than man. In contrast to the oath that we swore to the constitution, and that I would also have sworn without protest to the emperor, the specific content of this oath ("to be loyal and obedient to the leader of the German Reich, Adolf Hitler") seemed and seems to me to rule out anything "self-evident." It seemed and seems to me to envisage not merely dubious obligations that might arise in the future but an obligation that along with my *whole* future there is included my present too, my "existence" as such. You declare yourself to be in agreement with the thesis that the obligation of an oath is always to be construed in the sense of the one to whom it is sworn. I have adopted here this basic hermeneutical rule. I have interpreted the oath to represent 100% National Socialism as it intimated itself openly enough in

August after the death of Hindenburg (I recall the statements of State Secretary Lammers), and as it may be plainly recognized to be the intention and will of the modern state from the words as well as the deeds of our present rulers. The intention and will of National Socialism is that in Adolf Hitler we have to do with a Czar and Pope in one person, or, as one must undoubtedly put it theologically, with an incarnate God. An oath to Hitler according to the National Socialist, and this is therefore the normative interpretation, means that the one who swears it commits himself hide and hair, body and soul, to this one man, above whom there is no constitution, right, or law, of whom I must be confident in advance and unconditionally that in all circumstances he knows and wills and will achieve what is best for the whole of Germany and for me, and concerning whom the mere assumption that he might lead me into a conflict in which he is wrong and I am right will already be treason, so that if I swear loyalty and obedience to him I either commit my whole person to him even down to my most secret thoughts or I pledge him nothing. A reservation in relation to this oath is not just not self-evident; it is impossible. By its very nature it pledges me in an absolutely infinite and unpredictable way. Since I have to interpret the oath along these lines, you will concede that I cannot take it as it stands (to Adolf Hitler instead of the constitution or the "predictable" monarch). One can accept on oath only a predictable obligation. But this oath requires of me that which I can give in faith only to God. To that extent it is a novelty compared to what has previously been required in my official relationship. If I do not have the good fortune to be a 100% National Socialist who can recognize his own intention and will in that of the state that demands this oath, what option have I but either to refuse the oath altogether or to seek an amendment which will set it under a proviso, making a demand of the National Socialist state in relation to which it might not be able to tolerate or even to want officials who are not 100% National Socialists, expressly rejecting in the oath of office the true and strict interpretation of the "name" of Adolf Hitler, and thus pledging officials to Hitler only as they were formerly pledged to the constitution or the emperor, in short, to an "authority" that is not incarnate deity? I did not take the path of complete refusal, but suggested my reservation because I think it important to demand this of the National Socialist state—or to elicit a declaration that it will not accept this demand, that in accordance with its words and deeds thus far it is resolved to be in truth a "totalitarian" state. If it does not remove me on account of this clause, then it goes on record that the totalitarian state that it has in view is not so bad. It will reduce itself to the position of an "authority" in the sense of Rom. 13. But if it removes me, it goes on record—and this clarification might be worth pondering—that it wants to be understood in an anti-Christian sense, though naturally I do not regard it as patently anti-Christian just because it rejects my "Christian" amendment, but because it seeks to establish its claim to absoluteness, i.e., the religious significance of the name of Hitler. I can indeed conceive of the idea that one person might ask for an amendment because of his scientific conscience, a second because of his legal conscience, a third his artistic, and a fourth his human conscience. It is perhaps a little surprising that in the land of poets and thinkers this has obviously not happened, that at least in the field of university professors only poor "theological" existence has thought that it should protest at this point. But however that may be, assuming protests like mine came in every color of the rainbow, would the resultant absurdity of such a varied breaching of the rule really have to be ascribed to those who made the protests and not wholly to the state which necessarily causes the absurdity with its absolute claim?—the state which is not content to be an "authority" but wants to be the good Lord himself. I cannot agree, then, that my protest is even *formally* absurd, i.e., because of its subjectivity. It would be this if the state that requires the oath presupposed some protests as necessary and self-evident. But this state does not do so. Inevitably, then, subjectivity arises against—no, *for* it. For it, inasmuch as with its protest it asks the state to become an "authority" and therefore a real state again. On the assumption that the purpose of the oath is the absolute incorporation of those who take it into the Führer's totalitarian state, it is beyond dispute that my protest is not *materially* absurd but is the only incisive protest in this matter. You complain that with my course of action I treat others as though I regard them so to speak as less conscientious Christians. To this I might say first that it is *not* a matter of "conscience," which I do not mention in my formula. Primarily and in the foreground it is a matter of how we view the reality of National Socialism of which this oath is a part. In the background it is a matter of the responsibility to the gospel in which we stand with this specific view. You for your part do not think we have to understand the National Socialist claim in the oath, and take it seriously, in the way that I see it, and therefore your responsibility to the gospel is different. As regards the first aspect of the matter, I might tell you how the National Socialist rector and the investigating judge in my disciplinary hearing expressly confirmed my presupposition. But in relation to responsibility to the gospel we must and will sincerely believe the best of one another, though this should not prevent divergent decisions from raising a question or even more. And am not I as an individual in a harder place than all of you, who in your agreement might find it easier to be sure that your position in this deliberate decision is right? There is certainly a danger that an individual who does as I have done might be mistaken and thus bring others falsely and unnecessarily under the question or even the accusation why they have not done the same—but it does not follow from this danger that there never ought to be individual initiatives in any circumstances.

The truly abnormal factor in the whole situation seems to me to be that the Evangelical Church in distinction from the Catholic (Fulda!) has refrained from any declaration to the effect that no oath, including that of the Third Reich, can pledge a man to opposition to the command of God. If the church had challenged the totalitarian state in respect of the oath, and the state had not protested, then the situation would be clear to me too. The self-evident proviso would be in force without any need for me to state it personally. But since the Evangelical Church has been silent thus far, and has perhaps recognized the totalitarian state in this way, I must reply personally when personally questioned, doing for the church what the church ought normally to do for me. I do not know whether you have heard that the administration of Marahrens has been asked on all hands to make a public declaration to this effect, and according to my information yesterday a decision is expected today. If it takes a form that I find acceptable, and if the state remains significantly silent for a time, and if my disciplinary hearing is not already over by then, I would indeed be able to relate to this fact and take the oath unaltered. And it would be an odd coincidence if the abbot of Loccum were to turn out to be my savior in distress. But this has not happened yet and there are not a few "ifs," as you can see.

I have nothing whatever to do with the fantasies of the *Basl. Nachr.* concerning the founding of a free theological university.

I am sending a copy of this letter to Mr. Bultmann, who has written me to much the same material effect as yourself. From not a few letters I see that many people—even among those who have already taken the oath—are quite glad that someone has belled the cat.

With friendly greetings,

Yours respectfully,
KARL BARTH

31

[A letter from Pastor Hans Bruns of Marburg to the Council of the Evangelical Church in Germany and Bishop Theophil Wurm of Stuttgart]

Marburg, 7 May 1947

[Pastor Bruns is worried by the teaching of Bultmann and wonders whether the church ought not to consider founding its own seminaries. On 26 February 1947, for example, Bultmann referred to "the legend of the empty tomb," and "the marvel of the resurrection." Bruns has already complained of this denial of the facts of salvation history to Bishop Wüstemann of Cassel, who will do all he can at least to set up a second NT chair. He is now approaching the Council because, in reply to a personal approach, Bultmann has stated that "there is hardly a scholarly theologian who does not regard the story of the empty tomb as a legend," and even though this is not true, the mere fact that he can say it characterizes the situation. President Asmussen and Bishop Hartenstein both support this move by Bruns. He thinks that the time has come to decide whether theological students are still to be confused or the church will show the faculties that it does not depend on them but can place the instruction of pastors in other hands by setting up new schools like Bethel and more recently Heilbronn.]

32

[A letter from the President of the Council of the Evangelical Church in Germany, Bishop Theophil Wurm, to Karl Barth]

Bromerhof/Isnyberg, 20 May 1947

[While on leave in Bromerhof/Isnyberg, Wurm has received both a mimeographed discussion of the impact of the resurrection and also the letter from Bruns of Marburg. He wants advice on the issue from Barth. He himself as a theological student was influenced by Karl Weizsäcker's work *Das Apostolische Zeitalter,* which, under the impact of Baur but seeking a middle path, tried to show that Paul's message of the resurrection did not include or presuppose the facticity of the empty tomb. In this way he and others had been able to handle the difficult resurrection narratives without hurting the congregations. Yet in view of I Cor. 15 they had had to decide for or against the facticity of the resurrection itself. They were not helped by the innocuous insistence of positive theology that the resurrection was "one of the best attested facts of world history." Barth in his work on I Corinthians does not seem to think that the facticity of the resurrection is the same as that of other events either ancient or modern. Scripture and Kantian epistemology agree that metaphysical facts and processes cannot be established by human reason but are open only to people of spiritual discernment. Bultmann, if he understands him correctly, aims to emphasize this by viewing "the NT records as testimonies to a naive religious thinking which can talk about the salvation event in Christ only in mythological form." Yet this can hardly apply "to the total witness of Paul to the fact of the resurrection," which is to the same effect as the resurrection stories of the Gospels, namely, that Christ's physical body was transfigured. "At this decisive point the church has no authority to teach otherwise than the apostles. I believe that the Bultmannian theory goes far beyond the concern for a sober assessment and solution of the epistemological problem to become a presentation which includes a negation of the fact itself, if not for him, probably for many of his hearers and for the community." Thus an ecclesiastical problem arises. If Bultmann cannot give his concern a form that is compatible with the creed, it is an urgent question whether the church should not seek new ways to give theological instruction. But the sentiments of leading theologians need to be discovered first. Direct contact should also be made with Bultmann for the sake of theological clarification. He is thus sending a copy of this letter to Bultmann to avoid any appearance of going behind his back. The letter itself is being sent through Asmussen.]

33

[A letter from Hans Asmussen, President of the Chancelry of the Evangelical Church in Germany, to Karl Barth]

Schwäbisch Gmünd, 23 May 1947

[In forwarding the letter from Wurm, Asmussen expresses his own doubts about Bultmann's teaching but also his conviction that nothing should be decided without a full discussion in the church.]

34

[Barth's reply to Wurm—a copy also being sent to Bultmann]

Bonn, 29 May 1947

Dear Bishop,

Your letter of 20 May reached me yesterday (the twenty-seventh). Permit me to reply to you directly. You will understand that I cannot deal with so important matter in just a few lines; but I will try to be as brief as possible.

I. At the beginning of the twenties Rudolf Bultmann was in the front ranks of those who were then attempting a reorientation of evangelical theology along the lines of a clear confrontation, brought to light in exegesis and systematics, between the human subject and the divine revelation that encounters this subject. It should be noted that he has remained true to this basic purpose to this very day. The different ways in which he, Gogarten, Brunner, and myself—to mention only us four—have tried to fulfil this purpose, and still do so, could be seen and evaluated in those early days as simply differences of nuance.

In my view the decisive and distinctive fact about Bultmann's way is that he regarded it as indispensable to base the reorientation on a (then the most recent) philosophical ontology or anthropology. He thought he could take from this ontology a definite "preunderstanding of man" which is normative for theology, too, and in accordance with which the confrontation of man with a distinct Other could be described as a general phenomenon of the uniqueness of human existence. From this standpoint we then have to understand what the Bible calls God's revelation as a specific—the Christian—determination of human existence. In contrast to the rationalistic, idealistic, romantic, and positivistic schemata of earlier theology, Bultmann believed that he had found in this, the existential schema, an adequate canon by which to expound the NT texts and understand their positive contents.

It cannot be contested that with the help and within the limits of this canon, supported by a philologically critical ability and schooling in which he has few equals, Bultmann has succeeded in shedding new and impressive light on important aspects of the biblical witness. Any assessment of Bultmann will have to reckon with the fact that in him we are dealing with a man of supreme scholarly seriousness and the leading German NT expert since Jülicher, who is also the most widely respected abroad. And apart from all else, some of the results of his NT work were undoubtedly what led him very naturally to take the right side from the very outset in the church conflict.

But the question remains whether that programmatic basing of theology on some philosophical ontology will not sooner or later, in some way or another, necessarily mean the overthrow of theology, and whether this has not actually happened in the case of Bultmann too. In my view this question has to be answered in the affirmative. What the Bible calls God's revelation, according to my understanding of its witness, is not to be explained as merely one determination of human existence. And the explanation of revelation as a determination of human existence is inevitably truncated and twisted when it is forced into the framework of that "preunderstanding," where it can have the significance only of a Christian instance of the general human encounter with some Other.

To this extent I could not and cannot find that Bultmann does justice at any rate to that which motivated me in the time of our common initiative early in the twenties. I believe that I must view Bultmannian theology more as a return to the theological method whose untenability was brought to light in Lessing, Kant, Schleiermacher, and De Wette (who is perhaps particularly close to Bultmann). For this reason, after similar developments in my earlier theological friends Gogarten and Brunner, I could not follow Bultmann in general or in principle, for all my gratitude to him for the instruction that I received from him in detail.

I myself believe that only the foregoing question of Bultmann's methodological presuppositions is either theologically or ecclesiastically serious and significant. What are now set before us for discussion are certain christological conclusions. I regard these as unavoidable on Bultmann's presuppositions. Within the "preunderstanding" which underlies his theological exegesis and systematics the only possible exposition of NT statements about the messiahship, the divine sonship, the vicarious death, the resurrection, and the coming again of Jesus Christ is one according to which these are to be seen as conceptual objectifications, influenced by the imagination of the NT age, of that which the encounter with God mediated through Jesus Christ signifies for man. I reject these conclusions along with Bultmann's presuppositions. I see in them a proof that (with formally different presuppositions) he is leading us back to Biedermann and beyond. I also do not hesitate to say that I have to regard them as "heretical," i.e., incompatible with the confession of the church. And those who adopt the presuppositions of Bultmann, or others like them, can hardly avoid his conclusions. It seems to me to be one of the greatest merits of Bultmann that he has not scrupled to maintain his cause faithfully and consistently. Those who do not want to finish up where he does must learn from this brave, learned, and perspicacious man not to begin where he does.

II. The accusation and complaint of Pastor Bruns is directed against certain sharp formulations of the negative conclusions which he heard in a lecture by Bultmann: the "legend of the empty tomb," "the marvel of the resurrection," and the like. I regard this way of bringing the case of Bultmann to discussion as profoundly unsatisfactory. Permit me to support this briefly.

1. Pastor Bruns does not seem to realize that the statements which—in a way that reminds us of poor precedents—he heard in Bultmann's class, and which he has repeated with an expression of his dissatisfaction, *could in themselves* be taken *in a good sense.*

The term *"legend"* may simply denote the literary genre of the

Easter stories of the Gospels (a *necessary* one in virtue of their unique content). The resurrection of one who is dead and buried, or his existence as one who is now alive, obviously cannot be reported in the form of a "historical" narrative but only as a "saga" or "legend." This term says nothing about whether what is reported really happened or not. A legend does not necessarily lack substance. It may relate to real history which took place in time and space but cannot be told "historically" (i.e., in a form which is demonstrable and illuminating for everybody). In this sense I, too, can and must describe the Easter story as a "legend." For myself, then, I would have to follow Bultmann's appeal to "most" of his colleagues—if I were not unfortunately aware that by the term "legend" (which, impermissibly in my view, he associates with the term "myth") he has in mind the idea that what the "legend" narrates never really took place. It is here that discussion should begin; the mere assertion that Bultmann used the term "legend" does not touch upon the truly serious question that needs to be put to him.

The same applies to the derogatory expression "marvel." This may simply denote the way that the resurrection message must look to unbelievers. I, too, might use the word to describe the impression that the message first has on us (even us "Christians"). I must assume that Bultmann meant it differently, i.e., that by means of it he wished to put the fact of the resurrection truly and definitively in the realm of credulous fancy. This and not the mere use of the term is what we need to discuss with him.

2. Pastor Bruns in his letter to you shows no realization of the fact that in Bultmann the statements of which he complains stand in the context of a negative conclusion that embraces the whole of christology. The "empty tomb" is in itself only one representative of that to which the NT writers bear witness: that the eternal Word of God really came in the flesh, that in the there and then to which they refer he came as a Jew to us Gentiles, that he suffered for us, went down to death, and was exalted to glory. The "empty tomb" is not on its own "a fact of salvation history." What must be confessed as a fact of salvation history in opposition to Bultmann and to so many docetic or docetizing heretics both old and new is the living Lord Jesus, the Christ of Israel, who is as such the Savior of the world—in contrast to a principially timeless Christ-idea which is embodied in this Jesus but can also be abstracted from him. That this confession is not possible with a denial of the "empty tomb" but only with (incidental!) recognition of it—this *context* and this alone can make the "empty tomb" a worthy theme of theological discussion. This is what is not expressed in any way in the accusation and complaint of Pastor Bruns.

3. Pastor Bruns obviously does not know the decisive presupposi-

tions of Bultmann's theology, or he knows them only at a distance. He does not perceive that the trouble in Bultmann begins much further back than where it comes to his attention in the exposition of the NT. He sees where Bultmann is going, but not where he comes from. He does not see that one must attack Bultmann, if at all, on the basis of his combination with a specific philosophical ontology. I do not know how strictly Pastor Bruns and perhaps many other critics of Bultmann have been asked whether they are not much nearer to Bultmann in their presuppositions than they think, whether they have an inner right, then, to complain about him. This gives to the accusation and complaint against Bultmann something of the nature of the outcry of the monks of the Nitrian desert against Origen or of the style in which certain "positive" church groups at the end of the last century and the beginning of this one used to argue against the "Liberals," or rather to protest and agitate somewhat hollowly against them. I am pleased, reverend bishop, to gather from your letter that you do not want to extend a hand to any renewal of the false fronts and fruitless tactics of that period. For my own part, notwithstanding all that I have on my heart against Bultmann, I have no wish to give strength to this monkish outcry.

III. In the disposition and direction indicated by the letter of Pastor Bruns no controversy should be initiated between the church and the theology of Rudolf Bultmann. The harm that would be done thereby would be incomparably greater than what is to be expected from Bultmann's writings and teaching—whose original purpose and positive qualities should not be forgotten for a moment because of his "heresy." A contesting of heresy which misses the essential point, well-meaning though it may be, has always been more dangerous to the church than the heresy in question. The existence of the extreme critic in Marburg, who is himself the occasion of so much criticism, and who works in a rather humorless place that seems to find pleasure in criticizing, will certainly not ruin the Evangelical Church in Germany, which in the rest of Germany is encompassed by many scholars and teachers of a sufficiently different mind and orientation. I even conjecture that the existence of a "heretic" like Bultmann, who is so superior to most of his accusers in knowledge, seriousness, and depth, might be indirectly salutary to the church as "a pike is in a pond of carp." On the other hand, the rise of a clerical group that hands out censures or doctrinal judgments with neither true vision nor reflection, no matter how orthodox it might aim to be, can only bring about destruction.

You will perhaps recall, reverend bishop, that in 1933–34 I argued emphatically that the confession of the Confessing Church, to be forceful and credible, would have to oppose not only the manifest errors and misdeeds of the DC [German Christians] but also the underlying false development of a whole theological epoch. I was only partially successful in my view at that time, and an awareness of the broad basis on which we then wanted to move on to "confession," at least in part, has maintained itself even to this day among only a very relatively small number. But now again, in the matter of Bultmann, I can give no other advice than either to go into the matter in its totality or to let it be.

As regards the establishment of church seminaries advocated by Pastor Bruns, I do not expect salvation from this either in this matter or in any other, nor from a new professorship on the existing Marburg faculty after the manner of university politics in royal Prussia.

You were good enough, reverend bishop, to refer in your letter to my little Easter article written for a Swiss paper. I did not speak about the "empty tomb" in this article, but about the fact that we need to take with literal seriousness the message of the bodily resurrected Jesus Christ if we are to find ourselves in a new life, in a new world. If Rudolf Bultmann were surrounded by a church which in its preaching and order, in its politics and relation to state and society, in its whole way of dealing with modern problems, were to put into practice even a little its belief in the Risen Lord, then not only would it be practically immune against the heresies of the Bultmannian conclusions and theses but it would also have in reply to Bultmann the one argument which could perhaps cause him to abandon his basic position, with its tying of the gospel to a pagan ontology, and make him a free expositor of the NT freely speaking for itself. I desire no less than that he should become and do this, gladly renouncing those bothersome theses. But I do not see what can make him do so, nor how the church can immunize itself against his false negations, so long as it is not clear in practice whether the church stands where it ought to stand in the light of its confession of the Risen Lord, so long as trains of thought are operative and even dominant in it which are only too closely related to the presuppositions of Bultmannian theology, so long as it is perhaps only a lack of intellectual strength and integrity that prevents countless numbers of its responsible members from concluding with Bultmann that Christ is *not* really risen. What guarantee do we really have that a church seminary or a new professorship at Marburg would really espouse the church's doctrine of the *Risen* Jesus Christ and thus offer an effective check to Bultmann?

Please understand, reverend bishop, that my view is not that in face of the Bultmann problem we should retreat to an inner line and let things take their course. We should ask other NT scholars to enter into professional debate with Bultmann, as Prof. Schniewind has already done in exemplary fashion. If the situation in Marburg proves to be as perilous as Pastor Bruns makes out, we should send the best pastors available into the community there and do everything else that is possible to see that Bultmann and his students are encompassed not only by a "believing" but also by a living community. If it is thought that his unfortunate theses are causing confusion in wide circles, we should take steps—though without starting a witch-hunt or mentioning Bultmann by name—to pronounce an anathema against them with a well-considered *Si quis dixerit. . . .* If there is the theological confidence to do it, a statement should be made, in a commentary on the first thesis of the Barmen Declaration authorized by the Council of the Evangelical Church in Germany, that implicitly this thesis covers any canonization of a philosophy. It seems to me, of course, that such measures do not need to be taken, and even ought not to be taken to the extent that the church itself is in order or brings itself back into order. The proper action of the church in the face of the Bultmann problem can consist only of the church really *being* the church, in practice and not just in theory, at the very point of Bultmann's attack. Certainly the presence, as I see it, of an intellectual and spiritual error in the theology of Bultmann cannot be met by the mechanical measures that Pastor Bruns has in view but only in the freedom of the Spirit—the Holy Spirit and the human spirit!

You will consent if I send a copy of my letter to Professor Bultmann.

Thanking you for the confidence in me displayed by your approach,

Yours respectfully,
KARL BARTH

35

[A letter from Bishop Theophil Wurm to K. Barth]

Stuttgart, 1 June 1947

Honored Professor,

On returning from vacation I received your letter of 29 May, which made it from Bonn to Stuttgart in the astonishingly quick time of two days. I first need to thank you for the great seriousness with which you have answered my query in this difficult and important matter. Your presentation will be a great help in our attempt to find the proper spiritual way to overcome the threat of a new theological division in the Evangelical Church.

The day after tomorrow I shall have a chance to present your reply to brothers Niemöller and Asmussen and to confer with them.

Taking the liberty of sending you an address that deals with a related problem,

Yours truly,
DR. WURM

36

[Plan of Rudolf Bultmann's tour in the United States in 1951]

ITINERARY (Tentative)

Yale University, Shaffer Lectures (4) — 15–19 Oct.

Boston Area — 21–27 Oct.
- Wellesley College (nondenominational)
- Andover-Newton Theological School (Baptist-Congregational)
- Episcopal Theol. School
- Boston University School of Theology (Methodist)
- Hartford Theological Seminary (interdenominational)

Free Week — 28 Oct.–3 Nov.

New York Metropolitan Area — 4–10 Nov.
- Princeton Theol. Seminary
- Lancaster Seminary (Ev. Reformed)
- Drew University School of Theology (Methodist)

Chicago — 11–17 Nov.
- University of Chicago
- McCormick Theol. Seminary (Presbyterian)

Vanderbilt University (Nashville)

Cole Lectures (6) — 18–24 Nov.

Free Week

Union Theol. Seminary, New York — 2–8 Dec.

37

[Rudolf Bultmann's Report to the Marburg Faculty of Theology on his U.S.A. tour. 2 October–20 December 1951]

Report of the Lecture Tour of Professor R. Bultmann in the U.S.A. in the Months of October, November, and December

On 2 Oct. arrival in New Haven (Conn.). A stay there of three weeks, during which the so-called Shaffer Lectures were given in the Divinity School of Yale University on the theme "Jesus Christ and the Modern Interpretation of the New Testament."

From 21 Oct. to 1 Nov., lectures were in the "Boston Area," namely, at Wellesley College, my base, at Andover-Newton, the Episcopal Theological School at Cambridge (whose Dean, Dr. Charles Taylor, is a Marburg graduate), and the University of Boston. The subjects of these lectures were problems arising in the Shaffer Lectures and also "Humanism and Christianity" and "The Significance of the Idea of Freedom for Western Culture."

On 2 and 3 Nov., participation in the conference of a theological group, of which Paul Tillich, e.g., is also a member, at the College of Preachers at Washington.

From 4 to 10 Nov. at Nashville (Tennessee), where the Cole Lectures were given at Vanderbilt University, the theme being the same as that of the Shaffer Lectures. The president of Vanderbilt, Dr. Branscomb, is also a former student at Marburg.

From 12 to 17 Nov., lectures at the University of Chicago and McCormick Seminary and also Lutheran General Seminary, Maywood, near Chicago. The subjects here were much the same as before. In Chicago I met Dr. Amos N. Wilder (brother of the poet Thornton Wilder), who is well known in Marburg for the addresses he gave here in the summer semester of 1950.

After a rest in New Haven there followed lectures at Princeton, Drew, and Hartford, 26–30 Nov. At Princeton I met Prof. Lehmann, who was a guest professor at Marburg in the summer semester of 1950 and looks back on that semester with great pleasure. The president of Drew is Dr. Craig, another former student at Marburg. At Hartford, with which Marburg has been in regular contact for some years, Dr. Frick and Dr. Schimmelpfeng, further Marburg alumni, are still remembered. From 5 to 7 Dec., lectures at Emory University in Atlanta (Georgia). Here I met Prof. Hocking, an exchange professor at Frankfurt in 1950 who came from Frankfurt to give lectures at Marburg.

My last lectures were given at Union Seminary in New York from 8 to 13 Dec., during which period I also gave a lecture at Crozer Theological Seminary in Chester near Philadelphia. In New York I met Prof. Reinhold Niebuhr, who is well known in Germany and highly regarded in the U.S.A. for his understanding of Germany. On the Sunday I visited Paul Tillich, who was enjoying a "Sabbatical Year" in his country house on Long Island and writing the second volume of his dogmatics.

My welcome was warm everywhere, the hospitality was overwhelming, and there was much openness to the questions dealt with in the lectures, as shown especially in the ensuing discussions—both in smaller circles with colleagues and larger ones with students. The response to the work of German theology is the more gratifying as it springs from a justifiable sense of being the response of an equal partner. If German theology today takes up many questions earlier than does American theology, many fields are covered in American theology which are not tackled, if at all, with the same energy in Germany, and which in the present situation can be tackled only inadequately because of the lack of means and numbers. Thus the relation is one of mutual give and take.

It is a particular delight to experience the affection with which the many American students who once studied at Marburg look back on their time there. We find them almost everywhere, and in the preceding survey I have been able to name only a few. Among the older generation Wihelm Herrmann, Adolf Jülicher, and Karl Budde are particularly remembered.

I cannot fail to mention the many meetings with earlier German colleagues of various faculties who had to leave Germany in the Nazi period and who are now highly esteemed and have found a new home in the U.S.A. Their relation to modern Germany is a special problem about which I cannot speak in a few short words. It may be said, however, that even if they do not contemplate a return to Germany they have the destiny of modern Germany very much on their hearts. They proved this by their sacrificial assistance during the worst period after the war. And it is a consoling thought that their work in the U.S.A. is indirectly to the benefit of Germany too.

38

[Autobiographical sketches of Karl Barth from the faculty albums of the Faculties of Evangelical Theology at Münster (1927) and Bonn (1935 and 1946), first published in E. Wolf, In Memoriam Karl Barth. Rede, gehalten am 4. Juni

1969 bei der Gedenkfeier der Rheinischen Friedrich-Wilhelms-Universität Bonn für ihren einstigen Ehrensenator, *No. 31 of* Alma Mater. Beiträge zur Geschichte der Universität *(Bonn, 1969), pp. 26–35. Reprinted by permission of the Verlag Peter Hanstein GmbH, Bonn]*

I. Münster, 1927:

I belong to Basel, and was born on 10 May 1886 as the eldest son of Fritz Barth and Anna Barth (née Sartorius). My father, previously pastor of the Aargau community of Reitnau for seven years, was at the time a teacher in the Evangelical School of Preachers at Basel. In 1889 he began to teach on the Faculty of Theology at the University of Bern, where he later became Professor of Church History and New Testament and served for twenty-three years.

It thus came about that I spent my youth among the people of Bern, not without some opposition to a temperament and drift of mind from whose paralyzing resistance I already saw my father suffer not a few times. What annoyed me later became understandable *ceteris imparibus* from the experiences of Calvin with the same people. We then lived on the extreme outskirts of the city, so that forest, field, and garden belong to my earliest and deepest recollections, along with the arcades, fountains, and towers of the old city, the lakes and valleys of the Bernese Oberland, and not least the regular trips to Basel to our much loved grandmother Sartorius, which were always a festival.

"Boys go to school, soldiers to the field, and let each see to it. . . ." I can still hear my father singing this encouraging verse the evening before I was to enter the primary school of the later Free Gymnasium, a well-known private "Christian" institution. From the first day I was never good at arithmetic and my handwriting has always been poor, but I did become a bookworm. My fundamental and often reread text was Niemeyer's *Book of Heroes,* a bloodthirsty account from 1818 of the wars against "Buonaparte," who could not be condemned too severely. Told to give a sentence with an accusative object, even in tender childhood I could thus give the prompt answer: "Napoleon founded the League of the Rhine," which completely astounded my teacher. And I have later been accused of selling "history" short in my theology!

Both secretly and openly, martial interests were at the center of my intellectual development up to my sixteenth year. Playing toy soldiers was something my brothers and I did constantly and seriously. In a cadet corps which existed in Switzerland in those days, and still exists in part today, I received fairly regular military training for four years and in spite of poor achievements in shooting, made the rank of sergeant. At the same time, strangely enthused by the iambics of Schiller's "Wilhelm Tell" and Körner's "Zriny," I was for many years a suspiciously productive dramatic poet, though my efforts with the violin, in spite of the active musical life of our household, were less than fruitful. Technical accomplishments of any kind, e.g., gymnastics, I had long since left without envy to others. But my imaginative enterprises in the open and at home, in which I used to ask my brothers and friends to take part, make it seem not improbable that in other circumstances I might have developed into a dramatist or the like.

The offerings and requirements of lower and upper high school, on the other hand, affected me more like an unavoidable cross. I never reached more than second position in my class, and not often that. Even today my aversion to the emphasis placed at that time in Bern schools upon the mathematical and scientific disciplines sometimes pursues me in my dreams. Regrettably we were never so well instructed in the older languages as they usually are in German schools. I really devoted myself fully only to history and the writing of essays, in which I could outstrip all my rivals in every class.

In 1901–02 I attended with much pleasure the confirmation classes of Pastor Robert Aeschbacher, well known in Germany, too, for his sermons. In keeping with the style of the turn of the century, he was very apologetically inclined, but brought the whole problem of religion so closely home to me that at the end of the classes I realized clearly the need to know more about the matter. On this rudimentary basis, I resolved to study theology. I did not know then what I was undertaking, and now that I know this sphinx more closely I do not think that today I would have the courage to take the same step.

In the autumn of 1904, I took the examinations for my certificate, just stumbling through chemistry, physics, etc., with a second class. A trip to Frankfurt and Cologne as a reward for enduring the torture introduced me with astonishment to the vast domain of Germany. Directed and advised with kindly zeal by my father, I then began to study at Bern University. I industriously absorbed, though without gaining any real insight, the solid but rather dry wisdom of Professors Lüdemann, Steck, and Marti. With incomparably more empathy, but not without looking for new paths of my own, I followed the lectures and assignments of my father. The first book that really moved me as a student was Kant's *Critique of Practical Reason,* from which I shortly after found my first theological refuge in Herrmann's *Ethics.* At this time I spent much time, money, and energy in the student union Zofingia; it was not in the least enervated by the first beginnings of the youth movement of those days. I have later found friends in different ways, but because of my happy and colorful recollections of it, I do not regret this episode.

After taking my examinations in the fall of 1906 (philosophy, the history of religion, church history, and Bible knowledge) I was ready in Swiss fashion to go abroad. I wanted to go to Marburg, but my father would have preferred to see me at Halle or Greifswald. The result was that I went to the more neutral Berlin, where I wisely avoided Seeberg, unfortunately in my folly took no notice of Holl, and heard Harnack with such enthusiasm (and with a little less zeal Kaftan and Gunkel) that apart from the work I did for his seminar in church history I almost completely neglected to make use of the many facilities for general education that were available in that foreign city. After a summer semester in Bern that was almost fully taken up with "work" as president of my society, and after a four-week assistantship in a big congregation in the Bernese Oberland, in the winter semester of 1907–08 I obeyed the stricter authority of my father rather than my own inclinations and went to the University of Tübingen, where I heard Schlatter with great reluctance, Haering with astonishment, and only the church canonist F. Fleiner (now in Zurich) with pleasure. For my required examination in Bern I composed a vast work on the self-selected topic "The *Descensus Christi ad inferos* in the First Three Centuries." I often visited Bad Boll, though with no basic understanding, and took part in many student allotria as a guest of the "Royal Society."

Finally in the summer of 1908, various circumstances brought it about that I was able to visit Marburg, which I had earnestly wanted to do because of Herrmann. I was now able to hear whom I wanted; apart from Herrmann I particularly attended the classes of Heitmüller, though Jülicher was less to my taste. In the fall, tolerably well prepared, I took my second (systematic and practical) examination, then did an independent assistantship, this time in the Bernese Jura, and finally spent a second year on the banks of the Lahn, kindly provided by Rade with a post as assistant editor of his *Christliche Welt.* These three semesters in Marburg easily form my happiest memory as a student. I absorbed Herrmann through every pore. I thought I acquired a sound theological foundation by an intensive study of Schleiermacher and Kant. Through my work on the *Christliche Welt* I came into very interesting contact with the theological and church movements of the day. In particular I found two friends who are still my friends today and will remain so: Eduard Thurneysen (now in St. Gallen-Bruggen) and Wilhelm Loew (now in Remscheid). The name of Troeltsch, then at the heart of our discussions, signified the limit beyond which I thought I must refuse to follow the dominant theology of the age. In all else I was its resolute disciple (as *Z.Th.K. Jahrg.* 1909 shows).

In the fall of 1909 I took up practical work as suffragan pastor of the German Reformed congregation in Geneva, to which I had to minister alone for half a year because the chief position was vacant. Perhaps it was the presiding genius of the place (I had to preach in Calvin's auditorium every Sunday) that led me, along with the continuous reading of Schleiermacher, to plunge into Calvin's *Institutio*—with profound impact. I did not undergo a sudden conversion, but thought I could easily unite idealistic-romantic and Reformed theology. Along these lines I allowed to be printed a large treatise on faith and history which would have been better left unprinted.

In Geneva I became acquainted with Nelly Hoffman, who became my wife in 1913. Obstacles both within and without prevented me from achieving my purpose of taking the Licentiate of Theology at Marburg. The more I had to preach and teach, the more the pursuit of academic theology began to become "in some way" alien and puzzling to me. This became especially true when, in 1911, I came to the Aargau like my father before me, to the peasant and artisan congregation of Safenwil. There, partly under the influence of the message of Kutter and Ragaz, which was then at its peak, the social question and the social movement became urgently important to me. In the class conflict which I saw concretely before me in my congregation, I was touched for the first time by the real problems of real life. The result was that for some years (the death of my father in 1912 may have contributed to this) my only theological work consisted of the careful preparation of sermons and classes. What I really studied were factory acts, safety laws, and trade unionism, and my attention was claimed by violent local and cantonal struggles on behalf of the workers. A change came only with the outbreak of World War I. This brought concretely to light two aberrations: first in the teaching of my theological mentors in Germany, who seemed to me to be hopelessly compromised by their submission to the ideology of war; and second in socialism. I had credulously enough expected socialism, more than I had the Christian church, to avoid the ideology of war, but to my horror I saw it doing the very opposite in every land.

In this hopeless impasse, I first found illumination in the message of the two Blumhardts, which was oriented in principle to the Christian hope. I owe my acquaintance with their thinking to my friend Eduard Thurneysen, who for seven years was a pastor with me in the Aargau, and with whom I had at this time innumerable anxious discussions. I still thought and preached along the old lines. I still regarded it as obligatory to belong even outwardly to the Social Democratic Party. But beyond the problems of theological liberalism and religious socialism, the concept of the kingdom of God in the real, transcendent sense of the Bible became increasingly more insistent, and the textual basis of my sermons, the Bible, which hitherto I had taken for granted, became more and more of a problem. On a certain day in 1916, Thurneysen and

I very naively agreed to go back to academic theology to clarify the situation. If we had known what was to happen we would not have found the *parrhesia* ["confident audacity"] to do this.

The following morning, surrounded by a stack of commentaries, I found myself before the Romans of the apostle Paul with what seemed to me to be the newly put question of what was really in it. From the notes that I then made on Romans, there arose what became later the well-known, controversial book. More than I myself realized, it was strongly influenced by the ideals of Bengel, Ötinger, Beck, and (by way of Kutter) Schelling; being under their influence, the book later could not convey what really had to be said. In the first instance, I wrote the book only for myself and for the private edification of Eduard Thurneysen and other concerned people. Even in 1918 I had no inkling of the repercussions which would follow when, with the help of a friendly business man, I had it published in a Bern house, where it was preceded by a little volume of sermons composed in conjunction with Thurneysen. That I had thought and expressed things for which I would have to answer before a wider public first began to be clear to me when, in September 1919, I was invited to give an address at the Religious Social Conference at Tambach (Thuringia) and for the first time saw the completely altered situation in postwar Germany. Here I first met the Stelzendorf pastor Friedrich Gogarten, who in *his* village had in a very different way been caught up in concerns and considerations similar to my own. Here I suddenly found a circle, and the prospect of further circles, of people to whose unrest my efforts promised answers which at once became new questions in the fresh contacts with these German contemporaries. The greeting of more than one of these people who were hungry for reality took me by surprise and caused me to put afresh the question of the biblical meaning of the kingdom of God. This new questioning was stimulated by the posthumous publications of Overbeck, by Kant, whom with the help of my younger brother (now teaching philosophy at Basel) I had come to see differently in the light of Plato, by Kierkegaard and Dostoevski, whom as yet I know only selectively, and by a better knowledge of Paul himself through a series of sermons I preached on Ephesians and II Corinthians. This stimulation came independent therefore, of the older Württemberg and all other speculative theology, and in what I now realized and stated to be open opposition to Schleiermacher, whose unserviceability was later consistently demonstrated by Emil Brunner. The first evidence of this change is the address on "Biblical Questions, Insights, and Prospects" given at the Aargau Conference of 1920. Things now began to snowball. *Romans* passed to a Munich publisher who better understood the kairos, but from whom I had to retrieve it after the first edition was sold out in order to subject it to complete revision.

In the middle of this task, I was surprised one morning in February 1921 to be asked by old pastor Heilmann, later of the Prussian Ministry of Culture, whether I would be willing to accept the honorary professorship of Reformed theology being established at Göttingen. I can now admit, six years later, that at that time I did not even possess the Reformed confessional writings, and had certainly never read them, quite apart from other horrendous gaps in my knowledge. If I agreed after very short consideration, this was because of the immediate sense that as things were my place was among the theological students of Germany and not elsewhere, and in the blind confidence that things would somehow work out both in relation to my scholarship and also my growing family. In October, then, fourteen days after the second edition of *Romans* was ready, to the accompaniment of all kinds of tumultuous events within my congregation, we moved to the distant city of Albrecht Ritschl, where with an assurance that is inconceivable to me today, I took up the books on whose contents I had to give academic lectures and opened them at once with no chance to prepare. Fortunately my theology, such as it had been, was more Reformed and Calvinistic than I realized, so I could devote myself to my special professional task with pleasure and a good conscience. The imprecision of my teaching commitment meant that I could acquire step by step the necessary materials which, not foreseeing the future, I had previously neglected. It was very comforting and encouraging to me when in February 1922 I received with surprise the news that I had been nominated for the D. Theol. degree by the Faculty of Theology at Münster. And I was more grateful than they knew for the thanks of many Göttingen students with which I soon found myself to be surrounded. The book on I Corinthians arose out of lectures that I gave in Göttingen in 1924.

These were, of course, difficult years, for I had not only to learn and teach continuously but also, as the champion of a new trend in theology, I had to vindicate and protect myself in the form of lectures and public discussions of every kind. And good care was taken that as an alien from a neutral country, I should learn to know postwar Germany through the period of inflation and the debate about the Ruhr, which was particularly lively in Göttingen. The publishing of the new journal *Zwischen den Zeiten* in concert with Georg Merz, Thurneysen, and Gogarten (from 1923) brought new possibilities but also new worries, responsibilities, and attacks. But I always returned to Germany and the Germans from my vacations in Switzerland where I have a second home in the "Bergli" of my friend Rudolf Pestalozzi by Lake Zurich. At the end of the summer semester of 1925, when I had my first three-semester course of dogmatics behind me, I received the news that the Evangelical Faculty of Münster had successfully put my name forward for appointment as Professor of Dogmatics and NT Exegesis. Again, having been sometimes (though not too much) disturbed by a certain constriction in my external position at Göttingen, I had no reason not to accept with assurance this vote of confidence, and to this day I do not regret having done so. May this feeling be mutual. In my own view, I will always be a rather difficult case needing both collegial and Christian patience in more than one respect.

Münster, 26 March 1927 KARL BARTH

II. Bonn

A. 1935

More briefly than my predecessor, I recall that I was called to Bonn in 1930, suspended on 26 November 1934, dismissed by the Cologne court on 20 December 1934, relieved of this sentence by the higher court of Berlin-Charlottenburg on 14 June 1935, retired by Minister Rust on 22 [21] June in accordance with §6 of the relevant statute, and on 25 June 1935 appointed a professor at the University of Basel by the administrative council of the canton of Basel city.

Basel, 11 July 1935 KARL BARTH

B. 1946

The deluge passed in 1945 as it had come in 1933. In the summer of 1946, I was invited to return to Bonn from Basel for a guest semester; I will now supplement my criminalistic reports of 1935 in this book with a few more peaceful words.

The man to whom I undoubtedly owe the presuppositions of my later relation to theology was my father, Fritz Barth (1856–1912), who by the quiet seriousness with which he applied himself to Christian things as a scholar and as a teacher was for me, and still is, an ineffaceable and often enough admonitory example. I think I owe my direct impulse to study theology to the confirmation preparation that I received from my Bern pastor Robert Aeschbacher. Among my academic teachers those who influenced me most strongly and fixed the early phase of my career were H. Gunkel, A. v. Harnack, W. Herrmann, W. Heitmüller, and the church canonist Fritz Fleiner. I wanted to become a pastor and was so for twelve years, without regarding myself as either called or adapted to the office of academic scholarship and teaching. Directly out of the problems of my pastoral ministry I found myself compelled—at about the age of thirty—to revise my theological foundations insofar as I had received these at the universities. The very strong influence of Christoph Blumhardt, mediated to me by the gifted Zurich pastor Herman Kutter, first led me back simply to more concrete biblical exegesis.

At this stage I received a call to become the Honorary Professor of Reformed Theology at Göttingen. By accepting this, I was led to a new and more basic study of the reformers and to controversy in principle with Schleiermacher and the modern theology determined either directly or indirectly by him. I then traversed many a complicated path in Göttingen, Münster, and Bonn and received several new impulses through the attentive hearing and questioning of my German students. At this time (1921–1935) I had also to go through many a hectic conflict, so I was fairly well prepared for the battles that began in 1933. Also at this time, gradually or more visibly, I came to learn, along with a great centralization of what was material, to move and express myself again in simple thoughts and words. I learned also to put criticism (which is, of course, necessary) more in the background than positive exposition; I did so more than I had done in the twenty years or so of my liberation from the traditional system of the eighteenth and nineteenth centuries. In Bonn in 1932 I began to give form to my *Church Dogmatics,* which had already been fairly extensively drafted, and on which I worked in Basel after the events of 1933–1935. I hope to spend the time that is left to me after reaching my sixtieth birthday on its continuation. But the work of young theologians in 1946 interests me so much that I am sincerely sorry that I cannot double myself and make a contribution here to the reconstruction of church and state.

Bonn, 12 August 1946 Karl Barth

39

[Rudolf Bultmann drafted an autobiography on 28 January 1959 at Syracuse University, Syracuse, New York. This was first published in English in his Existence and Faith, *ed. S. Ogden (New York, 1960), and then, with an extended conclusion, in* The Theology of Rudolf Bultmann, *ed. C. W. Kegley (New York, 1966), pp. xix–xxv.]*

[Bultmann first tells of his birth on 20 August 1884 at Wiefelstede, in the then Grand Duchy of Oldenburg. His father was an Evangelical Lutheran pastor, Arthur Bultmann, whose father, born in Freetown, Sierra Leone, had been a missionary. His mother Helene, née Stern, was the granddaughter of a pastor. He went to school at Rastede and Oldenburg and had an early taste for the Greek world, German literature, music, and the theater.

In 1903 he began the study of theology at Tübingen, then moved to Berlin, then Marburg, being particularly indebted to the church historian Karl Müller at Tübingen, Hermann Gunkel and Adolf von Harnack at Berlin, and Adolf Jülicher, Johannes Weiss, and Wilhelm Herrmann at Marburg. Weiss encouraged him to take a doctorate and begin teaching at Marburg. For his Licentiate in Theology he wrote *Der Stil der paulinischen Predigt und die kynisch-stoische Diatribe* (1910), and after composing his *Die Exegese des Theodor von Mopsuestia* (1912) he was accepted as a teacher. He became friendly with Wilhelm Heitmüller, who had succeeded Weiss in 1908, and also with Martin Rade, becoming a member of the "Friends of the *Christliche Welt*" and learning much from the discussions of this group.

In 1916 he was appointed to a professorship at Breslau, where his first two daughters were born and he experienced the hardships of the later war years. Here also he wrote his *Die Geschichte der synoptischen Tradition* (1921). In 1920 he was called to Giessen, where he enjoyed lively exchanges with his colleagues. In 1921 he returned to Marburg to follow Heitmüller, and although he received an invitation to Leipzig in 1930 he remained at Marburg until his retirement in 1951.

In Marburg his third daughter was born in 1924 and he took great pleasure in working among the students. The Hitler regime, however, brought suspicion and mistrust in 1933. During the war his only surviving brother died in a concentration camp, and with many others he regarded the defeat of Hitler as a liberation. He had belonged from the very first (1934) to the Confessing Church and had worked with von Soden to uphold academic freedom so far as this was possible.

The burden of the postwar years was lightened by gifts from abroad, though mistakes on the part of the occupying powers delayed political and social reconstruction. Yet there was a good relation with the Americans, and he was especially grateful to those who helped to reestablish the University of Marburg.

His first colleague in Marburg had been Jülicher, who retired in 1923. Von Soden had replaced Jülicher and taught until his death in 1945. With both of these men Bultmann enjoyed a good relationship. The same applied to the OT scholars G. Hölscher and K. Budde and also to W. Baumgartner, though tensions with R. Otto, Herrmann's successor, led to lively discussions among the students, especially when visitors like Gogarten and Barth gave lectures at Marburg. Bultmann also profited from his friendship with the philosophers N. Hartmann and M. Heidegger, the philologist P. Friedländer, the classical scholars H. Dahlmann, F. Müller, and C. Becker, and the historian F. Taeger.

His publications while at Marburg may be found in the bibliography in the *Theologische Rundschau* 1954 (cf. *Exegetica. . . ,* ed. H. Dinkler

[Tübingen, 1967], pp. 483–507). Prior to the war he lectured in Scandinavia, Britain, Holland, and Switzerland. He paid another visit to Sweden in 1947. In 1951 he made his American tour, primarily to give the Schaffer Lectures at Yale, which were later published as *Jesus Christ and Mythology* (New York, 1958). In 1955 he was in Edinburgh for the Gifford Lectures *History and Eschatology* (Edinburgh, 1957; ET *The Presence of Eternity* [New York, 1957]). In 1959 he came to Syracuse University to lecture in the Department of Bible and Religion.

All these and other exchanges forwarded both his NT work and his theological thinking in general. He had a personal part in the great theological and philosophical revolution which began with Barth's 1919 *Romans,* Gogarten's address "Die Krisis unser Kultur" (1920), and the founding of *Zwischen den Zeiten* (1923). He himself contributed to it with his essays "Die liberale Theologie und die jüngste theologische Bewegung" (*GuV,* I, 1–25) and "Die Bedeutung der 'dialektischen Theologie' für die neutestamentliche Wissenschaft" (*GuV,* I, 114–133), and also with his articles for *Zwischen den Zeiten* 4 (1926), 385–403; 5 (1927), 41–69; 6 (1928), 4–22; 7 (1929), 9–43 (*GuV,* I, 65–84; 85–113; 134–152; 153–187).

The truth in this revolution seemed to him to be that Christian faith is no mere phenomenon of religious history and therefore theology is more than a religious or cultural phenomenon. Christian faith is "the answer to the Word of the transcendent God who encounters man" and "theology has to deal with this Word and with the man who is reached thereby." Yet this did not entail for Bultmann a superficial condemnation of liberal theology. His own work was a continuation of the historico-critical research pursued in this theology and an attempt to make it fruitful for contemporary theology.

Existential philosophy, learned from Heidegger, was also of crucial importance for Bultmann. He found in it concepts appropriate to human existence and the existence of believers. His concern to use it in theology led to opposition to Barth. Bultmann was grateful to Barth for the decisive things he had learned from him and did not think their relation had really been clarified, through he found a beginning of such clarification in Heinrich Ott's *Geschichte und Heilsgeschichte in der Theologie Rudolf Bultmanns* (1955). In contrast, his kinship with Gogarten became increasingly clear.

Concerning "demythologization," he first used the term in 1941 in an address entitled "Neues Testament und Mythologie" (published in *Offenbarung und Heilsgeschehen* [Munich, 1941]; cf. *KuM,* I [1948], 15–53). The ongoing debate might be traced in the volumes of *Kerygma und Mythos,* ed. H. W. Bartsch (from 1948). The exchange with Karl Jaspers was published under the title *Die Frage der Entmythologisierung*

INDEXES

1. LIST OF LETTERS

[Postcards are marked by an asterisk and the letters and postcards that are summarized are marked by a dagger.]

2. LIST OF DOCUMENTS

[Documents summarized are marked by a dagger.]

3. SCRIPTURE REFERENCES

4. NAMES

Holl, Karl 153

5. PLACES

6. SUBJECTS

7. GREEK WORDS

8. WORKS OF BARTH AND BULTMANN

BARTH

BULTMANN

9. WORKS BY OTHERS

Books mentioned by Barth and Bultmann

Barth's desire to break through the schema of 18th-19th century Theology. i.e. relating of theology and philosophy.
Letters 58, 90, 69, 67, 48

- his critique of Bultmann for not breaking out of this theological scheme, his return to "the bondage of Egypt".

Bultmann's critique of Barth for "falling prey to an outdated philosophy" Letters 47, 94

- on relation of church to theological scholarship. p. 125 f.

Barth's perception of where their paths part company: Letters 67, 58, 95. p. 143

Bultmann: 89